Engaging College and University Students

Engaging College and University Students outlines creative and effective course organization and teaching-learning strategies for higher education courses. By describing specific instructional best practices, rather than addressing general questions about teaching in higher education, the author presents a valuable resource for educators to consult in the moment. The author explores the challenges of engaging students in online settings and draws comparisons with face-to-face strategies of engagement. By organizing the strategies according to course progress, and offering corresponding rubrics for assessment, this guide for instructors offers a solid foundation for an ever-changing teaching and learning landscape.

Ken Badley is Research Professor of Education at Tyndale University in Toronto, Ontario, Canada. He has taught in secondary, undergraduate, graduate, and doctoral programs in Canada and the United States, and has worked extensively with teachers in Kenya. He is the author of many books and articles related to curriculum, instruction, and the teaching vocation.

GW00771331

If you are designing a new course or want to change one you have taught for years, this book is for you. I am recommending it to new and seasoned faculty who want to increase student engagement. Badley offers up a storehouse of ideas with sufficient details for immediate implementation. New ideas and reframed techniques categorized according to their best purpose provide the reader rationale for selecting a particular strategy. This book will stay open on my desk!

Pam Nordstrom, Provost, VP Academic,
Ambrose University, Calgary, Alberta, Canada

Ken Badley generously shares with us his tried and tested practical strategies for learning-centred instruction. More importantly, he shows us how engaging student learning can be fun for everyone involved, even when it is online. Ever the realist, Ken imagines the best, takes the edge off the worst of the stress, encourages us with humour, and gifts us his own experiences. This not a tirade against lecturing; this is a wonderful overview of strategies that enrich learning and teaching. Ken anticipates the criticisms of lethargic or anxious faculty and invites instructors and learners past the tyranny of 'covering the content'. If you or your faculty want to move from good, to better, let Ken guide you through learning-centred instruction. Buy and share your copy of *Engaging College and University Students* widely.

Beth Green, Provost, Tyndale University,
Toronto, Canada

What makes an engaging lesson? In this captivating book, Ken Badley provides professors with a vast toolkit of methods to engage their learners. Reading this book will help teachers in higher education as they work with curriculum, assessment, and instruction. Badley writes with wit, wisdom, and humor. This incredibly practical book is based on Ken's extensive experiences in the world of teaching and learning. While the primary audience of this book is professors, anyone who engages students in the world of learning will benefit greatly from the lessons contained within.

Adam Paape, Professor of Education, Concordia University,
Wisconsin, Mequon, Wisconsin, USA

How can I inspire each of my students to be actively involved in their own learning? This is obviously the most important question asked by the most memorable or the most influential teachers. That's the question that kept Ken Badley awake and led him to create a wonderfully enthusiastic, encouraging book for teachers in higher education. This book immediately resonated with my own professional questions energized me, even though I work half-way around the world.

The book provides readers with a balanced overview of the principles of learning-centered education while offering a rich bank of strategies. In concrete, clear and inspiring ways, Badley opens up space for colleagues to provide students with unforgettable study experiences, experiences that will bring them joy as they acquire new knowledge and skills. *Engaging College and University Students* offers readers ideas about how to approach all phases of the teaching process—from course design and detailed planning of the start of the course, to students' learning experience through the semester, to assessment and feedback. Badley addresses the range of students' senses by offering strategies related to reading, writing, discussion, and even the arts.

Dana Hanesová, Faculty of Education, Matej Bel University, Banská Bystrica, Slovak Republic

KEN BADLEY

Engaging College and University Students

Effective Instructional Strategies

Illustrations by Kristen Badley and Sophie Chardon

Routledge
Taylor & Francis Group

NEW YORK AND LONDON

Cover Design: Kristen Badley

First published 2023
by Routledge
605 Third Avenue, New York, NY 10158

and by Routledge
4 Park Square, Milton Park, Abingdon, Oxon, OX14 4RN

Routledge is an imprint of the Taylor & Francis Group, an informa business

Library of Congress Cataloging-in-Publication Data
Names: Badley, Kenneth Rea, 1951- author.
Title: Engaging college and university students : effective instructional
    strategies / Ken Badley ; illustrations by Kristen Badley and Sophie
    Chardon.
Description: New York, NY : Routledge, 2023. | Includes bibliographical
    references and index.
Identifiers: LCCN 2022007285 (print) | LCCN 2022007286 (ebook) |
    ISBN 9781032195247 (hardback) | ISBN 9781032195230 (paperback) |
    ISBN 9781003259596 (ebook)
Subjects: LCSH: College teaching. | Effective teaching. | Instructional
    systems–Design.
Classification: LCC LB2331 .B33 2023 (print) | LCC LB2331 (ebook) | DDC
    378.1/25–dc23/eng/20220316
LC record available at https://lccn.loc.gov/2022007285
LC ebook record available at https://lccn.loc.gov/2022007286

ISBN: 978-1-032-19524-7 (hbk)
ISBN: 978-1-032-19523-0 (pbk)
ISBN: 978-1-003-25959-6 (ebk)

DOI: 10.4324/9781003259596

Typeset in Joanna MT
by KnowledgeWorks Global Ltd.

To long-time friends, Dave and Marilyn Hedlund (Regina, Saskatchewan), Brenda and Randy Babich (Moose Jaw, Saskatchewan), Diane and Sandy Ayer (Calgary, Alberta), and Claude et Annette Demaurex (Lausanne, Switzerland). You have enriched my life beyond measure.

Contents

In late 2020, after Covid-19 had upended so much of our work as higher educators, a number of professors and teachers met with me in a series of workshops about how to engage students more deeply in online courses. As I met with these colleagues over several weeks, it became apparent that the challenges of engaging students in online settings did not differ too significantly from the challenges of engaging them in face-to-face settings. It also became apparent that many higher educators want to make their courses more engaging. Most don't want to show PowerPoint slides, deck after deck, day after day. Most want lively conversation with their students. They want critical engagement with readings and ideas. They want students free to do their most creative thinking.

How? That is the question many professors are asking. How do we get that engagement, that critical thinking, and that creativity? In this book, I catalogue some of the ways I have answered that question. Other professors have developed myriad ways to engage students and to foster creativity. But with a page limit and finite energy, I offer here about a hundred strategies to increase student engagement.

Believing that we're all in this together, in a sense, I have written this book in a personal tone, as if we were talking in a room and you, my reader, had asked me how I do such-and-such. Therefore, I use first- and second-person personal pronouns. I use contractions … and ellipses. I make only sparing reference to the research related to most of the topics I treat herein. I make a few snide remarks here and there.

In one sense, this volume can stand alone. But in my own writing trajectory, it is book five in a series of six. The first volume, *Curriculum Planning with Design Language: Building Elegant Courses and Units* appeared in 2018 as my homage to architect Christopher Alexander, whose idea of pattern languages revolutionized my approach to course and curriculum design years earlier. I advertise that book regularly in these pages.

Another homage of sorts, to Mihaly Csikszentmihalyi, appeared in 2020 as *Generating Tact and Flow for Effective Teaching and Learning*. To complete this project, my colleague Susanna Steeg Thornhill and I collected narratives of great classes from dozens of educators. Our goal was to understand how what Csikszentmihalyi calls flow happens in classrooms and in what ways, if any, we can create the conditions for it. As was the case with Christopher Alexander and his design principles, I also make repeated references in this volume to Csikszentmihalyi and flow.

The third book in this intended series, a co-edited volume, appeared in 2021 with the title, *Joyful Resilience as Educational Practice: Transforming Teaching Challenges into Opportunities*. My colleague Michelle C. Hughes and I wanted to remind educators of the many people who support our work. We started the book before the pandemic, but as it turned out, it was timely because educators needed a reminder that they were not working alone.

In 2022, my co-edited volume with Margie Patrick, *The Complexities of Authority in the Classroom: Fostering Democracy for Student Learning*, appeared. I do not refer to it as much herein as I do to the first two books I named, but the ideas in that book run though this volume, especially the idea of shared classroom authority or epistemic authority, the question of whose knowledge counts. I remain deeply committed to the view that we learn with our students. The final volume, which I plan to work on next, addresses questions of educational vocations. I keep playing with the title, *How Good Teachers Last: Flourishing Long Term in the Classroom*, but I should probably focus on getting the book written before worrying too much about the title. I provide this partial auto-bibliography to help frame the work I have done in this book. The strategies I include here are not stand-alone even though I stated above that the book can stand alone. The strategies I offer here are underwritten by a specific philosophy of education, they reflect a specific epistemology, and they fit best in a certain kind of context.

One more caution is warranted in the Preface to a book on teaching strategies. Business guru Peter Drucker is usually credited with having originated the phrase that culture eats strategy for breakfast. In truth, the origins of this clever saying remain murky. But its truth is clear. As I apply it in this volume, attempts to employ engaging strategies to enrich a specific class here or there may not work well, or perhaps not at all, if the culture—what I usually call the ethos or the climate—of that class is professor-centered rather than learning-centered. The strategies I catalogue in this book reflect an epistemology markedly different from the dominant epistemology in many higher education classrooms. The strategies I offer here reflect an understanding of the professor-student relationship at odds with the kinds of relationships considered normal in higher education. The strategies in the chapters that follow rest on assumptions about the classroom as a kind of communal space, where professor and students work together to deepen their understanding of the subject matter. None of these sentences implies that I do not view myself as an expert, that I disregard professional boundaries, that I care less than others about curriculum, assessment, and learning objectives, or that I don't take seriously how much students pay per clock hour to be in my courses. These things matter deeply to me. And because these things matter deeply to me, I want to be in a classroom where my students and I together create a culture that enriches their learning by increasing their engagement, that offers them variety, and that gives them opportunities to learn in the ways they learn best. Neither does my advocacy of shared authority imply that I hold in a kind of contempt from below those colleagues who deliver engaging lectures to packed classrooms and lecture theaters. I have great respect for such professors. But I believe they constitute a smaller percentage of the population than many want to think.

Having warned that these strategies may not work well if they are simply dropped into a course ordinarily grounded in a professor-centered epistemology and view of authority, I should add a codical. In *The Nicomachean Ethics*, Aristotle claimed that we can learn or adopt a disposition by repeatedly engaging in the practices that would ordinarily flow from that disposition. The same may be true of adopting an epistemology or a view of classroom authority. If someone ordinarily committed to the lecture were to try a few learning-centered methods for a semester, perhaps they would move toward a more learning-centered program overall. In light of Aristotle's claim, I offer the strategies in this book to all, regardless of their preferred instructional methods, hoping that those who stick their toes in the non-lecture waters will find themselves and their students enjoying the university classroom more than was previously the case.

I like trying new things. My T-shirt should likely say "Bores Easily." So, to prevent boredom, I keep trying new things in my classes. Most of what appears here has grown out of my own practices. Because I teach education, some of what appears herein I have actually learned from my own students. I have tried to give credit to the others who told me about other strategies.

Ken Badley
Calgary, Alberta
January, 2022

Acknowledgments

First, I acknowledge the many university students who have laughed with and at me as we worked through my first faltering attempts to use some of these strategies. Their many suggestions for improvement have helped me become a better educator. I blame my remaining weaknesses as a professor on rock and roll, teenagers, seniors, the weather, or the government, depending on the day of the week. I also acknowledge the many colleagues, known and unknown, who originally developed many of the strategies I describe here.

Thanks go to Kristina Hedlund who, in September 2021, worked patiently with the Table of Contents from my original proposal to Routledge to organize 450 pages of materials in more than 100 files so I could focus on writing instead of searching on my hard drive for the material for each chapter. Also, thanks to Greg Burbidge who enriched Appendix B by contributing several pages on educational applications of gaming.

My thanks go as well to Matthew Friberg at Routledge in the US and Jessica Cooke at Taylor & Francis in the UK. Without their expertise, guidance, encouragement, and trust in me, this book would not exist. I also acknowledge the many editors, typesetters, and designers at Routledge who work behind the scenes to bring this project to completion.

As always, I am grateful to the many members of Team Ken who kept me going during the writing phase of this project. You know who you are. Kristen Badley, who produced the powerful cover and many of the internal graphics for this book, deserves thanks (and payment at higher rates than she charges). And thanks to Sophie Chardon, who created some of the internal graphics. For Jo-Ann Badley's influence on all my thinking about education, I am continuously grateful. Many of her insights appear uncredited in this volume.

As I have done in other volumes, I acknowledge the role of my B.Ed. students at both Tyndale University in Toronto and Mount Royal

University in Calgary who, over the last several years, have inspired me to keep looking for new teaching-learning strategies, new ways to share classroom authority, new ways to de-teacher the university classroom, and new ways to apply design principles to course and unit planning. Together, we have journeyed to discover what Parker Palmer calls the heart of teaching. Part of that journey has involved laughing with them at their amazing PowerPoint karaoke presentations, at my lame jokes, and at my pedagogical flops. But another part has been that they have taken the openings I have offered and produced research papers, songs, spoken word performances, social initiatives, a book about flourishing during practicum, board games adapted to curriculum units, videos, and websites of resources for teachers. I shared classroom authority with them and they shared their abundant talents with their classmates and with me. To complete their course requirements, they have done real work for a real audience in the real world. We are all richer for what they have brought. We have truly feasted together, both literally and metaphorically. For that, I will always remain grateful. Regardless of how much we enjoyed our shared work on campus, they have inevitably graduated and gone on to realize the dreams they had when they came to campus in the first place. They have continued to give me joy as I have watched them develop as competent and visionary professional educators who want to teach in amazing ways.

Ken Badley
Calgary, Alberta
January, 2022

Illustrations

Framing the Book
Section I

In the first chapter in this section, I situate the book, both in its immediate context of Covid-induced changes to our work, and with reference to the enduring questions of how students in higher education learn most effectively. The second chapter contains my effort to frame the rest of the book within a cluster of historical debates, contemporary questions, and concepts. In Chapter 3, I present several more concepts, which shape my educational work and which I tend to use almost as natural language in conversation and writing. Readers will be quite familiar with some of these and perhaps not so familiar with others. Chapter 4 includes my warrant for attempting to build classroom community and suggests ways to do that.

The material in this section can be rightly considered introductory to the many chapters on strategies that follow. But what I present here is nevertheless central to the dozens of strategies I catalogue in the remainder of the book. As I note at several points, the strategies on offer in what follows are not simply one-off activities that can be plugged into any kind of course. Rather, they are underwritten by and foster a specific (shared) epistemology, and they flow out of and contribute to a specific kind of classroom climate. I encourage you, my colleagues, to read these chapters instead of skipping ahead to the second section.

DOI: 10.4324/9781003259596-1

One

The first answer to the question in the chapter title is that I increasingly find myself in conversations with colleagues about disengaged and disaffected students. "They're in the back row on social media." "They say they can't get to the library." "They object to buying a textbook." And these conversations frequently turn from engagement to critical thinking. "They seem unable to think critically." "They believe anything they've read online ..." and so on. You and I both know that the word *they* in the above complaints does not mean *all*. Some students sit in the front and engage with us, even asking for more challenging material and more directions for their research. Some students love the library. Some students have a hundred sticky notes in their textbook by the end of term. Some students identify weaknesses in our favorite authors' arguments that we didn't see. But most of us have heard the kinds of complaints I listed. The *why* in my chapter title is thus a why of solidarity; I want to understand better how to teach so we engage all our students, and I want to find more effective ways to encourage critical thinking.

These conversations about engagement sometimes circle around to an expressed wish for practical advice on how to get students more engaged. The second reason I have written this book is to explore that question: "How do we engage students?" In the pages that follow, I offer some of the ways I have used to increase student engagement. I offer these without boasting; I learned most of these strategies from other educators, and I still worry before every class that my teaching will bomb, that I will bomb. I lose sleep over the students I somehow cannot reach. And negative comments on course evaluations stick in my brain for years. So this book does not come from on high. But some have asked what I do to engage students, so I catalogue and describe some of the strategies I have used to get my students interested in the course materials. I write only as one colleague to another. At that,

DOI: 10.4324/9781003259596-2

I write as a colleague who is still trying to figure out the mysteries of student engagement.

Because the chapters that follow are an extended answer to the *why this book* question, I have written in the first person as if we were simply colleagues on a break or in a workshop, talking with each other. Much of what follows is narrative (this is what I do) and some of what follows are directions (here is how to do this). The first and last sections of the book include some expository writing, but I offer only a minimum of that kind of text because I do not try in this book to persuade anyone to abandon transmission modes of teaching, notably the lecture. Rather, I want to assist those who already want to shift toward what I call learning-centered teaching. I know that some of what I offer here could enrich the lecture, but enriching the lecture is not my purpose (nor is attacking it). My singular purpose is to describe approaches to curriculum, instruction, assessment, and the classroom ethos that arise from an explicitly non-transmission philosophy of education.

Allow me to write autobiographically for a moment. I completed first and second grade in one year but then needed an extra year to repeat the grade 12 courses I failed the first time. Between those two bookends, I achieved my last "A" average in grade 8, under the guidance of a teacher who, as it turned out, worked a side gig as a professional clown. I discovered that detail only decades later and wonder in retrospect if there may have been a connection between his clowning and his success as a teacher at motivating me; he engaged us, he engaged me. When I look back at my elementary and secondary education from the perspective of a professional educator, I now see what happened between elementary school and age 18 that I did not understand at the time: I grew bored and I disengaged. I don't blame my teachers entirely for this, after all, I had the normal adolescent struggles, and my teachers taught in the way most teachers taught at the time—they wrote notes on the board, we copied them down, we fed them back on tests. In those circumstances, one might expect disengagement.

Arriving at university, to which I was admitted thanks to an optimistically-named "mature admissions" clause that made room for a few students with 60% high-school averages who waited one year, I discovered the same model in place. Mostly, professors talked and students listened. With many happy exceptions, that model has managed to stay largely in place in the decades since I finished my first degree. I mention those happy exceptions with joy; I now teach university students who tell me about professors who devised this or that amazing and engaging activity to help their students achieve a specific learning outcome. I will come back to these professors in a moment. But students also tell me about professors who show a new deck of PowerPoint slides every day, some of whom do not make time for questions, and, in some cases, who invite students not even to attend class if they prefer not to because the slides are posted on the course wiki.

Most of us know the justifications for a transmission mode of teaching dominated by a teacher talk. The educator has knowledge or expertise that students simply do not have. The educator's job is to transmit knowledge to students (a view in place for millennia). This or that particular course is content-heavy, and my students will not learn the material unless I lecture. I register no objection to the facticity of the first claim; I have worked hard through years of my own post-secondary education and my whole teaching career to gain knowledge and to develop expertise that most of my students lack. But I have questions about the second claim. What if instead of claiming that my task is to transmit knowledge, I framed my objective as helping students learn what they need to learn about this subject? That reframing might shed a different light on how we use class-time. Regarding the third claim, I want to register two objections. First, specialists in every field of knowledge could point to the intimidating volume of content in their courses. Thus anyone making the content-heavy argument may implicitly be insulting those in other disciplines and those who teach other courses. My second complaint about that claim is that it seems to rest on a similar false assumption to that underwriting the second claim: Because this course has a lot of content, the best way for students to learn that content is for me to lecture.

Even brief inspection reveals that these justifications all rest on a common assumption: Class time should primarily be given to the transmission or transfer of course content. In plain language, the professor should talk a lot. A second assumption may lie slightly below the surface in these arguments as well. That lecturing, with or without a deck of PowerPoint slides, is an efficient way to transmit information from one person to another. Again, I have not written this book to counter these arguments, and therefore offer only the brief criticisms above. I want to move as quickly as possible to the non-lecture strategies that seem to engage students most effectively. I offer what follows not to help those who would like to spice up lecture teaching but to support a different model altogether, one that starts with the question of what we want our students to learn, but does not assume that the best way for them to do that is for us to talk all semester long.

The Covid-19 pandemic connects to the third reason I have written this book. The switch to online teaching induced by the pandemic in the early months of 2020 meant that professors were denied access to some of the usual cues we rely on minute-to-minute to assess how our students are responding to our classes. Nevertheless, we could still observe enough to know that, overall, teaching in online settings presents challenges we typically do not face in face-to-face teaching. By the time of writing (December, 2021), the verdict has come in: Many students who already struggled with boredom in face-to-face, transmission-based teaching found that mode more boring in online teaching. In revealing this weakness of the transmission mode, Covid may have helped us see that the lecture enhanced by the slide deck projected onto a classroom screen still remained simply a presentation of information. The switch to online teaching forced on us by Covid perhaps helped us see that while computer slides may have enhanced the lecture, those slides did not change the essential character of the lecture or substantially improve it as a mode of teaching. To come back to the purpose of this book, some professors who suddenly found themselves teaching online saw the need to teach differently. They saw that they needed new ways to frame teaching in higher education, new approaches, and new strategies. For them, I offer what follows in this book.

THE ZONES OF TEACHING

In the background—but not that far in the background—of my thinking about the learning and teaching strategies I describe in this book is a continuum I call the zones of teaching. Some of my readers will be aware of the work of Lev Vygotsky and his phrase *zone of proximal development* (1978). Vygotsky was concerned that educators give enough support to students as they engage in new learning that they can succeed, but not so much support that the learning process entails no challenge. For some educators, the word *zone* immediately brings Vygotsky to mind. I need to make clear here that my use of the word

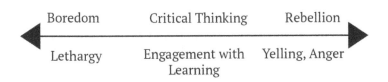

Figure 1.1 The zones of teaching.
Credit: Sophie Chardon.

differs from his (although there are obvious connections. Figure 1.1 illustrates what I mean when I use the word *zone*. I think one could situate the mood in any college classroom at any time on a continuum like that in Figure 1.1.

This continuum shows the range of student engagement. On the left end, students give no attention or energy to learning, and their critical faculties are not awakened. On the right end, some event or words have triggered one or more students so that frustration leads to anger and outbursts in class. What I call *the zone of critical engagement* is characterized by full attention and high energy for learning. I have no grounds or desire to specify precisely where the middle zone might begin and end but, framed correctly and presented in the right portions and ways, course materials, questions, problems, and professor-induced cognitive dissonance can hook students into engaging critically with what the professor has planned. Too little tension and students will not engage, too much and they give up or erupt.

Readers familiar with Phillip Schlechty's work on student engagement will recognize commonalities between his interests and my own, although I will not attempt to compare his five-level scale (Figure 1.2) to my continuum. Note that Schlechty distinguishes five levels of engagement and disengagement, from full engagement, through two levels of compliance, to retreatism and open rebellion. To use his language in a general way, in this volume, I focus on strategies to help students move upward

Engagement	Attention and commitment
Strategic Compliance	Attention and low commitment
Ritual Compliance	Low attention and commitment
Retreatism	No attention or commitment
Rebellion	Explicit disinterest

Figure 1.2 Phillip Schlechty's five levels of engagement.
Credit: Sophie Chardon.

on Schlechty's scale. Of course, in kentopia (my fantasy world where every student engages willingly with learning and teaching, explained further in Chapter 2), all students already function at Schlechty's top level. The students in real college classrooms—non-kentopian classrooms— might be anywhere on his scale.

In this book, I have set myself this task: Describe learning and teaching strategies that I have seen work effectively to invite or pull students into higher levels on Schlechty's scale and the middle zone of my continuum, what, throughout this book, I call *critical engagement*.

POSSIBLE TENSIONS ARISING FROM ADOPTING THESE APPROACHES

When professors give birth to an idea for a new teaching/learning strategy, develop that idea from scratch, try it in class, and revise and refine it, it truly becomes their own and can be said to be theirs. My concern with offering the strategies I offer in this volume is that professors who adopt these strategies will, in a sense, not be building their own program but will be reproducing someone else's program, possibly creating a kind of mismatch with their own view of knowledge and of how students learn best. That concern arises not out of some kind of selfishness or concern that others will try to teach the way I teach. Rather, it arises out of my concern that other people will not teach authentically … out of who they are.

On the other hand, for years I have recommended what I call the *adopt and adapt* approach to teaching strategies; I tell colleagues and pre-service teachers to adopt other educators' materials and strategies and then adapt those materials and strategies to their own purposes and teaching styles. I recommend this approach because it saves valuable time. Why invent something from scratch when someone else has already developed it and worked out the inevitable kinks? As I noted earlier, I myself have appropriated many of my go-to strategies from other educators. So, while part of me wants my colleagues to build their own teaching program from the ground up, I offer the strategies and approaches in this book to save them headaches and time. I expect that in the same way I have made other people's strategies my own, my readers—with some repeated uses and a share of tinkering—can make any strategies I suggest here integral parts of their own educator's repertoire. Eventually, these can truly belong to those who adopt them, their origins notwithstanding. Research into students' views of good teachers consistently reveals their concern for authenticity (for example, Intrator, 2004). I believe that professors who make other educators' approaches and teaching strategies their own can meet that criterion.

Some small clarifications about my language use are needed. The teaching and learning strategies I describe in this volume all work as part of an overall approach—my overall approach—to teaching, and I describe that approach as *learning-centered*. Many educators describe this approach as *student-centered*, but I refrain from that language here because, although I work hard to connect the course contents to my students' interests, I always try to keep us focused on the contents before us. I refrain from using this language for a second reason: Many hear it to mean that the educator has abandoned the curriculum contents to such a significant degree that students and educators alike are essentially wasting their time. I use the language of *learning-centered* to distinguish my approach from *professor-centered* teaching, the phrase usually used to designate the opposite of student-centered learning. I use the language of learning-centered for a second reason: To distinguish my approach from mischaracterizations of Dewey's claim that the starting point of teaching should be our students' interests. Dewey repeatedly clarified that claim by pointing out that their interests were the starting point, not the end point of our teaching (Dewey, 1902, 1938). The worst mischaracterizations of Dewey's ideas come from those who argue that experiential education ultimately leads to the most radical forms of constructivism—what I call *me-pistemology*—where others must take seriously anything I believe, even the patently absurd claim that Sacramento is the capital of France.

Finally, I use the phrases *teaching strategies* and *learning strategies* interchangeably. I am fully aware of the possible ways to nuance these differently, especially that the first phrase places more focus on what the professor does and the second focuses more on what the student does. An alternative usage, which I do use periodically in what follows, is *teaching-learning strategies*, which I consider clunky writing. Please take my word that regardless of which language I use to denote the strategies I discuss in this volume, my concern is to teach in learning-centered ways, ways that engage my students.

CONCLUSION

Because certainty that I should write a specific book or article so consistently eludes me, the warrants I have offered here may have been more for my own benefit than for my readers' benefit. Nevertheless, I hope what I have written in this chapter makes sense. I am tempted to plead, "Hey, I'm just trying to help." In truth, that is what I want to do with this book.

In the next two brief chapters I introduce several concepts and ideas that shape and underwrite the strategies I present in later chapters. Readers will already be familiar with some of these and some will be new. Those anxious to get to the heart of the book may want to jump ahead to Chapter 4, but I consider what I offer in Chapters 2 and 3 essential to understand what follows, and I recommend patience.

REFERENCES

Dewey, J. (1902). *The child and the curriculum*. University of Chicago Press.

Dewey, J. (1938). *Experience and education*. Macmillan.

Intrator, S. M. (2004). The engaged classroom. *Educational Leadership*, 62(1), 20.

Vygotsky, L. S. (1978). Interaction between learning and development (M. Cole, Trans.). In M. Cole, V. John-Steiner, S. Scribner, & E. Souberman (Eds.), *Mind and society: The development of higher psychological processes*, (pp. 79–91). Harvard University Press.

Two

I begin with what is perhaps an egregiously oversimplified question, meant to echo John Dewey's questions about various philosophies of instruction: Do we intend to bring the curriculum to our students or our students to the curriculum? (Dewey, 1902, 1938).

To me, *bringing the curriculum to the students* implies that we focus on the content, a view captured in the 1913 image of the Nuremberg Funnel (Figure 2.1), a German cartoon dating back to 1647 and meant to catch the view of education that focused on pouring knowledge into students' heads. The opposite view, *bringing the students to the curriculum*, implies that we attend very carefully to the ways we can invite students to engage with the curriculum contents, what throughout this book I call *learning-centered instruction*. Dewey expressed his concern that we approach the connection between students and curriculum by using the language of *students' interests*. Obviously, successful teaching cannot be either/or, but the distinction may help clarify the approaches to teaching I describe in this book.

My own epistemic frame for teaching is shaped quite strongly by Parker Palmer. In *To Know as We Are Known*, he presents the idea shown in Figure 2.2 (Palmer, 1983). The left side represents the transmission model of education by which the student must go through the educator to get to the curriculum contents. On the right is the model Palmer recommends we adopt (for which he does not provide a catchy name). In short, the students and teacher together work to understand what he calls the big subject.

That big subject could range across questions such as these:

- Does the U.N. still have a mandate?
- Should the Electoral College be abandoned?
- Do guaranteed minimum-wage programs work?
- Is harm reduction a good enough reason to fund injection sites?
- Why does X so consistently lead to Y?

DOI: 10.4324/9781003259596-3

Figure 2.1 The Nuremberg funnel, representing the view that educators pour knowledge into students' heads.

Credit: Public domain.

Student ⟶ Teacher ⟶ Knowledge

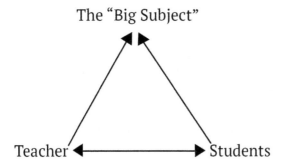

The "Big Subject"

Teacher ⟷ Students

Figure 2.2 The contrast between a traditional, teacher-centered view of classroom epistemology and the view Parker Palmer presents in *To Know as We Are Known* (1983).

Illustration by Sophie Chardon.

We expect that the professor knows more than the students about how to go about finding answers to these questions. But honest professors will admit that, despite their professorial subject-area expertise, even brilliance, some students disengage in classes dominated by professor talk, especially when that talk is primarily explanatory rather than discursive. The bulleted questions above and others like them are so complex that sometimes no clear answer emerges, regardless of how much information we have at hand. In Palmer's conception of teaching, we need to go at these questions with our students rather than simply give answers to our students. He perhaps approached the posture of *co-learners* that Carl Rogers identified half a century ago (1969). I suggest taking Palmer's approach while realizing fully that such a posture represents a departure from traditional understandings of the purposes of education and the epistemology implied in those understandings.

In my own courses, I openly admit to my students that while I am an expert relative to them on many questions, there is much I have not figured out yet and I would love for them to help me figure it out together.

PRIOR QUESTIONS FOR TEACHING

As part of the process of planning every course and every individual class session, I ask myself four questions:

- What do I want my students to know after they have studied this topic?
- Can they learn this without my lecturing?
- To provide them with some degree of security, can I use teaching and learning strategies (other than the lecture) with which they are already familiar?
- To pique their interest, can I use teaching and learning strategies they have not seen before?

These are powerful questions, first, because they tip on its head the traditional (transmission) approach to teaching and learning, an approach that can be summarized in two other questions: What section of my physical or metaphorical ring binder do I cover today? Will I have enough time to cover that section in class? These two questions reveal the assumption that the best way for my students to learn is for me to explain, to tell, to transmit.

I want to explore briefly each of the four questions I ask prior to every class session, beginning with what I want my students to understand by the end of class. I want to know how to help them become productively engaged with whatever material we need to study on a given day. Rightly, students now ask why they should pay good money to listen to a professor lecture when there are many engaging presenters—some of them more engaging that we are—on the same topic online (witness Sam Wineburg's 2018 title, *Why Learn History When It's Already on Your Phone?*). My question is consistent with the emphasis of a movement most commonly known as *backwards by design*. This approach can be summarized in three questions: What do we want them to know (what is the curriculum or what are the learning objectives)? How will we find out if they know (assessment)? How should we teach so they learn what they need to know (instruction)? Those questions show clearly that advocates of backwards by design want educators to begin at the end point (thus the word *backwards*) instead of simply asking, what is next in a ring binder or what is the next deck of slides. The first of my four questions above obviously reflects the backwards-by-design approach.

My second question focuses on whether (and how) my students can learn what I want them to learn without my lecturing. This question is key to understanding this whole book. Over my own career as a professor, I have moved almost completely away from lecturing to much more discursive and activity-based teaching. I know that some professors who primarily teach using the lecture mode succeed in engaging students in critical reflection, but I have informally observed what researchers in student engagement have repeatedly found: That students typically experience lower levels of engagement in lecture-based courses than in courses structured using other formats (Kelly et al, 2005; Denker, 2013; Heflin et al, 2017; Maphosa et al, 2017). A growing number of professors have found and reported on a variety of ways to increase student engagement while still using the lecture format (Fies & Marshall, 2006; Terrion & Aceti, 2012). In this book, I do not attempt to add to that growing body of literature. Rather, I describe other ways to increase students' engagement. Some of what I describe here would work with lecture-based classes, but I focus throughout on helping those professors who want to move away from lecturing. I need to be clear; I have not written this book to dismiss the lecture, but the strategies I describe herein are meant to stimulate critical reflection through discussion and other engaging activities.

The third question is obviously less philosophical than the first two but it is still important: What teaching and learning strategies are my students already familiar with because their elementary and secondary teachers used those strategies? In my view, familiarity with teaching strategies reduces students' anxiety and increases their self-efficacy. I call this third question important because most undergraduates today have had a very different school experience from most of today's professors, especially those professors in their middle years or older. Most of today's undergraduates have already spent thousands of hours in activity-based learning, in group work, and in research. They already know how to use some of the strategies I describe in this volume. Undergraduates' familiarity with these strategies has at least two implications. First, if you, my reader, read about a strategy here that you have never heard or thought of before, please do not think it sounds corny or that it could never work. If I have flagged it as a strategy undergraduates have likely used already, explaining how it works and getting them to engage with it will be simple. Second, your students' opinion of your teaching ability will likely go up when they see you using some of the same strategies used by their more engaging elementary and secondary teachers.

My fourth question really functions as a corollary of the third. I want to pique their interest and let them know I work hard to find new ways for us to do our academic work, so I appropriate or devise teaching and learning strategies they have likely not seen before.

If I were ever to add a fifth question to the list above, it would be this: How much attention do I give to students' prior knowledge in a field? At several points in this volume, I suggest strategies for getting answers to that question. Not to oversimplify, but those strategies mostly look like sophisticated ways of asking, "What do you already know about this?" Of course, the range of student knowledge in a typical class will vary, but our own task is clarified somewhat if we know the answer. When K–12 educators use the language of *prior learning* and *scaffolding new learning*, they are referring to the need to provide students with the necessary background to learn what comes next. Answers to this fifth question—however we get them—free us to build on whatever foundation our students already have.

VARYING INSTRUCTIONAL STRATEGIES

While asking about varying instructional strategies might qualify as another in the series of questions I have discussed above, I view such variation more as an assumption, or perhaps a necessary conclusion. The findings of the researchers I noted above bear out the view that students do not want to learn the same way every day. So I introduce variety. And I do not need other people's research to confirm my inclination; I do not want to teach the same way every way.

Having come to that awareness or arrived at that conclusion years ago, I have searched for, adopted, and devised as many ways as I could to build variety into my own instructional repertoire. But I do not view this variety as a means of supplementing or enhancing the lecture. As I noted in Chapter 1, the strategies I describe here are grounded in and represent a learning-centered view of the professor's work, not an information-transfer view. And they also reflect a view of shared epistemic authority or classroom authority, which I have argued at length elsewhere and will not repeat herein (Badley & Patrick, 2022). In short, most of the strategies I catalogue in this volume cannot simply be inserted into a transmission orientation to the classroom. I wish that sprinkling a few learning-centered strategies into a transmission-based course would work effectively (and some professors probably could make it work). But I remain convinced that the strategies I catalogue in this volume work best in the hands of educators who are committed to shared authority and student engagement with content. And what I offer in this book reflects such a commitment.

CONCLUSION: THE CHANGING TASK OF THE EDUCATOR

The tasks of the educator change over time. In an age of information scarcity, the task of the educator may justifiably be to give information to students. In such a time, transmission is a suitable means of instruction. Justifiably, the instructional focus could be on delivering content or covering material (a phrase I dearly want to put in quotation marks). In a time of information scarcity, it would be appropriate to assess students' learning afterward—what many now call summative assessment—to measure students' acquisition of content.

One could identify several distinct points in the transition from information scarcity to information surplus, an obvious one being the invention of the printing press. I will not repeat the whole history of that transition here but will say only that the transition has been completed very recently, some might argue since the 1990s. Therefore, educators who continue teaching as though we remain in an age of relative information scarcity can offer at least a partial defense if they end up in pedagogical court.

My granting that notwithstanding, we now live in a time of information surplus. In our time a suitable goal of education would be to create an educational experience in which our students learn to be wise sifters of information who possess good crap detectors. They need to become critical users of information. In a time of information surplus, students should engage in scaffolded critical interaction with materials. The educator's instructional focus should be on helping students use content critically and wisely. Although we still need to submit grades to the Registrar's Office, our assessment should be formative as well as summative. Our assessment of our students' work needs to be interactive, and it should lead us to continuous micro-adjustments to our instruction.

In Chapter 3, I continue framing the catalogue of strategies by introducing several more concepts, ideas, and even physical places. Some of these are widely known to educators and others are relatively unknown.

REFERENCES

Badley, K., and Patrick, M., Eds. (2022). *The complexities of authority in the classroom: Fostering democracy for student learning.* Routledge.

Denker, K. J. (2013). Student response systems and facilitating the large lecture basic communication course: Assessing engagement and learning. *Communication Teacher* 27(1), 50–69. https://doi.org/10.1080/17404622.2012.730622

Dewey, J. (1902). *The child and the curriculum.* University of Chicago Press.

Dewey, J. (1938). *Experience and education.* Macmillan.

Fies, C., & Marshall, J. (2006). Classroom response systems: A review of the literature. *Journal of Science Education and Technology,* 15(1), 101–109.

Heflin, H., Shewmaker, J., & Nguyen, J. (2017). Impact of mobile technology on student attitudes, engagement, and learning. *Computers and Education,* 107(April), 91–99.

Kelly, P. A., Haidet, P., Schneider, V., Searle, N., Seidel, C. L., & Richards, B. F. (2005). A comparison of in-class learner engagement across lecture, problem-based learning, and team learning using the STROBE classroom observation tool. *Teaching and Learning in Medicine: An International Journal* 17(2), 112–118.

Maphosa, C., Kalenga, R. C., & Chimbala, R. (2017). Displacing or depressing the lecture system: Towards a transformative model of instruction for the 21st century university. *The Anthropologist* 14(6), 555–563. https://doi.org/10.1080/09720073. 2012.11891281

Palmer, P. (1983). *To know as we are known: A spirituality of education.* Harper.

Rogers, C. R. (1969). *Freedom to learn.* Merrill.

Terrion, J. L., & Aceti, V. (2012). Perceptions of the effects of clicker technology on student learning and engagement: A study of freshmen chemistry students. *Research in Learning Technology* 20(2), 1–11.

Wineburg, S. (2018). *Why learn history (When it's already on your phone).* University of Chicago Press.

Three

Throughout this book I use several concepts almost as ordinary language, and I want to take this one chapter to explain some of those briefly for the sake of my readers. The concepts I list and explain here are central to my own way of framing teaching and of attempting to engage my own students. The concepts I treat in what follows are these: The engaging classroom, multi-modal teaching, shared classroom authority or epistemic authority (whose knowledge counts?), student self-efficacy, meta-cognition, kentopia, flow (from Mihaly Csikszentmihalyi), tact (from Max van Manen), critical reflection and critical thinking, the flipped classroom, and curriculum design. Only one of these is of my own invention; with the others, I credit the originators where their identity is known.

ENGAGING CLASSROOMS

A robust and growing body of research into engaging college classrooms is available to anyone interested in moving into a more interactive mode of teaching in higher education. A sizable portion of this research has focused on how to make lecture teaching more engaging for students. Clark (2018) suggests that the contents of lectures themselves have the capacity to engage students. Others have combined the lecture with problem-based learning (Delialioğlu, 2011), group discussions (Garside, 1996), co-operative learning (Cavanagh, 2011), student-response systems, such as clickers for quick classroom polling (Hall et al, 2005; Frick et al, 2020), and even magic tricks (Moss et al, 2017) in their attempts to increase student engagement during lectures. In my view, as commendable as these attempts to increase student engagement with lectures might be, those using them seem to be negotiating at the edges, so to speak, inasmuch as they remain committed to the lecture as the best way for students to learn curriculum materials.

DOI: 10.4324/9781003259596-4

MULTI-MODAL TEACHING

Without turning this chapter into a screed against the lecture, I want simply to suggest that replacing the lecture with other modes of instruction—if professors use those modes of instruction well—can produce dramatic increases in student engagement with the course contents. I need to emphasize that I mean *modes* plural, not with one other mode. In 2003, Edward Tufte offered this comic, searing critique of mono-modal lecturing when he wrote that "power corrupts and PowerPoint corrupts absolutely." My agreement with Tufte is not my point here; my point is that the professor who uses the same mode of teaching—any mode of teaching—day after day after day will end up with disengaged students. In short, we must vary the modes of instruction. In Chapters 4 through 14 of this book, I offer dozens of ideas about how to do that.

SHARED CLASSROOM AUTHORITY

In traditional education, where the professor transmits knowledge to students, epistemic authority rests largely with the educator. After all, the professor is the one with the expertise, as represented by several degrees, and the professor also has a contract with the university to teach. Students expect their professors to stand, to exercise control over classroom electronics and how classroom time is spent, and so on. In other words, there are expectations on all sides that the professor will have and exercise authority in the room. One researcher, in fact (Moustakim, 2007), found that students resisted his attempts to move into a more interactive mode because, in their view, he was the professor. I have experienced this kind of resistance myself, periodically having heard variations of "You're the one being paid, you tell us what's what."

Without repeating at length the contents of a recent book on classroom authority (Badley & Patrick, 2022), I will note here what I wrote there: I have consistently observed that students' engagement with course contents increases as a result of my having shared epistemic authority or what I call *classroom authority* with them. In other chapters herein I offer several specific strategies by which a professor can share authority with students. Here, I define it simply: Shared authority means that students have a significant measure of control over their learning and, as I noted in Chapter 2, that the professor and students approach the subject—what Parker Palmer calls the *big subject*—together

(Palmer, 1983). Figure 2.2 illustrates Palmer's approach to instruction, and by implication, to the contrast between two epistemologies.

STUDENT SELF-EFFICACY AND LEARNING POWER

Those not familiar with this phrase should see the work of Albert Bandura (1977, 1997). In summary, self-efficacy has two aspects: The student is succeeding academically and knows it. I don't think Bandura quite meant the level of bravado the "No Fear" T-shirt seems to imply, but he may have been close to the English phrase, "I've got this," as long as it's said humbly. I know my readers can think of two opposites of the picture Bandura draws. One, the student is not succeeding but does not seem to grasp that fact. Two, the student is succeeding but feels like a failure ("I only got 97%!"). Because the second section of this book (Chapters 5 and 6) is titled "Strategies for Building Student Self-Efficacy," I will not define or explain Bandura's work at great length in this chapter.

META-COGNITION—THINKING ABOUT THINKING

Most undergraduates will know this concept because many of their elementary and secondary teachers will have talked about it and have found various ways to implement it. Elementary teachers tend to use the language of *thinking about thinking*. Secondary teachers tend to use the phrase in the section title above. K–12 educators ask their students to think about what steps they took to complete a task, why they drew the conclusion they drew about a given topic, and why they gave that particular answer (right or wrong) on a test. Meta-cognition may be a kind of expanded form of the traditional expectation among mathematics educators that students show their work.

Throughout this volume, but especially with reference to assessment, I refer to meta-cognition because it connects to self-efficacy. Bandura and others have identified dozens of conditions for and correlates with student success. Because students' encouragement and ability to engage in meta-cognition regularly appear in such research, I have incorporated meta-cognition into my own language and practice.

KENTOPIA

This semi tongue-in-cheek concept refers to that time or place in higher education where all students engage fully with their professors all the time. In kentopia, these same students achieve what was once considered mathematically impossible: They all have above-average grades. In kentopian institutions, all meetings are organized and short, and all administrative procedures are simple, intuitive, and explained clearly. In kentopia, professors never receive or check their work email after 5:00. The IT department seems to understand intuitively professors' classroom technology needs, and all university-related software works perfectly. Even the courseware has all the features each professor wants and no others. Would stipulating that stacks of grading take care of themselves be a bridge too far?

FLOW

Mihaly Csikszentmihalyi's work on flow (1982, 2000, 2002), especially his *Flow:The Psychology of Optimal Experience* (1990), has deeply shaped my own thinking about how classrooms work best. His shaping on my thinking has been so thorough, in fact, that with my colleague Susanna Steeg Thornhill, I wrote at length about Csikszentmihalyi and flow in *Generating Tact and Flow for Effective Teaching and Learning* (2020). That shameless plug out of the way, I regularly refer to flow in this volume and will sketch the concept of flow here.

Briefly, a flow state has these qualities. Individuals in flow feel a sense of control, despite being somewhere near the limits of their abilities. The person in a flow state usually has a sense of the activity being its own reward or purpose. People in flow states lose their awareness of time and their self consciousness.

On Csikszentmihalyi's account, certain conditions must be in place for someone to get into a flow state and, as educators, these conditions are of special interest if we want our students to get into flow during our classes or while doing outside-of-class work for our classes. The first pre-condition he names is goal clarity. Is the purpose of the assignment or the class activity clear? He ties goal buy-in to goal clarity. Do our students agree with us about the purpose (and importance) of a given assignment? Is the student receiving clear feedback? I confess to being glad that Csikszentmihalyi did not place the caveat *and timely* on that condition because my turnaround times on students' work have not always been exemplary. Over the decades of his work on flow, Csikszentmihalyi's list of pre-conditions evolved, but two final conditions consistently appear: Concentration in the task at hand and the balance between challenge and skill. In the previous paragraph, I noted that people in flow have a sense of control even though they may be performing at or near the limit of their abilities. On Csikszentmihalyi's telling, one cannot get into flow watching television because there is no challenge. Likewise, one cannot get into flow if the challenge is far beyond one's skills, for example, when I play a world champion in tennis or when I try get Microsoft Word to work the way I want it to.

Three decades of following Csikszentmihalyi's work have led me as a professor always to want to plan a class session so that my students get into a flow state, what jazz musicians call the groove and athletes call the zone. In fact, with Susan Jackson, Csikszentmihalyi has written about flow in sports (1999).

TACT

In the book on flow and tact I advertised above, my colleague Susanna Steeg Thornhill and I offer classroom flow narratives from several dozen educators. We framed these stories with reference not only to Csikszentmihalyi's concept of flow but also with reference to Max van Manen's concept of tact (1991, 2016). I mention van Manen here because I also make reference to tact from time to time in this volume. With the word tact, van Manen refers to the ease with which some educators seem able to manage a classroom, initiate and sustain a discussion, understand and respond to students' questions, and so on. He refers to those among us who make it look easy. Whether I like it or not, as a Canadian I hear about great hockey players. Perhaps the greatest of them all, Wayne Gretzky, is reputed to have said that "the good player always knows where the puck is … and the great player knows where the puck is going to be." My understanding of van Manen's concept of tact is somewhere between the two parts of Gretzky's claim. To the point of this volume, I am convinced that teachers with high tact are more likely to end up with engaged students.

CRITICAL REFLECTION AND CREATIVE THINKING

In Chapters 1 and 2, I used the language of critical reflection and creative thinking without defining those terms. Throughout this volume, I use the phrases critical reflection and critical thinking interchangeably. And—as do many educators—I see significant overlaps between critical thinking and creative thinking. In Chapter 7, I return to these related issues with reference to the matter of classroom climate. Later, I focus on them for the whole of Chapter 15. I offer this brief introduction to them here with reference to two hotbeds of thought and creativity to which I refer periodically throughout the book: Building 20 at the Massachusetts Institute of Technology and the Skunk Works at Lockheed Martin Aerospace in Burbank, California. In sum, until it was torn down in 1995, Building 20 at MIT was a hotbed of interdisciplinarity, creativity, and invention for five decades (Lehrer, 2012). The Lockheed Skunk Works, still in operation, began about the same time as Building 20 and has a similar record of creativity and invention. I think both settings should interest educators because the people who worked in both settings somehow had their creativity unleashed so they could think what was literally unthinkable (using literally in its literal sense). For example, the Skunk Works developed aircraft that could not be seen on radar (stealth), an idea that was unthinkable at the time. My question—and it may be kentopian—how can we create classrooms where students do work and think thoughts of which they never would have imagined themselves capable under ordinary circumstances?

FLIPPED CLASSROOM

Most undergraduates will know the meaning of this phrase because they will have had a few courses or portions of courses structured this way during their secondary education. At its simplest, in the flipped classroom, students read and research outside the classroom and then use their class-time to process their new knowledge, ask questions of their teacher or classmates, discuss implications of what they have learned, and so on. Thus, class-time is put to other uses than transmitting information. Because an online search of "flipped classroom" (even with quotation marks) will generate millions of records, I will not explain it further here. But I will make reference to it periodically throughout this book.

CURRICULUM DESIGN

As I write this paragraph in late 2021, the idea of curriculum design seems to be still on the ascendency. Unfortunately, educators use the word in a bewildering variety of ways, and my own rather restricted meaning is not prominent among those ways. One use of the word warrants mention here: Universal Design for Learning (UDL). The core of UDL is that educators should take into account that learners come to class with a wide variety of needs and approaches to learning. We should plan—design—lessons to include all those kinds of learners. This emphasis has gained prominence in K–12 education and, at the time of writing, is growing in higher education. Without cataloguing the many other ways contemporary educators are using the word *design*, I will state simply that throughout this book I use the word with reference to the application of aesthetic and architectural principles to course, unit, and class planning. I noted earlier the important influence that Mihaly Csikszentmihalyi has had on my thinking about education. Architect Christopher Alexander has exercised a similar influence.

In his books on building and town planning (for example, Alexander et al, 1977; Alexander, 1979), he promotes and explains a set of principles which, in his view, should govern the design of the buildings we inhabit and the outdoor spaces we use. His principles include strong centers, clear boundaries, clear entrances and exits, green spaces, coherence, and harmony. I have found ways to apply these architectural and planning principles to the tasks of designing curriculum, courses, and the parts of courses. With reference to the earlier heading on multi-modal teaching (page 20), one design principle is the need for both repetition and variety.

At risk of having this chapter become a kind of running advertisement for my own books, I must note that I explored Alexander's ideas at length in the 2018 book, *Curriculum Planning with Design Language: Building Elegant Courses and Units*. I am grateful that that title is now being used as a textbook in graduate curriculum design courses. Many other educators have explored how Alexander's work with pattern languages might apply to course and lesson design (Goodyear, 2005; Goodyear & Yang, 2009; Mor & Winters, 2008; Olsen, 2008).

CONCLUSION

I have offered nearly a dozen concepts here, all of which inform the strategies at the core of this book. Recognizably, in some cases I use these in their standard senses. In other cases, I (or others) stipulate a meaning that varies somewhat from contemporary usage. In one case, I made up my own cheeky concept. I have given over three chapters to the foundation for what follows. In the next chapter I begin in earnest the core project of this book, the catalogue of strategies for engaging college and university students.

REFERENCES

Alexander, C. (1979). *The timeless way of building*. Oxford University Press.

Alexander, C., Ishikawa, S., Silverstein, M., Jacobson, M., Fiksdahl-King, I., & Angel, S. (1977). *A pattern language: Towns, buildings, construction*. Oxford University Press.

Badley, K. (2018). *Curriculum planning with design language: Building elegant courses and units*. Routledge.

Badley, K., & Patrick, M. (Eds.). (2022). *The complexities of authority in the classroom: Fostering democracy for student learning*. Routledge.

Bandura, A. (1977). Self-efficacy: Toward a unifying theory of behavioral change. *Psychological Review*, 84(2), 191–215.

Bandura, A. (1997). *Self-efficacy: The exercise of control*. Worth Publishers.

Clark, L. B. (2018). Critical pedagogy in the university: Can a lecture be critical pedagogy? *Policy Futures in Education*, 16(8), 995–999. https://doi.org/10.1177/1478210318787053

Cavanagh, M. (2011). Students' experiences of active engagement through cooperative learning activities in lectures. *Active Learning in Higher Education* 12(1), 23–33. doi: 10.1177/1469787410387724

Csikszentmihalyi, M. (1982). Intrinsic motivation and effective teaching: A flow analysis. In J. L. Bess (Ed.), *Motivating professors to teach effectively* (pp. 72–89). Jossey-Bass.

Csikszentmihalyi, M. (1990). *Flow: The psychology of optimal experience*. Harper and Row.

Csikszentmihalyi, M. (2000). Education for the 21st century. *Education Week*, 19(32), 64–66.

Csikszentmihalyi, M. (2002). Motivating people to learn. http://www.edutopia.org/mihaly-csikszentmihalyi-motivating-people-learn

Delialioğlu, Ö. (2011). Student engagement in blended learning environments with lecture-based and problem-based instructional approaches. *International Journal for the Scholarship of Teaching and Learning*, 5(2), Article 20.

Frick, H., Birt, J., & Water., J. (2020). Enhancing student engagement in large management accounting lectures. Having them use devices to answer multiple choice questions during a lecture. *Accounting and Finance*, 60, 271–298.

Garside, C. (1996). Look who's talking: A comparison of lecture and group discussion teaching strategies in developing critical thinking skills. *Communication Education*, 45(3), 212–227. doi:10.1080/03634529609379050

Goodyear, P. (2005). Educational design and networked learning: Patterns, pattern languages and design practice. *Australasian Journal of Educational Technology*, 21(1), 82–101.

Goodyear, P., & Yang, D. F. (2009). Patterns and pattern languages in educational design. In L. Lockyer, S. Bennett, S. Agostinho, & B. Harper (Eds.), *Handbook of research on learning design and learning objects: Issues, applications and technologies* (pp. 167–187). IGI Global.

Hall, R. H., Collier, H. Y., Thomas, M. L., & Hilgers, M. G. (2005). A student response system for increasing engagement, motivation, and learning in high enrollment lectures. *Proceedings of the eleventh Americas conference on information systems*, Omaha, NE, USA, August 11th–14th, pp. 1–8.

Jackson, S., & Csikszentmihalyi, M. (1999). *Flow in sport: The keys to optimal experiences and performances*. Human Kinetics.

Lehrer, J. (2012). Groupthink: The brainstorming myth. *The New Yorker*, January 30. https://www.newyorker.com/magazine/2012/01/30/groupthink

Mor, Y., & Winters, N. (2008). Participatory design in open education: A workshop model for developing a pattern language. *Journal of Interactive Media in Education, 2008*(1), Article 12.

Moss, S. A., Irons, M., & Boland, M. (2017). The magic of magic: The effect of magic tricks on subsequent engagement with lecture material. *British Journal of Educational Psychology 87*(1), 32–42. https://doi.org/10.1111/bjep.12133

Moustakim, B. (2007). From transmission to dialogue: Promoting critical engagement in higher education teaching and learning. *Educational Action Research 15*(2), 209–220.

Olsen, D. (2008). *Teaching patterns: A pattern language for improving the quality of instruction in higher education settings*. (Unpublished doctoral dissertation), Utah State University, Logan, UT.

Palmer, P. (1983). *To know as we are known: A spirituality of education*. Harper.

Steeg Thornhill, S., & Badley, K. (2020). *Generating tact and flow for effective teaching and learning*. Routledge.

Tufte, E. (2003). PowerPoint is evil: Power corrupts, PowerPoint corrupts absolutely. *Wired*. https://www.wired.com/2003/09/ppt2/

Van Manen, M. (1991). *The tact of teaching: The meaning of pedagogical thoughtfulness*. SUNY Press.

Van Manen, M. (2016). *Pedagogical tact: Knowing what to do when you don't know what to do*. Routledge.

Four

Much of what I describe here happens best in what I call a classroom community. By that I mean that I get to know my students and they gain some familiarity with each other. I will not specify some kentopian degree of familiarity but, ideally, I would like all my students to know at least a few others in the class by name. I focus in this chapter on strategies to build that kind of community. These are not teaching strategies *per se*; rather they are ways to build an ethos or climate in which students enjoy learning, to build a classroom to which students want to come. I see large overlaps with what Parker Palmer calls a community of trust (1998). In his vision, students can openly and safely express their views and the foundations of those views, and they do not have to hide their identities.

Building classroom community or a community of trust is a semester-long project with many aspects. In what follows, I note three major areas of focus: Hospitality, ownership of the class, and humor. There is much more to building community than these three aspects, and I raise other matters in later chapters. But we begin here, on the first day.

THE FIRST DAY

Semester Start Strategies, the third section of this book, begins with several strategies for building community. Because I treat them at length there (in Chapter 7), I will not include details here. But the four first-day, community-building strategies I recommend there are name tents, professor Q&A, the DNA strand, and students' learning objectives for the course. Very briefly, I ask students to make folded, card-stock name plates so I can begin learning their names on day 1. Professor Q&A is simple. I announce that because many of them do not know me, they can ask me questions about anything (and I reserve the right to decline answering). The DNA strand is a discussion starter. I draw a DNA strand on the board or show a slide of one I have prepared

DOI: 10.4324/9781003259596-5

that says "Curriculum" on one side and "Your Life" on the other. I ask my students what the protein bars are that connect the two. What do we need to do in this class to connect the class to your life? Finally, I ask students about their learning objectives for the course as a way to help them understand that the syllabus represents my beginning vision for the course but that we need to shape the course together and that doing so involves my hearing what they want to learn. I treat these four items in Chapter 7 but I list them here because they relate centrally to building classroom community.

HOSPITALITY

Research into showing hospitality to students is relatively recent and remains thin (Haswell et al, 2009; Schneider & Keenan, 2015; Kramer, 2016; Palmer, 1998; Smith, 2011; Smith & Carvill, 2000; Stratman, 2015; Tremmel, 1984), but more educators are recognizing the benefits hospitality pays to students and professors when classrooms become places where people are named, recognized, and heard. I have tried to show hospitality several ways.

Classroom Food and Drink

I own a classroom food operation that fits in one banker's box. It includes an electric kettle, a French press coffee maker, napkins, silverware, cups, ground coffee, and a wooden box with a variety of teas. I usually bring some baked goods as well, baking cookies myself once per term. A three-hour block can be challenging, and a bump in food energy can help students pay attention better and for longer. For any number of reasons, some students come to a morning class without having had breakfast or an afternoon class without having had lunch. They need blood sugar to attend fully. My hospitality helps them attend fully and their attention helps us all do the work we need to do in class.

Without implying any comparison of the physiological and affective dimensions of my bringing food to class, I do want to note that hospitality sends an important message about how I view the classroom space and our joint membership in the class. Several years ago, when one of my students accused me of bringing food and coffee to class simply because I wanted students to like coming there, I replied that he was exactly right. There's more to it of course, but I don't know of anyone who would argue against having students who want to come to class.

The logistics of offering hospitality at the basic level I have described are relatively straightforward. First, and of course, I have to carry my hospitality kit to class from my office. When I am assigned a classroom with a locked cabinet, I leave the kit in that room. Ordinarily, I arrive to class early enough to plug the kettle in, but someone needs to press the coffee down after the requisite time, so I usually ask if a student would be willing to do the coffee each week. Consistently, someone volunteers to serve the class in this way for the whole semester, often someone who has actually worked as a barista. This strategy would obviously not work in large classes. Adapting it to online settings is simple; I ask students to have a hot beverage in hand at the start of class.

Another strand of writing on hospitality approaches it as something apart from food or perhaps beyond food (Schneider & Keenan, 2015; Smith & Carvill, 2000; Smith, 2011; Stratman, 2015; Tremmel, 1984). In this wider framing of hospitality, the professor offers the class itself as an invitation to students. As is the case with the coffee, tea, and baking, students are invited to enjoy the intellectual food on offer but, of course, they may hold back if they wish. Understood this way, classroom hospitality implies a whole range of postures, gestures, and practices.

Greetings at the Door

From working with educator colleagues in Kenya on seven different occasions, I learned that the work of learning begins only after the professor has greeted everyone in the room. Many K–12 educators greet students at the door of the classroom as they enter, some of them in creative, humorous, and even heart-melting ways. Fewer professors do so, and I did not begin this practice myself until my first visit to Kenya. Full disclosure ... on my first day teaching on my first trip there, a Kenyan colleague expressed mild alarm that my Canadian colleagues and I had simply launched in, rather than beginning class with a round of greetings.

Greeting students does imply that unpacking, checking that you have all the requisite teaching materials ready, and preparing the classroom electronics will require you to arrive earlier than otherwise (and you may need to wait for another professor to vacate the room).

Welcoming Music

About 4 or 5 minutes before class is to start, I play a song through the classroom projection system. Essentially, this serves as my adaptation of my practice (from decades ago) of putting a cartoon on the overhead projector before class to pull students' eyes toward the screen and help them relax a bit before class started. My reasoning for this is simple: Almost everyone enjoys music and I find that students' anticipation of class increases when I play a song through the classroom's sound system. Playing music shows I have thought about my students, their feelings, and their having arrived early to class. Music reduces pre-class stress (Ferrer et al, 2014; Ploukou & Panagopoulou, 2018), and it allows me to test my laptop's connection to the classroom electronics. I time the start to the length of the song so the song ends at exactly at the class's nominal start time.

Given the variety of tastes represented in a typical classroom, I choose middle of the road songs. I always select pieces beforehand to make sure the contents and performance are acceptable for classroom use and that the recording has the requisite technical quality. In online teaching, I recommend using this strategy as students return from break (in a three-hour class), but at the start of class, I recommend having your camera on and chatting with those who have joined the meeting early. Of course, YouTube is my main resource for these welcoming songs. Students also respond well to fun performances of classics, such as these:

- "Beethoven students clapping" at https://www.youtube.com/watch?v=mh9Mf-nBvp4&t=56s
- "Train passengers sing Over the Rainbow" at https://www.youtube.com/watch?v=xctzp0dp9uc

Students also seem to love stars who share the stage with a fan. Search any pop singer's name in YouTube with "with fan" or "with audience member" to find such videos.

The Circle Meeting

Most undergraduates and some graduates will be familiar with the circle meeting because of its growing popularity among K–12 educators. It is also known as the *morning meeting*, *class meeting*, or *closing* circle (when used at the end of the day in K–12 education). In face-to-face teaching, it involves having students literally stand in a circle and respond to a prompt provided by the professor.

Why use this strategy? The circle meeting builds community among students, in part because they all can see each other's faces, which they cannot do seated in most classrooms. It allows those who rarely speak in class to speak, especially if the topic offered that day is on the light or innocent side. Some K–12 educators use it daily, implying that, while students might be surprised initially that a professor knows about it or uses it, they will know what to do and they will respond. Students will be familiar with rules such as "anyone can pass," "limit your comment to 10 words," or "everyone must say something." I sometimes work around the circle in order, but I find that tension is reduced if students are able to speak when they want to (or not at all). The procedure is simple: The professor offers a prompt and the students respond to that prompt. The professor may say thank you after students' comments but must thank every student who speaks or none.

Professors who find themselves resisting this strategy because they associate it with K–12 education or even with primary education should try it, even once. It may seem too soft for some classes or a waste of instructional time, but I include it in this book because of my observation that students who feel they are part of a classroom community engage more with the course contents than students who think of a class as simply something they need to do to graduate. That is, they learn more in the net time remaining than they would have learned if we had not invested the minutes in a circle meeting. Furthermore, the circle meeting is a way to recognize Native or First Nations epistemology ... that we are in a circle and we learn from each other.

Those wanting references and more resources can search "classroom morning meeting" on YouTube, where there are several examples. Most online examples relate to K–12 classrooms but they nonetheless illustrate how the meeting works. I do not know of a published resource focused on higher education. A variety of books are on offer, all related to K–12 classrooms.

On the recommendation of my colleague, Carla Nelson, I have repeatedly used a printed version of Peter Reynolds's children's book

Ish (2005) as a prompt for circle meetings in face-to-face classrooms. I usually have a student read the book aloud and then ask the class to respond to the question, "How teacher-ish do you feel at this point in the semester?" Later in the term, after students have developed some trust in each other, they usually feel free to report that they are feeling good about teaching, adrift and wondering, raring to go, and so on. For online classes, I use any of several online versions of this book. If "How teacher-ish do you feel?" is on the heavy side, then a lighter prompt might be along the lines of "What do people often comment on when they think about the town, city, or country you originally came from?" or "What did you do in the last seven days that was out of character?" Obviously a wealth of prompts for circle meeting responses is on offer in poetry, children's literature other than Reynolds's book Ish, and many other genres.

I also have used quotations from famous educators and lines from popular films, usually on a slide, and, of course, still shots from popular films with the prompt super-imposed on the picture. A still shot from a film allows the professor to open up a discussion of the contrast between the on-screen portrayals of professionals—reel nurses, reel chemists, reel archeologists, reel mathematicians—and the real nurses, chemists, archeologists, and mathematicians we hope our graduates become. I discuss the use of video clips at greater length in Chapter 12 and offer more help there on how to prompt such discussion.

Colleague Jon Coutts has developed a creative way to take attendance that fits under the umbrella of the class meeting or morning meeting. When he calls students' names, they are to respond not with "present," but with an answer to a simple question along the lines of "name one planet" or "name one singer." With this system, every student gets to speak before instruction begins, and always on a lightweight topic.

THIS IS OUR CLASS

Without doubt, the professor and the student do not enjoy the same status in the university as a whole or in a given class. I do not need to list the history or the details of those differences in status. However, those differences notwithstanding, the professor and the students share a common objective: That the students learn the contents of the course. In this brief section, I offer a couple effective ways to remind students of this common purpose.

The Language of We

Language is key to building classroom community. How we frame our work as professors powerfully influences how students frame their work as students in our classes. For example, the words *we* and *you* strike students' ears in very different ways. *We* connotes joint effort and sends the message that my job as professor is to help my students achieve the class's learning objectives. To refer to metaphors of teaching for a moment, *we* language fits with metaphors of teaching as coaching or teaching as guiding (Badley & Hollabaugh, 2012). On the other hand, *you* language may remind students of the differential power relationship between professor and students (which I know is real). Such language may strike students as my talking down to them or, to use contemporary language, my *schooling* them. Metaphors of teacher as judge come to mind here. I want to emphasize both to my students and to you, my readers, that I want my students to understand that, in my view, we are in the class together and I want them to succeed.

A Slide I Often Show on the First Day of Class

If you finish this course a worse person that you started, you should sue me.

If you finish this course unchanged, then you should get a refund.

If you finish this course a better person than when you started, then together we have succeeded.

Rather than the language of *class* or *this class*, I always use the language of *our class* to remind my students and myself that that we are working together toward a common goal; it is not me dragging them along and guaranteeing attendance by whatever stealthy means I can think of. There's much more to this than I'm saying here, but read Parker Palmer's *To Know as We Are Known* (1983) for a detailed explanation of the epistemology underlying my practice.

Not Reading the Riot Act

The first class after a major assessment (such as a mid-term exam) offers a key moment to underline that professor and students comprise a *we*. Some educators start that class by addressing the whole class about working harder, focusing, keeping up, and so on. I do not know the research on the efficacy of such exhortations, but one effect colleagues report to me is that students are usually quiet for the rest of that day's class. The question of whether learning and performance improve remains unanswered.

As an alternative to reading the riot act, as one colleague calls it, I organize a student-led *turnaround discussion*. The day before I return a major assessment, I ask for one or two volunteers to pick a recent coach movie and select the turn-around speech scene ("Yes, the members of the other team are all wealthy, good-looking, and so on, but we can do this because we have heart and skill!"). I ask that student or those students to come prepared to show the selected clip to class and to lead the conversation about what we need to do to improve in the second half of the semester.

A humorous list I often show to supplement the student-led non-reading of the Riot Act.

TOP TEN POSSIBLE MOTIVATIONS TO HANG IN THERE

10. Cash
9. Hanging in there is easier than dental work.
8. The old higher lifetime higher income argument.
7. Those who enter a contest for a free trip abroad.
6. The professor said to.
5. Cite examples such as Nelson Mandela who hung in there.
4. The Grand Vision speech ... all the DNA that ever existed so that blah, blah, blah ...
3. The professor promised to keep bringing food to class.
2. The psychotherapist said to.
1. Because you know we're all in this together and we have all the resources we need to complete this course successfully.

The day students get back a major assignment or gather for the first time after a mid-term exam is a significant opportunity to build the sense that professor and students comprise a team with a common learning task. Having students lead that conversation shows respect, not only for the students leading the conversation but for the whole class. Framing the question of improvement as a joint effort helps build a community of trust. We are in this together; I am their coach and supporter, not their monitor.

HUMOR

Despite my strong interest in humor, I have not read much research on the effectiveness of humor in the classroom. Some professors and some students believe that educators must be funny. I want to distinguish entertainment and comedy from having a sense of humor. Given the public character of our work, having a sense of humor is important; we must be able to laugh at ourselves and at our own mistakes. Still, the sheer number of successful educators who pointedly do not try to entertain their students ought to tell us all we need to know about the importance of that kind of funny: It is simply not necessary. My own attempts at humor range across a number of genres or styles. I make frequent television, movie, and music references but purposely get them wrong, asking for example, if Rachel and Joey ever managed to get together before the television series *Friends* finally ended. Botched cultural references offer a secondary level of humor because my students know I actually know who was supposed to end up with whom. I also work self-deprecating remarks into conversations about my lack of knowledge about technology, not knowing that "Free Britney" referred to a pop star's contract and not to an independence movement in western France, and not knowing that ISIS was not the acronym for the International Space Station. Also, from time to time, I hold up signs with sayings on them such as "Professor's Opinion," "Rhetorical Question," "Just Joking," and "The Truth!"

POWERPOINT KARAOKE

I have built a number of slide decks on different topics for use in PowerPoint karaoke (search that string on YouTube for examples). Simply, PowerPoint karaoke entails speaking or teaching from a set of slides one has never seen before. The origins of this form of comedy are murky, with some claiming that improv theater groups invented it and others suggesting that librarians were the inventors. Its origins aside, I ask students to nominate one or two people to "teach" that day's topic based on a set of 20 random slides. Students usually nominate classmates who talk a lot in class, so the chance of creating a traumatic situation for any individual student is reduced. Teaching through 20 slides in PowerPoint karaoke should take six minutes at most. The six-minute investment pays interest. That is, it piques students' interest in the day's topic and the higher levels of engagement result in greater learning.

THE HAKA: TRANSLATED

Most students are familiar with the haka, originally a Māori welcome ritual but adapted by the New Zealand national rugby team as a means of intimidating its opponents. At my request, a videographer added subtitles I wrote to a video of the New Zealand team's delivery of the haka at the 2019 World Cup. But the wildly erroneous translation I wrote is about how the All Blacks (Ōpango in Māori) lacked the courage and strength to be educators so they had to play rugby instead. My students find this both funny and encouraging. To my point here, they view it as my showing that I support them in their effort to become competent beginners in a difficult profession. Obviously, the haka can be mistranslated to encourage students in any academic discipline in anticipation of entering any profession. For that matter, one could produce a faux translation that focused simply on the challenges of being university or college students, without addressing any specific vocational aspirations.

The Haka Translated

Are any of you still teaching? No!
We used to be teachers, We used to be teachers
It was hard, hard, hard ... too hard
Much too hard, Much too hard, Much too hard
You must be stronger than a rugby player to teach school
You must have a mind like a steel trap, a steel trap
You must have reflexes like a snake, like a snake
And the strength of ten giants, ten giants
Rugby is for soft men and old people
Teaching is only for the strong
For warriors stronger than us.

Ken Badley

CONCLUSION

As I noted at the start of the chapter, building classroom community is a semester-long project. I have seen the postures and strategies, I suggest work consistently, but always as part of a much larger picture that includes varying instructional strategies, offering flexibility and choice in assessment, responding at length to students' written work, and dozens more elements. In short, in this chapter I offer some starting points, not a comprehensive plan.

REFERENCES

Badley, K., & Hollabaugh, J. (2012). Metaphors for teaching and learning. In K. Badley and H. van Brummelen (Eds.), *Metaphors we teach by*, (pp. 52–67). Wipf & Stock.

Ferrer, E., Lew, P., Jung, S., Janeke, E., Garcia, M., Peng, C., Poon, G., Rathod, V., Beckwith, S., & Tam, C. (2014). Playing music to relieve stress in a college classroom environment. *College Student Journal*, 48(3), 481–494.

Haswell, J., Haswell, R., & Blalock, G. (2009). Hospitality in college composition courses. *College Composition and Communication*, 60(4), 707–727.

Kramer, J. (2016). A Deweyan reflection: The potential of hospitality and movement in the classroom. *Curriculum and Teaching Dialogue*, 18(1/2), 75A.

Palmer, P. (1983). *To know as we are known: A spirituality of education*. Harper.

Palmer, P. (1998). *The courage to teach*. Jossey-Bass.

Ploukou, S., & Panagopoulou, E. (2018). Playing music improves well-being of oncology nurses. *Applied Nursing Research*, 39, 77–80.

Reynolds, P. (2005). *Ish*. Walker Books.

Schneider, D., & Keenan. E. (2015). From being known in the classroom to "moments of meeting": What intersubjectivity offers contemplative pedagogy. *The Journal of Contemplative Inquiry* 2(1), 1–16.

Smith, D. (2011). Hospitality, language pedagogy, and communities of practice. https://onchristianteaching.com/hospitality-language-pedagogy-and-communities-of-practice/

Smith, D., & Carvill, B. (2000). *The gift of the stranger: Faith, hospitality, and foreign language learning*. Eerdmans.

Stratman, J. (2015). What's in a name: The place of recognition in a hospitable classroom. *International Journal of Christianity & Education*, 19(1), 27–37.

Tremmel, R. (1984). Hospitality in the classroom: The teaching stance of the writers in the schools. *Journal of Teaching Writing*, 3(2), 191–200.

Student Self-Efficacy and Assessment
Section II

In Chapter 3, I briefly introduced Albert Bandura's idea of self-efficacy. Bandura first suggested this concept decades ago (1977a, 1977b) and continued to work on it and its implications for several decades (1986, 1997). With the passage of time, other researchers produced a robust body of secondary literature, with applications in politics, psychology, leadership, and education. With reference specifically to education, I will summarize Bandura's dual-aspect idea very simply: Students experience a sense of high self-efficacy when they are succeeding academically and when they know they are succeeding.

Bandura's stipulation of these two conditions may bring to mind two other scenarios. We have all taught high-achieving students who had difficulty believing they were doing well academically ("I cannot believe how dumb I am!"). The strategies I offer in these two chapters are meant to help such students. Most readers have also taught students who struggle to grasp the course contents but somehow believe they have everything in hand ("Yes, it's almost ready to hand in."). The strategies I offer in these two chapters are for these students as well.

This second section of the book contains only two chapters, the first of which I have simply called "Strategies to Increase Student Self-Efficacy." I want to support all my students' efforts to achieve Bandura's first criterion, that they succeed academically. That desire implies that I will challenge those students who seem to flourish naturally in academic work and that I will help and create appropriate structures for those students who find academic work challenging. I begin in Chapter 5 by offering ways to encourage students to believe that they can do well and to view themselves as capable learners. I am not naïve about my students' potential; not only are they all not geniuses, some will not even graduate, but I do want to encourage them all to believe they can improve.

DOI: 10.4324/9781003259596-6

Chapter 6 focuses on assessment. Assessment remains one of the key means by which students draw conclusions—rightly or wrongly—about their own academic abilities. We know this ourselves, quite deeply, because we have all been in the student role. In Chapter 6, I describe some ways to assess students' work that allow them to engage more enthusiastically and more critically with the course materials, while demonstrating that they have achieved the course learning outcomes.

Five

If dozens of people had co-written this chapter with me, it would contain many more strategies than the few I list here. At that, several of these ideas came from other professors' classrooms. These strategies all contribute to students' sense of confidence in themselves or their sense of control over what they are learning, and therefore to their success.

THE *DAILY FORECAST*

For decades, I have distributed some kind of daily plan document, which always includes a schedule of planned activities, any needed outlines or written materials, scaffolding and discussion questions for the video clips the class will discuss, links to online resources, and so on. My George Fox University colleague, Susanna Steeg Thornhill, calls her daily plan document a *forecast*, in recognition that things don't always go to plan. I liked the tone of that word so I changed the name of my daily handout from *Daily Plan* to *Daily Forecast* about a decade ago. Students consistently tell me they love knowing in detail where we are headed each day. Their knowledge of where we're going increases their sense of control over their learning for each class session and thereby their efficacy. Secondarily, it increases their confidence that I know where I'm trying to lead the class each day. A sample *Daily Forecast* sheet appears in Appendix A (pages 214–216) and illustrates what I distribute to students. Note in that example that I have placed housekeeping and administrative items at the end of the document—that is, at the end of the class session—and that I included there a note about the topic of the next class. I leave administrative and housekeeping to the end because I want to use my students' start-of-class energy for diving into our content, not for details about what comes next.

DOI: 10.4324/9781003259596-7

My rationale for using this strategy is simple: Increasing students' knowledge of what a given class will involve increases their confidence and their self-efficacy as learners. It also demonstrates to students very clearly that we are working from a plan that their professor has worked hard to prepare for what they will do that day. The professor who simply works through a deck of slides every day needs to distribute no such sheet, but in an activity-based classroom, professor and students alike need quick access to the same information and a document to help them judge their pacing against the time available. Professors who use *Daily Forecast* or *Daily Plan* sheets consistently receive comments about how helpful students find those sheets.

A *Daily Forecast* sheet adapts easily to online settings. With the reduced levels of non-verbal communication in online teaching, such a sheet likely becomes more important to both professor and students than it is in face-to-face classes. We may be unable to judge our students' engagement as easily in online teaching, but with such a plan, everyone always knows what we are supposed to be doing and what we will do next. *Daily Forecast* sheets for online classes should make clear what parts of the class are full-class online, breakout rooms or groups, or working alone offline. These different modes are illustrated by the sample in Appendix A, adapted without much modification from an online course taught in June and July 2020. In online settings, students appreciate receiving the outline in advance if possible; I usually aim to have it posted the night before class, even if I do not have all the details finished. In face-to-face classes, I usually distribute it at the start of class, but sometimes post it on the course wiki beforehand. For online courses that happen in single three-hour blocks, I recommend scheduling time when the whole class is not all meeting together.

HIDDEN GEMS

One way to build student self-efficacy is to remind students periodically that sometimes ordinary people do extra-ordinary things and that extra-ordinary people may be among us without our knowing. I address hidden gems in several ways. One is to recount ways that previous students helped shape the current course. Tell students that you adjusted the weight on an assignment or that you incorporated this or that class activity or assignment because of something a student said in a previous semester. Telling students about student contributions to your thinking about the course structure or contents sends several messages: you give credit where it's due, you listen to what students say, you are open to ideas and suggestions from others, you change, and you are always looking for ways to improve the course.

An enhanced version of the above strategy is to point students to stories about other students' exceptional discoveries and ideas. A good example comes from a British secondary student who discovered that the International Space Station was misinterpreting some of its data (search "British student solves NASA problem"). Without knowing all the details of that story, a professor and students can speculate about the classrooms that student sat in and the teachers who taught him. Did his teachers and classmates guess that they had a hidden gem in their classes? In Chapter 3, I mentioned Lockheed's Skunkworks and Building 20 at MIT, both useful for prompting class discussions about how university classrooms might be places where students could think the literally unthinkable.

Many professors get permission from former students to use their work as exemplars of good assignments. Permitted examples obviously can help students understand the purposes and parameters of an assignment. But to my point in this section of the chapter, showing such examples to students also communicates that the professor values students' good work

Showing YouTube clips of famous people performing in disguise offers another way to build students' self-efficacy. Search "Jimmy Fallon and U2 in NY subway" or "Jimmy Fallon and Miley Cyrus in NY subway" to find two such examples. I often show one of these clips in the second class session of a course, then I tell them that after the first class, I was so amazed that I get to teach such an amazing group of people, and that their strength was so obvious on that first day that I wonder if I should have to pay to be in class with them. My students and I both know this fiscal picture is not going to be realized but the looks on their faces when I express those ideas reveal one thing very clearly: "He thinks we're worth teaching!"

An inverse of the star-in-disguise approach also works. YouTube has lots of clips of talented audience members joining a star on stage. Search "Kristen Chenowith and Sarah Horn" for one such example.

After showing that clip, I make comments along the lines I noted in the paragraph above: "Wow, this is an amazing class and I get to teach you!" "You are like an undiscovered gem." "Does anyone else know how good you are?" "I am so excited about the work we can do together this semester." Later in the semester, once community is built and students know there's a humor layer in the class, you can say, "Of all the classes I've taught, you are definitely the most recent." Rigorous, stand-up, longitudinal research indicates that 91.48% of students get that joke.

In the next chapter, I describe how I offer several choices or *Tracks* for students to follow to complete a significant portion of their course assessment. I have periodically listed Leadership and Planning as one of the tracks. In those cases, I have four or five students meet with me regularly to reflect on how the course has been going and to discuss how to shape what is coming next. Because the grade for following this track is necessarily based only on participation, I assign those who select it a pro-rated grade based on their grades on their other work in the course. Students electing to follow this track participate in the meetings with me and at the end of the semester they write a reflection essay on their experience planning a university course. I never open this track to the whole class and do not list it in the syllabus, but I invite a group of students I already trust or who come recommended by my department colleagues.

Part of the Invitation for Education Students to Elect the Course Planning Track

Seriously, there's a lot in common between planning a class for K–6 and planning for a class here at the university. If you're interested in this track, please email me. We will meet Mondays at 12:30 in my office, reflect on recent classes, and think out loud for one hour about the contents and structure of the upcoming weeks. Working with me on this class might give you some insights into teaching adults. Like it or not, you will (ALL OF YOU, GUARANTEED) be cast in situations where you teach adults.

Finally, I produce classroom posters and mocked-up book covers based on students' comments in class. When students come to the next class and see an 11x17" poster on the wall with a picture and their own words printed as a *law* or an *observation*, their eyes light up. For example, a pre-service teacher said in class that we should add humility to the list of essential educator qualities. I cannot show the image here but I found a picture of actor Keanu Reeves sharing food and hanging out with a homeless man. I wrote: "We should add humility to the list of essential educator qualities" at the bottom of the picture and labeled it a law, with the student's name. In this case, the student was a mature educator, not in need of recognition by means of a poster on the classroom wall. Nevertheless, students wondering if their ideas are heard in class will feel affirmed on entering a physical classroom or Zoom meeting and seeing their name on a law or observation. Often, another student contributes a "but" to the discussion quite quickly after the initial comment. I often add so-and-so's "corollary," "codicil," or "caveat" on the same poster or on a separate one. Besides building student self-efficacy and, in a semi-humorous way, sending the message that the professor listens, these printed laws and caveats can also serve as prompts for review of a previous session's contents. Obviously, they also help build classroom community. Mocking up a book cover and showing it on the classroom projector works the same way. Sometimes, I make the whole class the authors of the book, sometimes only one or two students.

COURSE DESIGN STRATEGIES

In an earlier chapter, I introduced the work of architect Christopher Alexander (Alexander et al, 1977; Alexander, 1979), his idea of pattern languages, and my own attempt to bring his thinking about design to the tasks of course and unit design (Badley, 2018). In Chapter 3, I listed a few of his principles: Strong centers, clear boundaries, clear entrances and exits, green spaces, coherence, and harmony. Obviously, we need to plan our courses in view of the contents, canons, recognized procedures and tests, and hierarchies of concepts within our respective academic disciplines, what we might call the epistemological organization or the epistemological structure of the course. But our students will experience greater success if we also attend to design principles when we plan, what we might call the aesthetic structure of the course.

To refer to the principles I listed above, a strong center in a home might be the living room fireplace; in fact, the word *hearth* has the same root as the word *heart*, implying that the fireplace was once considered the center of the home. Likewise, a course or unit should have a clear center. "These are the main roles towns play in the economy." "These are the main structural and thematic features of Milton's three major poems." "Over the last century, two distinct lines of thought have shaped the ethical standards of professional practice in this professional field." In a course, or a unit, or even a single lesson with a strong center, students will know what they are supposed to learn, in English vernacular, they will know the point. Except for coherence and harmony, I will not expand on the other principles listed in the paragraph above. But I will introduce three concepts some educators have worked with to bring more coherence to their courses and thereby increase student self-efficacy.

We all face this challenge of building coherence and harmony—of tying the parts together—in a course that will run for the nine weeks of a quarter or the 13–14 weeks of a semester. A growing number of educators are now working with the concepts of threads, layers, and throughlines to build such coherence. Threads and layers can take the form of an idea that the class returns to repeatedly or an activity that the class engages in each day. My own students know that in every class, we will view a brief film clip and discuss its implications for our practice. I distinguish threads from layers somewhat arbitrarily on the basis of how much time we give. A thread takes a maximum of 10 minutes in a three-hour block. A layer is a more substantial part of every class. I consider my use of video and the discussions that ensue a layer, because we typically give that part of the class about 20 minutes. I will not offer an extended warrant here for using video, but I will note simply that video is a natural language for students and my own students consistently report that the video layer causes them to think deeply about the course contents.

In courses where students have a lot of choice in what assignments they complete (which I advocate in the next chapter), they can follow a thread or idea by selecting certain assignments from among the choices on offer. I lifted the following from the syllabus of a philosophy of education course where students were required to respond to a number of readings.

By selecting specific assignments, you can focus your reading in this course around any of these four threads:

Vocation and your vocation: 1, 3, 6, 7, 9a, 10, 11, 14, 16, 17c, 17d, 17e

Curriculum and classroom work: 5, 7, 8, 11, 13, 14, 15, 17a

The classroom ethos: 4, 5, 6, 7, 8, 10, 11, 13, 14, 16, 17b, 17d

Educational perspectives/philosophies: 1, 2, 3, 4, 5, 7, 9b, 13, 15, 16, 17b, 17c, 17d, 17e

Throughlines run on a continuum. In their strongest form, they function as foundational ideas for a course. In their weaker forms, they are themes that resurface throughout the course (Swanson et al, 2019). "Milton's theme of the struggle between good and evil appears again in this section." "We see these economic functions again when we look at Rosenheim (Bavaria), Germany (population, 63,000), Belleville (Ontario), Canada (population, 54,000), and Otavalo (Imbabura), Ecuador (population, 40,000)." "As it has done in all four cases so far, informed consent appears again in the case we examined today." The particular subject matter the class studies varies day to day and week to week but the throughlines bring continuity to our students' learning. A small sadness for me personally is that while elementary and secondary educators have developed the concept of throughlines, built throughlines into their courses, and witnessed their potential to bring coherence to students' learning and increase student self-efficacy, we higher educators have been slow to embrace them. To return to learning-centered classrooms (one of the throughlines of this book), if those of us in higher education could focus a bit more on how students learn in real life, we would likely be quicker to adopt and adapt some of the approaches that our K–12 colleagues have developed.

PULLING STUDENTS INTO INSTRUCTOR MODE

Students' self-efficacy increases when they become instructors or see their classmates in that role. Obviously, conditions apply; I do not mean that students take over a three-hour block in my course. But numerous ways offer themselves for us to pull our students into instructor mode for a few minutes at a time. Most professors do not set out intentionally to get time "off" from teaching, but those who involve students know that most students will rise to the occasion and will take over some of the content and time if given the opportunity and appropriate guidance.

The paradigm example here, obviously, is the presentation of the research paper at the 300- or 400-level. This can take several shapes:

- Individual students make their presentations to the class (with time limits strictly enforced) with or without a prepared response from another student. Given different students' ease with presenting, the grade should rest most significantly on the written paper, not on the presentation. If another student is to respond, that response should be for course credit. This works best in senior-seminar type classes of about 12–15 students (or fewer) or the presentations will eat up too many course days at the end of term.
- The panel presentation with people who wrote related papers presenting briefly. Panel members take about two to three minutes each to summarize their arguments and conclusions. Panel members respond to each other for a few minutes before inviting the class's questions. Panels should not have more than five members.
- Debates and speed dating, both of which I discuss in detail in later chapters. These strategies do place students in instructor mode but, in both cases, I register caution about them when I discuss them in more detail.

Besides these, there are many other strategies available to pull students into instructor mode. Many of these strategies also build classroom community. Briefly, here are several such strategies:

- When students have broken into pairs or small groups for discussion, assigning the leadership function or reporting function in advance adds a note of importance or formality and can help students move into instructor mode for the moments they lead the discussion or report to the whole class.
- Students who have completed a maker project or built a website can show their work.
- Late in the semester, after students have seen case teaching modeled, a student can write a case study and lead the discussion of it (Chapter 12).
- A student can serve as note-taker during a class discussion. This student's words are show on the screen during the class. The professor posts or emails the notes after class. Students who serve as

note-takers must understand that their task that day is to take clear notes for distribution, not to audition for *Saturday Night Live*.

- Toward the end of the term, I invite some students to take charge of the video layer, that is, to choose and prepare the film clip from a list I provide, to write the scaffolding for the discussion (that I will include in the *Daily Forecast* sheet), and to lead the discussion. I retain the right to suggest/approve the clips chosen and I ask to see the scaffolding and questions in advance, advising that I will edit.

- I ask students to illustrate their question, which I list as an arts strategy in Chapter 13, but which also qualifies as a discussion strategy. The artists among us could probably explain why any sentence's power increases so significantly when we present it on a poster. Part of the answer is that the image goes straight to the right side of the brain and so it grips more tightly than if the professor only said (or even wrote on the screen) "I wish I knew X but haven't learned anything about it so far in my degree?" The three minutes extra it takes for a student to load a draw program and produce this little picture pays off in much richer discussion of the question. To my point in this last section of the chapter, it also moves the student momentarily into an instructor mode.

- Peer coaching and peer consultants. Appoint "consultants" for each unit who will act as experts to explain assignments to other students. Students who are capable to lead in this way can be rewarded for their work with a portion of the course grade but, unless the course is pass/fail, that grade should be pro-rated according to their grades in the rest of their course work. If they are rewarded that way, course weight should be about 10–15% and should include a write-up about what they learned by doing peer-coaching, and how they might revise the program next year if they were the professor.

- Plan this course with me. The Leadership and Planning Track I described earlier in this chapter also works to pull students into instructor mode.

- "Not the Riot Act," as I described it in Chapter 4 (page xx), offers one or two students the chance to lead what I call *the turnaround discussion* after the return of a mid-term exam or a sub-par set of written assignments.

- PowerPoint karaoke (listed with humor in Chapter 4). This gives a student or a pair of students the opportunity to teach and entertain simultaneously.

- Online images meant to illustrate a concept related to the day's topic. Students select an online image and then lead a brief discussion about that image. For example, I ask education students to search the string *curriculum implementation*. A few students project the slide they have selected and begin the discussion by commenting on the strengths and weaknesses of the image. Following the presenting student's comments, that student leads a whole-class discussion with or without the professor's assistance. I return to this activity as a discussion strategy in Chapter 12.

- The last word. When a discussion feels like it is drawing to a close, I often ask if a student has a sense of what needs to be said in conclusion and is willing to say it to the class to wrap up the conversation. This invitation will surprise students the first time they hear it because our prerogative to end discussions not only is stated clearly in our contracts but is underwritten by educational history and classroom traditions. Inviting a student to offer the last word in a discussion radically shifts epistemic authority toward students in general and the particular student who takes up the invitation. We must say nothing beyond "Thank you" to the student who takes up that invitation or the invitation will seem false. I experienced a kind of vertigo or anomie the first time I issued this invitation to a class, but I believe that all students have gifts to share with the class, and sometimes that gift is words of wisdom.

- These strategies work but they are not the last word on pulling students into the instructor mode; they are only the first word. They require trust on both sides. We need to trust that our students will bring their best in the moments when we turn some class time over to them. And they need to be able to trust us that we will grade their work with charity, recognizing that they are students in our class, not veteran TED-talk presenters. Thousands of professors have discovered ways to build that kind of trust and thereby enrich the learning both of those who present and their classmates.

CONCLUSION

Some readers will be familiar with the Alexander technique, an additional strategy that does not fit easily into any of the four major sections in this chapter. Without claiming to understand acting or musical performance, I am aware that many public performers use the Alexander technique to improve their posture, confidence, and performance. I use it myself and have introduced it to many of my education students, sometimes simply as a stretching exercise during a three-hour class. Without checking the billion Google hits returned at the time of writing (for the string *Alexander technique*), I will conjecture that professionals in many fields other than drama and music are using the technique. I mention it in this chapter on student self-efficacy because it does work. Our students need to bring all the resources they can to their academic work and, while practicing this technique will not move students from failing to Great Distinction, it will increase their self-efficacy.

We all should do what we can to encourage our students. I say that, knowing that we work within professional boundaries and that we do not have unlimited energy. So when I say we should do what we can, I am thinking of the kinds of steps we can appropriately take in our classes. At the start of the chapter, I noted that if a dozen colleagues had co-written this chapter with me, it would catalogue more strategies than I have listed here. I add now that some of those strategies would likely be more effective than what I have offered. But those I have listed here have proven to be effective with students at all stages of their university education. In this chapter I have focused on self-efficacy, not on engagement, but the two are linked in important ways. When students feel like they are in control of their learning, they engage more fully with their course-work; we all end up glad to be in class.

REFERENCES

Alexander, C. (1979). *The timeless way of building.* Oxford University Press.

Alexander, C., Ishikawa, S., Silverstein, M., Jacobson, M., Fiksdahl-King, I., & Angel, S. (1977). *A pattern language: Towns, buildings, construction.* Oxford University Press.

Badley, K. (2018). *Curriculum planning with design language: Building elegant courses and units.* Routledge.

Bandura, A. (1977a). *Social learning theory.* Prentice-Hall.

Bandura, A. (1977b). Self-efficacy: Toward a unifying theory of behavioral change. *Psychological Review, 84*(2), 191–215.

Bandura, A. (1986). *Social foundations of thought and action: A social cognitive theory.* Prentice-Hall.

Bandura, A. (1997). *Self-efficacy: The exercise of control.* Freeman.

Swanson, P., Rabin, C., Smith, G., Briceño, A., Ervin-Kassab, L., Sexton, D., Mitchell, D., Whitenack, D. A., & Asato, J. (2019). Trust your team. *Teacher Education Quarterly, 46*(4), 67–91.

Six

Very few professors dispute the need to assess students' learning and submit grades to the Office of the Registrar. Assessment is simply a given. However, how to assess learning presents its challenges. Do our assessments authentically allow our students to show what they have learned? Can we be guaranteed that the work they submit is their own? Can we prevent cheating on tests? Regarding the middle question, thanks to the internet, students can easily find a pre-written term paper on many standard topics or they can hire a custom essay writer. In a corollary development, software helps educators identify some papers with these dodgy origins, but not all. The massive switch to online learning has brought the last question—about cheating— further into our collective foreground.

In what follows, I directly address the first question and implicitly address the second and third questions. That is, the approach to assessment and the assessment strategies I describe here encourage students to submit original work, although I can make no guarantees. Perhaps I live in some kind of kentopian dream, but I believe that most of the student work I grade authentically reveals my students' learning. Again, I cannot say that for certain. Nevertheless, in this chapter, I introduce and explain the seven principles that guide my assessment of students' learning. In each case, I list ways I try to realize those principles in practice. The principles are these:

- Make structures and expectations clear.
- Recognize students' strengths and learning styles.
- Give students flexibility and choice.
- Authorize students by critically examining assessment criteria.
- Develop a course philosophy of mistakes with students.
- Produce real work for a real audience in the real world.
- Make my own life more interesting but not more complicated.

DOI: 10.4324/9781003259596-8

Each of these principles becomes the basis of one of the major sections of this chapter.

This chapter purposely appears as part of the section of the book given over to student self-efficacy. That is, in my view, assessment should contribute to my students' sense that they are succeeding; it should help them judge their learning accurately, but it links at many points to the two chapters in the next section of the book. In Chapter 7, I offer strategies to use on the first day of class. This, of course, because students' primary interest on the first day is to find out what they must do to succeed in the course. Chapter 8 relates closely to the other first-day strategies inasmuch as it focuses on offering students a clear syllabus.

CLEAR EXPECTATIONS

For our students to succeed, we must make absolutely clear what work they must do and what criteria we will use to assess their work. Obviously, these are necessary conditions, not sufficient conditions, and some of our students will not succeed even if we consistently meet these two conditions. How does one improve syllabus clarity and accuracy? In the name of clarity and readability, I ask a designer to make improvements to the format and composition of my syllabus. In the name of accuracy, I ask several students to check its contents before the first day of the course. These are but two steps of many I take to ensure that what I finally distribute to the class is as clear and accurate as I can make it. In fact, syllabus clarity and accuracy are so important that I give the whole of Chapter 8 over to the syllabus. My treatment of "Clear Expectations" may be brief, but I list it first because of its importance, and I later give a whole chapter to it for the same reason.

STUDENTS' STRENGTHS AND LEARNING STYLES

Attention to learning styles largely began in the 1980s and grew out of the work of David Kolb (1984, 1985) and Kenneth and Rita Dunn (1986, 1992). Much of the Dunns' work focused on K–12 education, but others have applied both their work and that of Kolb to higher education settings. The concept of multiple intelligences originated with Howard Gardner, who now works with the Harvard Graduate School of Education. In *Frames of Mind* (1983), he posited the existence of seven kinds of intelligence: Mathematical, musical, visual/aesthetic, verbal, kinesthetic, interpersonal, and intrapersonal (reflective, self-aware). In

Intelligence Reframed (1999), he added a category related to intelligence about nature and he suggested something like existential or spiritual intelligence but, as an atheist, noted his uncertainty about it as a category. Gardner did not initially focus his work on students and classrooms, but educators responded to his ideas very quickly, and *multiple intelligences* and its abbreviation MI became common language among K–12 educators.

In my view, taking a few minutes of class time for students to use one of the many online instruments meant to help people identify their learning strengths has two benefits. First, the instrument itself will likely help students think about why they prefer some kinds of learning activities more than others and why they do better work on some kinds of assignments than others. That benefit alone would justify the class time given to the exercise. But giving time for students to answer a few questions and to discuss as a class how people learn and how we might structure the class so that students succeed sends students the message that their professor is interested in their success and in how they learn as individuals, not only in getting through all the course contents before the end of the semester.

Talk about learning styles and multiple intelligences—especially with reference to higher education—has its critics, but I do not attempt to answer them here. My own acceptance of and work with the ideas has led me to two important conclusions. First, we need to vary the kinds of instruction we use to approach the course material (the subject matter of most of this book). Second, to the point of this chapter, we need to create opportunities for student choice in assessment. I encourage my readers to explore these two areas and to consider giving a few minutes of class time for students to complete one of the many online surveys and for the classroom discussion that naturally follows.

FLEXIBILITY AND CHOICE

In light of my recognition that students have different strengths and learning styles, I offer them a degree of choice regarding how they will be assessed. Of course, my students do need to demonstrate that they have met the learning objectives of the course, but, in the words of my colleague Michelle C. Hughes, they do not all need to demonstrate their learning in the same way or on the same day. Thus, I offer multiple ways for students to show what they have learned.

Table 6.1 An assessment schema that combines common assignments with student choice.

Assignment & due date		Common assignments	Course weight
1	Sept 10	Personal course objectives	5%
2	Sept 13	Response: Kairos Canada's *Winds of Change* 2018 Report Card	10%
3	Sept 20	Assessment of and response to Whitehead's *Aims of Education*	15%
4	Oct 11	Choose one from 4a to 4e related to the 2015 Truth and Reconciliation Report	20%
5	Nov 1	Reading response to ch 1 or 2 of the text: *Pedagogy of the Oppressed*,	10%
Total from specified, common assignments			**60%**

Assignment & due date		Elected assignments	Course weight
6	Nov 15	One of assignments 6a to 6d based on *Pedagogy of the Oppressed*	20%
Tracks assignment: Complete one from 7a to 7f, or 7g + 7h			
7	Nov 29	7a, Performance; 7b, Gaming; 7c, Maker	20%
	Dec 6	7d, Final exam; 7e, Research paper; 7f, Service, practices, mentoring	20%
	Dec 6	7g: Writing Center workshops	10%
	Dec 6	7h: Responses to readings	10%
Total from elected assignments			**40%**

Recognizing that some students simply want to be told what work they need to complete to get credit for the course, I require some common work for all students. For example, assigning work to all students related to the textbook's contents yields a baseline of understanding. Table 6.1 illustrates such a mix of common and chosen assignments. The table is adapted from a Sociology of Education, Fall/2019 course at Mount Royal University in Calgary, Alberta.

Notice in Table 6.1 that the first three assignments are common to the whole class. Assignment 4 has all students working with the final *Report* of Canada's Truth and Reconciliation Commission, but students can choose from among five different assignments to meet that requirement. With the common understanding students will have gained by having completed some common work, we can make effective use of our class time when we address the TRC's report together. This assignment also illustrates the flipped classroom (Chapter 3). Recall that in the flipped classroom, students worked through the learning materials on their own time to free up class time for discussion, questions, and consolidation of learning. By the end of Assignment 4, which was due the second week of October, students had done common work but already had five possible routes through that portion of the course. The last principle I explain in this chapter relates to my keeping my own life interesting but not creating a paper-work or grading nightmare for myself. To help meet that condition, assignment 4 has a fixed course weight, regardless of which choice students make.

Note also in Table 6.1 that Assignments 5 and 6 also offer students choice but will yield a common base of understanding to facilitate our work during class. Assignment 5, with two choices of reading, moves students into the course text. Likewise, Assignment 6 gives students a choice of four more assignments related to the course text. With reference to student choice, the total number of routes through the course to the end of Assignment 6 is now 40. With reference to my sanity, the grading schema remains fixed.

In Assignment 7 in this course, I offered students ten tracks, again with a fixed course weight of 20% regardless of which track any given student elects to follow. Thus, at a minimum, students could select any of 400 pathways through that sociology of education course, without my needing to engage in any custom grade calculations. At that, each of the tracks listed for Assignment 7 allows more room for students to select the topic and approach they wish to take to their chosen assignment.

Credit for the idea of Tracks goes to my wife, K. Jo-Ann Badley, who came up with that label in the early 2000s. For some years, I had used the labels Basket 1 to denote work required of all students, and Basket 2 to denote the portion of a course where students could choose among a list of options. Those labels worked but not always that well. But Jo-Ann defined and refined the concept of Tracks in ways that brought more clarity to course syllabi. Below are brief descriptions of the work required to follow the Tracks listed as Assignment 7 in Table 6.1. These appear as they did in the course syllabus. In the Rubrics Document posted on the course wiki (on Blackboard) for that course, students had access to much more detailed descriptions and to grading rubrics for the work in each track.

- **Research paper:** Write a 1,200–1,500-word research paper [students who express interest in writing a major paper can eliminate other assignments from the course, so the course weight can move to 40–50%].
- **Performance:** Song, spoken word, reader's theatre, lunch with a theorist.
- **Gaming:** Adapt a popular board game to increase understanding of one or more important concepts related to this course.
- **Maker:** Using your own equipment or a maker space, build a physical model to illustrate one or more concepts related to this course.
- **Final exam:** Using your exit slip or email, submit at least one exam question based on every class from week 2 through to week 12. Answering these questions satisfactorily should require both knowledge of course contents and critical thinking. The final exam will include some of your suggested questions but also others.
- **Service, practices, mentoring:** Volunteer in a service setting for two hours each week for at least ten weeks. Write 400–500 words in which you explain how your service changed or did not change your perspective on the subject matter of this course.
- **Writing Center workshops:** Attend at least four writing workshops given by the Academic Development Center and submit the form or brochure certifying that you attended. Your grade on this track will be based on the rest of your work in the course.
- **Summaries and critical responses to two journal articles:** Read and respond to two journal articles from the list provided in the syllabus. These should be about 500 words each and should include any suggested revisions you would make to the article's abstract.

In other courses, I have offered students several other Tracks. In the Film Review Track, the student writes a review of one film, chooses an appropriate clip from the film to show the class, and leads the class discussion of that clip. If two students elect to co-lead the discussion of a film, they still must write individual reviews. As I noted in Chapter 5, this track allows students to move into instructor mode, increasing their self-efficacy. Preparing for and leading a class discussion also increases their sense that they are important parts of the classroom community.

One time only, I listed a Book Project Track. Eight students (out of 31) elected that track and we produced a book that remains available on Amazon. The course weight for those eight students was 50%, which the student writers involved considered appropriate and fair. I have not listed this track again, mainly because Covid-19 upended so much of my own work, but I would like to do it again. Chapter 11 contains more detail on the Book Production Track.

At various times, I have listed Video Production and Legomation, but have had no takers so far, likely because students know that 20% course weight does not reflect the time needed to follow those tracks. On the other hand, students regularly elect the Poster or Tri-fold Brochure Track, both of which require an accompanying viewer's guide of 500 words. Also, a number of students have elected to build websites where they listed and annotated resources related to a specific topic of interest to researchers or school teachers.

A couple times, I have invited a few students to work with me in what I called the Leadership and Planning Track, which I describe in more detail later in the book. Their role was to assess our progress as a class and, in light of our conversations, to help me plan what should come next.

Finally, a benefit of including Tracks in a course is that the professor can easily add another assignment choice at some point in the semester. Almost always, a classroom discussion leads to a new question that piques a few students' interest. In a grading schema where 100% of the assessment genres and topics are fixed in advance, most professors do not want the logistical headaches of substituting in an assignment for a handful of students. This resistance is understandable. Most professors are already juggling the 40% teaching, 20% service, 30% research, 20% grading, 20% administration, and 15% advising challenge; they don't need more details to keep track of simply because two students found something interesting. I have no clever name for this, but when these questions or topics arise and a student says, "I would like to be able to work on that in a paper," I reply that the Research and Reading Track is perfectly suited for their purposes.

Separate from tracks, but another way to offer students some choice, but still have a baseline of common knowledge for in-class discussion, involves specifying the dates of a larger number of assignments than you require but allowing students to complete those they choose on the specified dates. The list below and the rather stern instructions following it illustrate this model, in which 11 assignments are available, but only a specified number are required. In different courses, I have required as few as three and as many as seven assignments.

Complete five of these readings:

September 15	Reading response #1
September 22	Reading response #2
September 29	Reading response #3
October 6	Reading response #4
October 13	Reading response #5
October 20	Reading response #6
October 27	Reading response #7
November 3	Reading response #8
November 10	Reading response #9
November 17	Reading response #10
November 24	No reading due
December 1	Reading response #11

Regarding this schedule, please understand that the due date is the due date. Assignments are due electronically or on paper at the start of class. There are no lates or extensions. If you do not complete enough assignments by the due date of the final assignment, then those you did complete on time will become the basis of the grade on this portion of your coursework.

In this plan, starting in week 2, each week has one designated reading response due. Students are to submit a specified number of such responses during the 12 weeks of term but no late submissions are allowed. I agree that this is a tautology but in this schema the assignments students complete are the assignments they complete. The plan allows students choice, not only among contents but also with reference to their own calendars. It also makes them responsible to manage their work. Because some students will flounder with such freedom, it may be wise to require that students complete, for example, two assignments by October 20 in the schedule above.

This scheme pays dividends for the professor inasmuch as work comes in over the whole term, not in whole class sets at a time. The class benefits because there will consistently be a few students who have read and responded to material related to a given week's content. Finally, and obviously, reading responses are not the only possible kind of assignment that could be used in this attempt to build in flexibility.

Some professors who use this model calculate students' grades based on the best three or four assignments submitted, even though they may have required students to complete a larger number. In this case, syllabus language could be along the lines of: "Your highest three grades on your six assignments will go into your course grade calculation."

CO-DETERMINING THE RUBRIC

Throughout this book, I work with the assumption that my readers will provide rubrics for all assignments. I recommend that professors post all the rubrics and assignment instructions (beyond the basic instructions included in the syllabus) in a single document on the course wiki. Here, I suggest inviting students into the revision of a rubric. Why? Millions of students write a major paper or research essay every semester. As professors who have both written and graded our share of these essays, we may assume that our students know as well as we do what quality of paper warrants an A grade, a B grade, and so on. But that assumption is almost certainly wrong, for reasons my readers know and which I do not need to catalogue here.

Here is one strategy I have used to help my students understand what I consider to be a good assignment: I invite them to edit and revise the rubric with me (after making clear that I have veto power). This process usually takes a few minutes in two successive class sessions. On the first day, I give out instructions along these lines:

> Here is last year's rubric for this assignment. In groups, discuss this rubric and add any lines (criteria) you believe are missing from the rubric. You may not add columns; the four columns and their titles are fixed. If you wish, suggest different weights for the different lines to reflect your group's conversation. Turn the paper rubric back in to me when I call the groups back (15 minutes).

After a brief discussion, which is not meant to move us toward any conclusions, I collect the edited rubrics from the groups. I work through the rubrics outside of class and at the end of the next class day, I project on the screen a table showing what the students produced. I then send the students back into their groups with these instructions on the screen:

> Here is a table with the individual scores for each line from every group, and the means for each line's weight (rounded up or down to the nearest 5%). Go back into your groups and, using the paper copies, discuss each line and the class's mean weight for that line, providing written reasons why your group believes any line's weight should be increased or reduced. You do not need to provide reasons if you believe the class's mean weight for a line should remain where it is. I will consider your input tonight and bring a final, revised rubric to the next class.

Some may view co-determination of the rubric as giving the store away. I see it as an effective way to get students to reflect on the nature of good work, not just on the criteria by which I grade their assignments. Perhaps the most interesting outcome of this exercise in co-determination—and I dearly want to type this in all upper-case—their numbers almost always match my starting numbers. A typical total of 30 minutes of class time produces a dramatic increase in their awareness of the criteria by which I assess their assignment and an increased sense of ownership of the respective rubric.

At some points, I have incorporated rubric awareness into a separate assignment: Based on the published rubric, students write a prose summary of the criteria an assignment must meet to be considered excellent. Co-determining rubrics function as one small part of what I call authorizing students or sharing epistemic authority, which I described briefly and for which I provided a warrant in Chapter 3.

A PHILOSOPHY OF MISTAKES

We need to remember, especially in the first weeks of the term, that our students worry about how successful they will be in our course. For this reason, at some point in the first two weeks of the semester,

I introduce the idea that our class needs to develop what I call a *philosophy of mistakes* (although it is really a philosophy of learning). I want them to know that as we approach what Parker Palmer (1983) calls *the big subject* together, we will all be learning; we will all be exploring, trying to figure out what's going on (to quote 20th-century epistemologist, Marvin Gaye). Explorers sometimes find their way straight to where they want to go. Other times, they do not. I want my students to understand that in my class we will treat mistakes as sources of information we actually need if we are to find our way forward. I want to reduce their fear of failure and increase their sense that they can succeed, their self-efficacy.

Some students will have encountered this idea during their elementary or secondary education, perhaps because one or more of their teachers used the phrase *fail forward* or had a classroom wall poster along the lines of Figure 6.1. Some students arrive at university

Figure 6.1 A concise summary of a classroom philosophy of mistakes that hangs in many elementary and secondary classrooms.
Credit: variously attributed; Art credit: Sophie Chardon.

understanding and welcoming the view of learning embedded in this saying and expressed on posters like that shown. Other students, arriving after long conditioning into another view of school and learning, simply want to know their grade or if they gave the correct answer.

Those students who have already learned to learn from their mistakes will welcome the news that one of their university professors follows this developmental approach to mistakes. Some of those who are new to a philosophy of mistakes or have resisted it in the past may be willing to adjust their thinking if we present the idea in the right way. My own approach has been to use one chapter from *The Perfect Wrong Note*, William Westney's (2003) excellent book on piano pedagogy. The gist of his argument is this: The piano student who makes a mistake actually meant to play the passage correctly, so let's find out why it came out wrong; let's find out what's happening behind the mistake. Besides having a great title, Westney's chapter "Big Juicy Mistakes" expresses the core of his philosophy very clearly.

I offer my students three reasons for developing a philosophy of mistakes. First, at university we are still learning how to learn, not just learning subject-area content. Second, we recognize that we are only human, that we make mistakes. Third, one of the ways we attend to self-efficacy is by remembering that learning is a journey.

Searching online for talks about learning from mistakes or failing forward will yield millions of hits, including talks by actors such as Will Smith and Denzel Washington. At many points, the learning-from-failure conversation seems to veer off into self-help, but perhaps such a change in direction is to be expected and even accepted. After all, students wanting to understand their failures and grow from those failures do need help.

To honour Westney's intellectual property, I do not distribute the chapter; I summarize his argument, post a few agree-disagree questions on the screen and open up discussion (Chapter 12 contains a detailed description of how to use Agree-Disagree sheets as discussion prompts). The five questions below illustrate the kind of questions I use to generate discussion about how we will treat mistakes in our class.

Please decide whether you agree or disagree with each of the following statements and be prepared to discuss your thinking.

1. In our class, students should intentionally make mistakes so we can all come to understand the subject matter of our course better.
2. Rock-climbers have a saying … that if you're not falling, you're not climbing at your limit. We should apply this saying to our class as well.
3. It is not possible to apply Westney's philosophy of mistakes in a class with this many students who are learning at different speeds and in different ways
4. Final exam grades are like autopsy results.
5. A professor who takes class time to discuss a philosophy of mistakes or a philosophy of assessment is wasting students' time.

We move from the Agree-Disagree sheet to a discussion of how such a philosophy might work in our class. I recommend that anyone using questions like those above have students discuss in pairs or small groups first so that those who prefer not to speak to the whole class still get an opportunity to share their views. After a few minutes in pairs or small groups, move to whole-class discussion. To make whole-class discussion more effective, ask people to report what their partner or someone else in their small group said, not to repeat what they said in their small group.

The power of developing a philosophy of mistakes—which is really a philosophy of learning—becomes powerfully clear in a story told me by Julie Owens, a colleague and school principal in Washington State. This story originally appeared elsewhere (Steeg-Thornhill & Badley, 2021, p. 57) but the author permitted me to use it here as well.

Working with children provides many opportunities for hitting the "perfect wrong note," (from Westney, 2003) where things don't go as expected but it's just as it should have been. I've found that sharing my reading with my students is very enlightening. The students in my classroom see me as a reader, as well as a writer. Having the opportunity to be purposeful about my reflections in this book provided many rich conversations I may not have normally taken the time to have. One of my students' favorite parts was about making "juicy mistakes." When a child makes a mistake either in our spelling practice or in a shared reading experience, the other children now encourage them by reminding them it is okay to make mistakes, and we should make them "big, fat, juicy ones."

This past week, I made one of my own in the classroom. Students had just finished their writing work sample for me to grade, and one child had put his on my work station right next to my freshly filled water bottle. While working with another child on animating herself as she speaks, I knocked over the bottle, spilling water all over this child's work sample. Mortified, I quickly jumped up to retrieve paper towels to clean off his work sample he had worked so hard on. The other children saw the commotion and asked what was wrong. I responded that water got spilled on a work sample and the boy instantly came over. The look on his face was a lot softer than I would have expected from a child whose paper was just ruined. He patted me on the shoulder and said, "It's okay Ms. Owens, it was a really big, fat, super, juicy mistake. Remember we all make mistakes." He then said that most of the pages were fine and that he would re-create those that were ruined. I learned so much that day about forgiveness and how even the young can teach us this so well.

If first-graders can work through Westney with their teacher and co-develop a philosophy of mistakes with her, surely we can do the same in higher education. Some might object that giving class time to such a conversation is losing class time that could be given to subject-area content. I frame such a discussion in investment language. Investing a few minutes in this conversation in the first or second week pays dividends for the rest of the semester and, in fact, for the rest of students' lives.

REAL WORK

As much as possible, I want my students to do real work on real problems for a real audience in the real world. I learned this language from Justin Cook, an Ontario colleague who focuses his work on the professional development of K–12 school teachers. I realize how idealistic this sounds. Some university subjects simply cannot meet this standard. Larger class sizes prevent the ground-shift that this standard would typically require. These are real constraints.

Still, the idea that I should be the only one who sees my students' work fits exactly what Harry Frankfurt complained about in his 2005 essay, *On Bullshit*. In his little book, Frankfurt describes a game we all learn to play in higher education. Students give the professors what they want, get the credit, and get out of there with a grade. Even if we can't reach Justin Cook's standard in every assignment—that our students will do real work on real problems for a real audience in the real world—can we at least keep his idea in view? Can we move a few degrees away from Frankfurt's critique?

I would love to list this principle first in this chapter because it is the one principle that rules them all. And I would love to claim that I have reached column five ("redefines expectations") on a four-column rubric, a rather oblique reference to the "dial it up to 11" meme. However, I have not yet succeeded. But, from time to time, a student asks my permission to do this project, build that resource website, or initiate that program, and reminds that I said I wanted to see real work on real problems for a real audience in the real world.

This section ends with a story, one told to me by Justin Cook. He related the story of a kindergarten teacher in Edmonton, Alberta, who led her students through a project where they met Justin's criterion in spades. For many years, Alberta's kindergarten social studies curriculum included a major unit on community. The teacher in question led her students into a project that both celebrated and recognized the people who help build community in Edmonton. This teacher had her pupils produce thank you cards for all the snow-plow drivers and truck-drivers who work hard for the months when Edmonton has to deal with snow. She took the cards to the Transportation Department office so they could be distributed. Several drivers contacted the school, one claiming he had not been thanked once in 25 years of driving a snow-plow and who now kept his thank you card from a kindergarten pupil on the dash of his snow-plow. Frankly, the drivers were overwhelmed at the thoughtfulness of these kindergartners, some of whom could not even write yet. The Department organized a trip to the school ... with a small parade of snow-plows and trucks. The drivers met—and thanked—the children and showed them their snow-plows and dump trucks. Granted, not many descriptions of school projects can pull one's heartstrings the way this story does. But term on term, I want to take up Justin Cook's challenge and I want to aim for the standard of creativity shown in this project and the depth of meaning it had for pupils and civic employees alike.

A MORE INTERESTING LIFE WITH NO PAPERFLOW NIGHTMARES

In the preceding sections of this chapter I have advocated that we offer some choice and flexibility to our students. I now stipulate a very important condition on that advocacy: It must not result in more work for professors. Choice and flexibility in assessment should not create an administrative or mathematical nightmare for the educator. In view of this stipulation, I do not open the assessment doors wide.

Most students view the kind of flexibility and choice I give them as a gift, and they respond positively. But I have discovered that this kind of flexibility comes as a gift to me as well. I still assign work common to the whole class and therefore am required to read dozens of similar chapter summaries or book reviews. But where students elect their assignments because I gave them choice, I get to read on a wide variety of topics, making grading less burdensome and far more interesting for me.

To refer to Table 6.1 again, common assignments ensure a common knowledge base for analysis of the textbook or other materials. Week to week, a class can gain that common base without the professor having to grade a whole set of assignments that address the same aspect of the same issue. That is, the course has continuity and students enjoy coherence in their learning. Class time has a focus. But students enjoy some choice. And professors retain their sanity. In the second half of the semester especially, elected assignments allow students greater choice. They are able to dig deeply into areas of their interests and strengths. In some cases, they will move into instructor mode. As long as the grading schema has some fixed parameters, the professor can grade a variety of work without getting bored.

CONCLUSION

Of course, one could add other principles to this list. For example, students regularly express their concern that assessments are fair. Educators have extracted from this concern a principle: Fairness and the appearance of fairness. Another example relates to self-assessment, a principle which helps shape the practice of many educators. According to this principle, students should be constantly assessing their own work, not simply relying on their teacher's or professor's judgment of its worth. A third principle comes from the work of Mihaly Csikszentmihalyi, that feedback should be clear and constant (Csikszentmihalyi, 1990, 2002). While recognizing that more principles shape our work (and my work) than I have catalogued here, I offer these seven and want to note, without boasting, that students respond positively to assessment practices shaped by these principles. Students regularly report to me that they find their assignments meaningful and they enjoyed doing (some of) them.

As I noted earlier, one of those principles—the clear syllabus—gets all of Chapter 8 in this volume. Thus, while this chapter ends, the question of assessment strategies remains open.

REFERENCES

Carbo, M., Dunn, R. S., & Dunn, K. J. (1986). *Teaching students to read through their individual learning styles.* Prentice-Hall.

Csikszentmihalyi, M. (1990). *Flow: The psychology of optimal experience.* Harper and Row.

Csikszentmihalyi, M. (2002). Motivating people to learn. http://www.edutopia.org/mihaly-csikszentmihalyi-motivating-people-learn

Dunn, R., & Dunn, K. (1992). *Teaching elementary students through their individual learning styles: Practical approaches for grades 3–6.* Pearson.

Frankfurt, H. (2005). *On bullshit.* Princeton University Press.

Gardner, H. (1983). *Frames of mind: The theory of multiple intelligences.* Basic Books.

Gardner, H. (1999). *Intelligence reframed: Multiple intelligences for the 21st century.* Basic Books.

Kolb, D. A. (1984). *Experiential learning: Experience as the source of learning and development.* Prentice Hall.

Palmer, P. (1983). *To know as we are known: A spirituality of education.* Harper.

Westney, W. (2003). *The perfect wrong note.* Amadeus Press.

The First Day and the Syllabus

Section III

The first chapter in this section suggests ways to assure students that the class will be a good place to be for the semester. Because students expect professors to dive quickly into the course syllabus, Chapter 8 addresses the syllabus in detail. But before Chapter 8, Chapter 7 picks up where Chapter 4 (on building community) left off by suggesting that professors begin with the people in the room rather than with the grading schema for the course.

DOI: 10.4324/9781003259596-9

Seven

This chapter focuses on the first day of the semester, the day students begin forming their impressions of the course and its professor (Buchert & Laws, 2008). I divide this chapter into four parts, beginning with the first minutes. In the middle two sections of the chapter, I offer guidance for discussions about students' sense of ownership of the class, their responsibility for its success, and the character of the class. Because some students will enter a course expecting what they consider the usual—taking notes on the professor's lectures—these conversations can play an important role in shifting students' expectations and thereby helping them gain some energy for what lies ahead. I call the last section of the chapter "Last Minutes," but not to be clever. Professors impress students when they plan well and end the class with obviously planned activities rather than being caught mid-something by the clock. The last section of the chapter offers three strategies for ending the first class of the semester well.

THE FIRST MINUTES: START WITH THE PEOPLE

Both students and professor come to the first class session in a term wanting to deal with the syllabus. In many courses, the syllabus takes up the whole first day of class. I do not dispute the need to deal with the syllabus. But I always start my semester with the people, both my students and myself. In this first section, I describe three practices meant to signal my recognition that we are people in the room and thereby to help build community.

Name Tents

Immediately after making my welcome remarks, I ask students to make a tent or name card with their names printed in large enough letters to

DOI: 10.4324/9781003259596-10

see across the room. Because name tents made with ordinary printer paper usually collapse, I always bring markers and enough sheets of colored card stock with me so that my students can make substantial name tents that will remain vertical once folded. Name tents allow me to address students—even those I don't yet know—by name on the first day, a powerful way to make students feel included and to build classroom community.

In Chapter 5, I dealt in some detail with Bandura's work on self-efficacy. I will not repeat that material here but I do want to note my observation that starting the first day with the people instead of the syllabus contributes to student self-efficacy. Starting with the people helps students sense that they are part of a learning community, and feeling like community members strengthens students' self-confidence as learners. That is, the affective dimension influences cognition.

First Day Circle Meeting

Chapter 4 includes a description of the purposes and various forms of circle meetings. Most undergraduates will have participated in many such meetings during their K–12 years so they will be quite familiar with the protocols and the various ways educators might organize the circle meeting. In my first-day circle meeting, I usually require that everyone respond to a low-temperature question or prompt along these lines:

- Something I did in the last week that was out of character for me.
- Where I was born and how long I have lived where I live now.
- An interest or hobby of mine.
- My major, if I have already declared it, or a possible major (if I have not).

Offering more than one prompt reduces tension for those students who prefer not to speak aloud in class. These low-temperature questions allow students to speak. Seeing each other's faces allows both students and professor to begin framing the weeks they will be together differently than if they simply launched into the syllabus.

Many students have never had a professor offer them an open Question & Answer opportunity on the first day of a course. My public defense for this practice is simple: We get to find out about our students, so why should we not let them find out about us? My private warrant is likewise simple: I want to build a classroom community. In light of that objective, I view the specific questions students might ask, and my answers to those questions as less important than my concern that I want them to know something about my person besides the fact that I will be teaching them this semester. I usually say something semi-snarky, along the lines of "Because you spent a lot of money for this class, and we're going to be working together all semester, maybe you had better check me out!" I typically get softball questions about my hobbies, my birthplace (Saskatchewan), my educational background and current work, and my family. But I've also had "What do you think is the difference between an ideology and a worldview?" and "What would you say to your 19-year-old self if you had the chance?" (read Dostoevsky sooner). To give credit where it is due, my wife, Jo-Ann Badley, adopted this practice years ago and told me about how warmly students responded to it, so I adopted it.

Perhaps because they are so surprised, and their socialization into the professional boundaries of the university has been so successful, students are sometimes hesitant to ask any questions. But, with encouragement, someone will start and things usually roll from there.

WHOSE CLASS IS THIS?

As I noted in my discussion of building a classroom community (in Chapter 4), I want my students to think of our class as our class, not simply as my class which they attend. The first day presents a major opportunity to begin helping my students frame our class that way. Here, I present three first-day strategies for creating community.

The Language of Shared Ownership

Starting on the first day and continuing throughout the term, I consistently use language meant to project a sense of shared work, that my students and I have the same purposes, and any success we experience is shared success. The key distinction here, as I pointed out in

Chapter 4, is that between the language of me/I/my/mine and you/your/yours compared and we/us/our/ours. I need my students to understand that, in my view if they succeed in learning, then I have succeeded in teaching; if they fail, I have failed.

In normal campus discourse, professors say things such as "I have two sections of 100 this semester, and one section of 265." And students normally say things like "I'm taking so-and-so's 301 and I'm taking 341 from so-and-so." The possessives—have in the first sentence and so-and-so's in the second—are in fact normal speech, and in normal speech they therefore go absolutely unnoticed. But those bits of normal speech and other phrases like them illustrate an important truth about campus life and how we frame our teaching work. Our classes are, in fact, ours. Even if our assignment in a given year includes two sections of an introduction where eight other sections are on offer and all who teach that introduction are expected to use the same textbook and teach the same content, we still think of our sections as ours. Complaining about such language patterns would be useless, but I try to nudge my students toward a reframing of course ownership. I want them to think of the courses they take with me as our courses, as courses we own together. If the course is our course, and we succeed, then we all succeed.

Please do not misread the paragraphs above. I am not abandoning my responsibility to teach and to submit grades. I am not putting my students in charge. I am not ignoring my subject-area expertise. On the contrary, I am trying to get my students to take some responsibility for the success of the course and to think of it as a shared enterprise. I have adapted one specific strategy and developed another to foster this shared sense of responsibility and to help students think of my classes as their classes ... as our classes. The first of these involves using a DNA strand as a metaphor and asking about the protein bars in our course DNA.

The DNA Strand

My British colleague Ruth Crick (only a distant connection to the similarly-named co-discoverer of DNA) introduced me to this metaphor decades ago. It still makes sense and students still respond positively to it. On the first day of class I show or draw a DNA strand like that in Figure 7.1. One side of the strand is labeled The Curriculum, and the other side says Your Interests and Questions. I explain that I deeply want

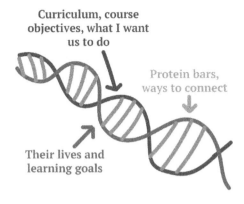

Curriculum, course objectives, what I want us to do

Protein bars, ways to connect

Their lives and learning goals

Figure 7.1 A DNA strand used as a prompt for discussion about how to connect course contents with students' lives.

Credit: Sophie Chardon.

to connect the course material to my students' interests and questions. After a brief explanation I ask, "So what are the protein bars? How do we make these connections?" I have had secondary students tell me that they hoped I would use film clips or bring food to class (literal protein bars) as they had heard I had done in previous semesters. And I have had one doctoral student tell me she had just had her $70 million school district budget drastically cut and that she hoped our ethics in education class would help her navigate the fiscal waters she had never dreamed she would encounter.

Semester after semester, I use this strategy to contribute to my students' sense that I care about connecting the course subject matter with their lives. Regardless of the subject matter at hand, the course contents have relevance to life. I want them to understand that I do not view the course as a venue to transfer the contents of my hard drive to their hard drive by the least efficient means possible. Rather, our class is a place where we will collectively discover amazing connections between university and what many in education call the real world, as if the world of the campus somehow does not deserve the honorific adjective of "real." At several points, I have talked about authorizing students and a shared classroom epistemology. Because it gives them a channel for input into course design and planning, discussing course DNA is one means of authorizing students.

Discussion of course DNA usually runs about 15 minutes but can easily go longer. I usually ask a student to take notes and email them to me (so I can post them on the course wiki) allowing me to focus on the conversation and demonstrating that I sincerely want to hear my students' views on the question. In online courses, I prepare a labeled slide in advance (like Figure 7.1) and share it on the online screen to introduce the question.

Personal Course Objectives

A natural follow-on to the DNA discussion is to ask students to articulate their own objectives for the course. I often require that students provide two or three personal course objectives in light of their reflection on our DNA discussion and these three components of the syllabus: The official paragraph description appearing at the top of the syllabus, the course objectives I have listed, and the outline of the course contents. Designating 5% course weight for personal course objectives (as shown in Table 6.1) is typical, but I have given as little as 3%. My purpose in giving course weight to this small, initial, easy assignment is to encourage my students to recognize that this is our course, not only my course.

CLASSROOM CLIMATE CHOICES

Decades of practice have shaped both professors' and students' expectations about university courses in general and the first days in those courses in particular. Recognizably, what I have suggested in the first section of the chapter and what I will suggest in this section run against some of these deeply entrenched expectations and the practices that sustain them. Nevertheless, in what follows I offer three more strategies I use to build student-efficacy, increase student engagement, and build classroom community.

Lockheed Martin's Skunk Works and MIT's Building 20

Most students have never heard of Lockheed Martin's Skunk Works (Burbank, California) or Building 20 at MIT (Boston), which I introduced in Chapter 3. For somewhat different reasons, both these places became great centers of creativity and innovation and, as a professor, I want to understand and I want my students to understand what conditions fostered the creativity and innovation at work in the Skunk Works and Building 20. The first was quite intentionally established as a research and development center whose creativity would depend in part on the brilliance of the select few chosen to work there and in part on the principles by which it originally operated (known as "Kelly's 14 rules"; Lockheed Martin, n.d.). The second—Building 20—simply evolved. Intended as a temporary, wooden structure, it was erected hurriedly during World War II for military research purposes and, following the war, was colonized by various MIT departments. Because Building 20 was to be torn down any time (but remained in use until 1998), senior administrators at MIT apparently allowed those who occupied it to do what they pleased with the building. By most accounts, it became a center of interdisciplinary research and a hotbed of innovation and creativity (Lehrer, 2012).

My introduction to these two sites has been briefer here than it is in my classes. When I introduce the Skunk Works and Building 20 in class, I usually show a few slides to give my students some initial familiarity with the two centers, and then I ask half the class to conduct some quick research (singly or in pairs) on each of the two sites and report back to class what they think the conditions were that led to the great creativity characteristic of whichever site they researched. The Wikipedia articles on both places are good starting points, as is Lockheed's website (Lockheed Martin, n.d.). The "Stickies on the Wall" discussion strategy (Chapter 12) works well for the reporting-in portion of this activity. Once all who want to report have done so, we make the transition to this question about our university classroom: "How do we structure a university class so that similar levels of creativity can be unleashed?" Discuss in small groups what class practices or structures would allow that kind of creativity to flourish in class.

Over many years I have heard both good and bad ideas in response to that question. Many students have suggested strategies I had planned to use anyway. But by giving them an opportunity to suggest these strategies, I bring them into the process of shaping the course, and I show them in yet another way that I want the course to reflect their strengths and their wishes.

Creativity was the founding purpose at the Skunk Works, and it happened rather serendipitously in Building 20. In university classrooms, unleashing creativity does not simply happen; teachers must structure curriculum, instruction, and assessment to unleash it. Students must understand that the class welcomes ideas further than two standard deviations from the mean. Most classes have a few persistent and ultra-creative students who would flourish even if they were taught by zombies, but most students need a push. When we ask our students to speculate about how Kelly's 14 rules might apply in a university classroom or how we could create some of the flavor of Building 20 in our classes, we invite them to view our class as a research center rather than simply as a site for transmitting information.

Csikszentmihalyi and Flow

Early in the semester, often in the second class session, I tell my classes about the work of Mihaly Csikszentmihalyi on flow, the pre-conditions he names for flow, and my desire to help create those preconditions (introduced in Chapter 3 herein; Csikszentmihalyi, 1990). After listing the preconditions (concentration, finding the challenge–skills balance, goal clarity and buy-in, and feedback clarity), I spend a few minutes exploring with my students his concept of the challenge–skills balance. By *challenge–skills balance*, Csikszentmihalyi meant that we are likeliest to get into a flow state when we are working close to the limits of our abilities but are experiencing success in our work. As a class, we discuss ways that we could create the preconditions for flow in our class and especially where the challenge–skills balance might be for our class.

The tension here between finding the challenge–skills balance in a university class and achieving Skunk Works or Building 20 levels of creativity is obvious. We are dealing with college and university students—mere mortals—not with seasoned and accomplished specialists. Our students' socialization into academic life has not encouraged them thus far to take risks, because risks lead to failure and failures have an impact on their grades. I could list more reasons we or our students might think that in any given class we should restrain ourselves and go on with business as usual. But to refer again to the tracks portion of the grading schema I described in the previous chapter, otherwise ordinary students in my classes have produced extra-ordinary work. Several of the eight students who chose the Book Project Track in the January semester of 2019 (Chapter 11) have told me they had never imagined sharing authorship of a book and finding their names on Amazon. For me, the key words here are *never imagined*.

Aerospace engineers had never imagined an airplane that could not be seen on radar. And then someone imagined it. So, yes, I recognize the tension between discussing the challenge–skills balance with students and then asking them to imagine class as a Building 20 or a Skunk Works. However, I believe that many students typically perform well below their capacity because they so rarely encounter an environment that demands the best of them.

Light Videos about Epistemic Uncertainty

I often use light-weight videos to underscore the point that I do not have all the answers and we will not always get resolution to the questions raised in class; some mysteries are going to remain unsolved. While we will not get everything sorted by the end of the semester, we are going to experience real joy as we think deeply and honestly with each other about the course contents. I use two videos (on YouTube) to underline this approach to the uncertainty that will characterize our work: "Building the plane while flying it" and "Herding cats." Both were produced by the same advertising agency for the same technology company. I know that the sense of loose or uncertain process portrayed in these short videos is not to everyone's liking, but students consistently find them easier to understand than the "Heisenberg" article in Wikipedia.

A Classroom Climate Matrix

As a university student, I once witnessed a professor use these words to cut a student off before she had completed her class presentation: "It's one thing to be boring but boring and useless I will not tolerate. Please sit down." This unnecessarily rude comment led me to produce a four-cell matrix—referred to in the privacy of my home by the professor's name—that can serve as a highly effective discussion prompt about classroom climate. For decades, I have asked students which way they would prefer their professors to fail, given that they will inevitably fail from time to time. No one wants a class to be boring and useless. Classes will not always be interesting and useful. On the days represented by the question marks in Figure 7.2, would students prefer that their classes be interesting and useless or boring and useful?

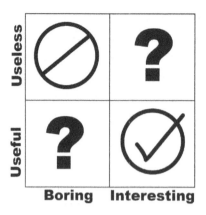

Figure 7.2 The Class Climate Matrix, representing a useful pair of distinctions for thinking about classroom climate.

Art credit: Sophie Chardon.

I recommend using this matrix to begin such a conversation but I can never predict where that conversation might lead. We will always have a few students who tell us they just want us to give them what they need to know for the exam. And (I hope) we will always have at least a few students who know that people who worked in the Skunk Works and Building 20 probably did a few interesting things that initially looked useless but later became the key to a major advance.

A discussion of classroom climate may also range over some of the topics I raised in Chapter 4 about building classroom community. How do shared authority and co-determination shift responsibility onto students? What does a community of trust imply about the safety to express our views and the foundations of those views? What does hospitality imply for the ways we might disagree with each other?

LAST MINUTES: THREE STRATEGIES

Students and professors alike have enough administration to attend to during their first week that they are justified if they want to exit the first class quickly. With my students' schedules more in mind than my own, I move to administration and housekeeping well before the end of class, giving myself enough time to accomplish these three tasks: Distribute and collect exit slips, take some head-shots of my students, and collect the name tents they produced earlier in the class.

The First-Day Exit Slip

Every post-secondary student who finished high school in the last decade will know what exit slips are and how to use them, so no professor has to explain them. I distinguish several kinds of exit slips, as follows:

- First day variant, where students address some or the following topics: Lightweight personal information such as their birthplace or favorite food, their preferred email, address, their preferred name for use in class, what program they are in, how this class fits into their program, their goals for the course, and so on.
- Regular day versions, where I typically ask students to talk about something they still don't understand from that day's class, something they wish we had spent more time on, or a question that that day's content raises, etc. In K–12 education, this is the most common usage of the exit slip.
- Exam-question variant (which I mentioned in Chapter 6 with reference to the Final Exam Track), where I ask students to identify a suitable exam question related to that day's content. Wording the question is important so that students refrain from submitting simple recall questions. I usually word my exit-slip prompt this way: "What exam question would appropriately test the material in today's class? This should be a question that requires critical thinking."

Ordinarily, I permit students to submit an exit-slip without their name but I encourage them to sign their name, stressing that we are a community of learners and I am trying to find my way forward in the class just as they are. In online settings, I ask for a volunteer student to serve as a clearinghouse for those who wish to submit anonymously. Obviously, on the first day exit slip, I need students to include their names. The textbox shows a first-day exit slip from a face-to-face, first-year education course at Mount Royal University in Calgary. Spaces for students' answers have been removed here but the original slip was photocopied on 8.5x11" paper.

First Day Exit Slip – EDUC 1231

Your last name on my class list.

Your preferred first name.

Other courses you are transferring to Mount Royal University, if any?

From what university or college?

The best class (name the subject, not the teacher) you've had in your life so far … K–12 up to and including any other higher education courses.

What made that class great?

Is there anything in the syllabus that remains unclear that I should address by email, on the blackboard, or in our next class.

Is there anything on the syllabus that remains unclear that I should address on the course site or in our next class?

Thank you for joining our class and for submitting this exit slip to me. I am excited about the work we will do together this semester.

I will return to the exit slip again in Chapter 14 with reference to assessment of our own teaching, and again in Chapter 15 when I address what I call the mid-course correction, the brief diagnosis I usually conduct with my students at about the half-way point in the semester.

The Photo Directory

In settings where the Registrar's Office does not provide a photo directory, I assemble my own because I want to learn my students' names and connect those names to their faces. After explaining to my students that my knowing their names is essential to our building the kind of classroom community I want us to build together (and build and community are the terms I use), I ask them either to email me a picture from their phone right then or to allow me to take a head shot while they hold their name tents so I can assemble a class directory. For various reasons, some will not want their photo taken but most will allow it. To save time, I invite them to let me photograph them in groups of two or three (holding their name tents) and I separate them out later on my computer. I assemble the directory and print it in color after the drop/add date. I carry this paper directory with me to class until I have learned everyone's name. On a slightly different note, I keep my old directories in a binder called "Former Students" to help me remember who's who when students send me reference requests or on those rare days when I wonder if I have been a good steward of my teaching vocation.

Gathering the Name Tents

I usually ask my students to leave their name tents with me to increase the likelihood that those tents will come back to our next class. Collecting them actually does more than that; it gives me an opportunity for more contact in the key final moments of our first class. I can say my students' names as I thank them for their name tent and for registering in my class.

CONCLUSION

The research on semester start-up procedures is unambiguous: Students form lasting impressions on the first day (Buchert & Lewis, 2010) or even before the first day of class (Legg & Wilson, 2009). I am aware of the urgency of dealing with the syllabus and with students' questions about the assessment schema in place in a given class, and I give the whole next chapter to syllabus clarity. The importance of the syllabus notwithstanding, I strongly recommend investing time in the practices and some of the conversations I have described here. Such investments pay significant dividends throughout the semester in student engagement, in the quality of student work, and in professor satisfaction.

REFERENCES

Buchert, S., & Laws, E. L. (2008). First impressions and professor reputation: Influence on student evaluations of instruction. *Social Psychology of Education*, 11(4), 397–408.

Csikszentmihalyi, M. (1990). *Flow: The psychology of optimal experience*. Harper and Row.

Legg, A. M., & Wilson, J. H. (2009). E-mail from professor enhances student motivation and attitudes. *Teaching of Psychology*, 36(3), 205–211.

Lehrer, J. (2012). Groupthink: The brainstorming myth. *The New Yorker*, January 30, 22–27. https://www.newyorker.com/magazine/2012/01/30/groupthink

Lockheed Martin. (n.d.). Kelly's 14 rules. file:///C:/Users/Owner/AppData/Local/Temp/kellys-14-rules.pdf

Lockheed Martin. (n.d.). The Skunk Works origin story. https://www.lockheedmartin.com/en-us/who-we-are/business-areas/aeronautics/skunkworks/skunk-works-origin-story.html

Syllabus Strategies

Eight

Students root their perceptions of the character of a given course and their expectations regarding that course in several kinds of soil: Their professor's reputation, their interest in the subject matter, and even the time slot in which the course is being offered. Obviously, the syllabus also contributes to students' perceptions. In what follows, I suggest strategies to engage students with the syllabus and to make the syllabus more accessible to all students. In the first section following, I describe steps we can take to ensure that our syllabi are as free of errors and are as understandable as possible. The second half of the chapter focuses on planning the course in such a way that its overall structure fits our students' actual calendars, and offering a simple calendar in the syllabus that reveals that structure at a glance.

CLARITY

The clear syllabus gives students a sense of control of the course and thereby contributes to their self-efficacy. Students cannot produce their best work if they feel like they do not know what is expected of them. I usually take the following steps to ensure that the syllabus is clear and to build my students' sense of control, often expressed as "I've got this."

Pre-Inspection by a Graphic Artist

My first strategy for achieving syllabus clarity is to have a graphic artist look over my syllabus for layout and format problems. In my own case, the graphic artist (or website user-experience specialist) who furnished most of the illustrations in this book looks over my syllabi for readability and visual properties. She looks at page layout, sectioning, the heading hierarchy, and font choices, asking at every point about whether the formatting is likely to diminish or increase students' sense of control. A good question to keep in mind with

DOI: 10.4324/9781003259596-11

syllabi is this: How would a student with ADD or dyslexia respond on seeing this syllabus? I ask my designer (who happens to be my daughter) to format for increased accessibility for the many kinds of learners I am likely to have in my class. She always sends my syllabi back to me looking cleaner and easier to read than when I sent them to her. I recommend that all professors find a graphic artist or typesetter to help make their syllabi more readable and accessible.

Pre-Inspection by Students

Second, I usually have some students check the syllabus in advance of the first day of class. If I don't know anyone on my class list, I ask colleagues to identify students on my list whom they think would do a good job on such a detailed task. With only rare exceptions, those students who do their classmates and me this service come back with legitimate questions and objections. They discover an assessment schema that adds up to 95%, a due date on a national holiday, or an unclear assignment. They also raise questions about the weights I have allocated to various assignments. I fix these errors and address their concerns before posting the syllabus on the course wiki or taking it to class, and thereby prevent confusion and frustration for my students and embarrassment for myself. A minor benefit of this process is that the handful of students who agreed to check the syllabus now have a greater degree of understanding and ownership of the course. That understanding obviously benefits them but it also pays dividends on the first day of class because they can help their classmates understand bits of the syllabus I have difficulty explaining clearly.

One of three emailed responses to a Sociology of Education syllabus sent to students a few days before the start of a course:

Hi Ken,
I've looked at the syllabus and I think overall it looks great. I once again love how students have some control and get to choose which track interests them the most, similar to your class that I took this past year. I've added some comments on the doc in red front and have included some more general comments below... I'm hoping none of it sounds too critical...

- It needs to be clearer that students are required to be doing assignments 1–7 and then choose one track from assignment 8 (e.g. subheadings). Make it clear to choose only one track.
- I really like the idea of services and practices... However, the first thing students are going to ask is if they can use practicum visits for this (especially for the 2nd years, since they have the same number of visits for the semester anyway).
- Under the "major assignment areas" box ... I absolutely love the idea of researching a topic and participating in a panel. I remember the last class of your course last semester, students actually seemed to want to discuss some ideas. Unfortunately, it seems like uni students are hesitant to discuss unless it's required. But I have participated in some classes where debating/being in a panel is required but students were actually very, very eager to do it. I think it's a great way to ask thought-provoking questions that may actually shape teacher-candidates' teaching philosophies/views on social issues. Is there some way we could try to integrate this as an actual assignment? Or is there some way we could build it into student lessons. (I realize there is already some planned discussion attached to this, but I think a required, structured panel would be really great.)
- Overall, I think the assignments are weighted very fairly. I also like how the tracks are weighted... 30% doesn't seem like a lot, but I think the tracks will really make students learn and realize they're here to learn, not just to earn their 30% and leave.

The Second-Last Draft

For the same reason that I ask a few students to look over the syllabus in advance, I always call the posted or distributed syllabus the second-last draft. That signals to students my own sense that I am capable of error and that I want to hear my students' views about what the syllabus contains. Because this is the second-last draft, students do not need to have a melt-down if they see a mistake. Even when a few students have inspected the syllabus, errors sometimes remain. Working through the syllabus together fits with my comment in Chapter 7 about using language that demonstrates my belief that this is our course, not just my course. Because the syllabus came from a human being, not from on high, we inspect it together and we fix it where needed, a posture consistent with a class philosophy of mistakes and also with the architectural principle that the places we inhabit seem more human when they show the patina of human occupation (Alexander et al, 1977; Alexander, 1979).

The Grading Schema

When we look at the syllabus, whether online or face-to-face, we should look as a class at the grading schema first, even though our own reasons for being in the room are likely best expressed in the course objectives. As my readers all know from experience, the first thing students want to know is what they need to do to succeed in the class (with the word *succeed* defined in a variety of ways). The official course description paragraph near the top of the syllabus and my course objectives are of little interest to my students compared to their interest in the assessment schema, so we turn there first. But I do not read through the listed assignments. I ask different groups of students to take a few minutes to examine the descriptions of the various tasks and then, in turn, to explain to the class their understanding of each respective assignment, to raise their questions, to note what they consider to be the important features of each assignment, and to interact with those classmates who may have their own questions. In these conversations, I see myself more as a resource than as the final arbiter or all things. I usually ask someone to take notes for me about mistakes and items that need clarification in the final draft. As I noted in Chapter 7, I also invite students to flag any remaining ambiguities on their first day exit slip.

My next strategy is simple: Produce an understandable grading schema. All syllabi have the potential to foster confusion among students, in part because of their own elevated stress levels on the first day of a course. Building flexibility and choice into a course's assessment schema has more potential to lead to student frustration … "So *what exactly* is it you want us to do?" As I demonstrated in Chapter 6, it is possible to build flexibility and choice into a course and still offer students a clear grading schema.

Rubrics

In Chapter 6, I advocated co-determining the rubric with students. I will not repeat my argument here but will point out simply that co-determining the rubric serves as an effective way to increase student understanding and ownership of an assignment. Because most students now expect to see published rubrics for their assignments and because rubrics inflate the page count of a syllabus, discouraging reading, I post a single *Rubrics Document* on the course wiki. Having all the rubrics in a single document simplifies answering my students' question (and sometimes my own), "Where is the rubric for that assignment?"

QR codes

One small detail worth noting is that with paper syllabi, some students will find QR codes useful wherever links appear to resources or online documents. You can produce QR codes simply by copying a URL into a field at https://www.qr-code-generator.com/. Regardless of how many students take advantage of your having included QR codes in the syllabus, including them signals to the whole class that you have not remained frozen in some kind of techno-coma since the Beatles announced their breakup.

Syllabus Humor

For syllabus content you consider especially important, make slides with humorously threatening messages on them. For copyright reasons, I am unable to show two slides I always project at key points in our discussion of the syllabus. The first, with an easily-recognizable picture of Justin Bieber, says "Remember, if you submit an assignment as a pdf instead of as a Microsoft Word document, he writes another song." My second poster, with a picture of Nickelback, reads this way: "Remember, if you submit your paper as a Google doc or via another cloud service instead of as an email attachment, these guys tour again." Students laugh, but these slides are not foolproof. A few students forget how I want their assignments submitted, but almost all of them remember my rule.

The Course Objectives

With the time pressures on the first day's class and students' justifiable interest in the course grading schema, the course objectives may get less attention on day 1 than they deserve. After all, they are the reason the course is on the books and they are the reason professors come to work. Asking students to write their own objectives in light of the published objectives works effectively as a way to get students to examine the part of the syllabus that they did not immediately turn to when they first looked at the syllabus. I repeat from Chapter 7 that assigning students' personal objectives something in the range of 3–5% at the start of the course means that they will look at the course objectives in a way they likely did not or would not do on day 1. Also, if what they submit is graded on a pass-fail basis, then they will already have completed some of their course work by session 2 (or, as some would put it, "already have some grades in the bank").

COURSE DESIGN AND SCHEDULE

Professors can do themselves and their students a favour by attending to what, in Chapter 3, I called the design of the course. Recall that I have expressed concern throughout the book that we think of our courses as places where we address both the curriculum content and questions of how our students learn best. That latter condition implies that we think of the weeks of the semester not simply as a succession of weeks of course content but rather as a succession of weeks in our students' real lives. In what follows immediately, I address that question. Following that, and knowing that most syllabi contain a detailed schedule, I suggest that we include a very simple semester schedule in the syllabus so that students can grasp the course structure easily. I then argue that we should also take into account that some students come to our class with apprehensions about what assignments they may have to complete. I argue that we should apply the architectural principle of the setback to reduce those apprehensions, that on the first day we should not reveal all the details or the full scope of the biggest assignment.

Natural Divisions in the Term

Most undergraduates view the acronym irl—in real life—as natural language. I use it here to draw attention to the natural breaks in a semester, breaks that are very important both to students and to professors, their friends, and families. Indeed, in what we might call the national mind, these breaks demarcate parts of the calendar year and, implicitly, the academic term. In this section I argue that we should view these breaks not as disruptions to the flow of our instruction, but as natural divisions between parts of our course. Whether or not we are willing to plan our semester for students' real lives has the status of a line of demarcation between educators whose first concern is to transmit their course contents to students and those who begin with the question, "What are the best ways for my students to learn this material." I deal at much greater length with my concern that we work with rather than against natural course divisions in the book I introduced at the end of Chapter 3, *Curriculum planning with design language: Building elegant courses and units* (Badley, 2018).

A Simple Calendar

A clear and simple semester calendar also reduces student confusion. My own observation over decades reveals that as syllabi have grown to include more and more boilerplate paragraphs from the university, students have become less and less interested in reading anything in syllabi except the course requirements. At the time of my writing this, the news networks are carrying the story of Kenyon Wilson, a department head at the University of Tennessee at Chattanooga, who noted in his syllabus that he had placed $50 in a locker for the first student to read that far in the syllabus. That student was to go the locker, use the combination Wilson had listed in the syllabus, and claim the money as their own. That no one read his offer in the syllabus does not surprise most of us who work on syllabi only to have students ask only about the grading schema for the course, perhaps even asking, "What do I gotta' do to pass?" In light of students' declining interest in tackling a 10–20-page document, I usually include a simple calendar like this one from a January semester course that met for three-hour blocks once per week. The calendar is simple, with just three rows: The week, the date, and each week's contents.

Week	1	2	3	4	5	6	Spring break
Date	Jan 8	Jan 15	Jan 22	Jan29	Feb 05	Feb 12	
Contents	Introduction			*The Courage to Teach* (text)			

	7	8	9	10	11	12	13
	Feb 26	Mar 05	Mar 12	Mar 19	Mar 26	Apr 02	Apr 09
		Ethics in teaching		Presence, shared authority		Presentations & conclusions	Wrap up

Students repeatedly thank me for providing a simple calendar like this one. The topics for each week are clear. To refer to architectural and design principles again, the entrances and exits of the course demarcations are clearly marked, as are the boundaries. The centers, by which I mean the main topics we will try to understand, are clear. Appendix A includes a more detailed calendar (pages 216–217), one of which I also include in every syllabus, but this abbreviated calendar gives a capsule of important information to students and increases their sense of control over their learning. The calendar above also illustrates a structural term used by K–12 educators much more than it is used by higher educators: The unit, which I discuss at length in the next chapter. For now, simply note that the course in question has four or five distinct topics or parts and that, from the first day of the term, my students will know the specific topic for each class session.

The Setback

This concept from architecture has an important application in course design and in how we introduce our assessment schema to students. The setback in architecture refers to the practice of hiding some of the volume of a building from the sidewalk view so that those looking at the building are less intimidated by its size. The Empire State Building in New York City illustrates the setback perfectly (Figure 8.1). My application of the setback to the syllabus is simple: Hide some of the course's volume on the first day so that students feel invited into the course rather than becoming convinced that they cannot possibly succeed. Perhaps this cliché has no basis in reality but some of my readers will have heard of professors who announced on the first day of term that only one in two will pass the course or that, with 50% of the course grade riding on such-and-such an assignment, students had better take it seriously. Intimidating students in this way likely produces its share of cortisol in students' brains but does little for their grades. My goal in employing the architectural principle of the setback is to produce less cortisol and more student self-efficacy.

In the curriculum design book I seem to advertise so persistently (Badley, 2018), I deal at length with the setback as a curriculum design principle. Here I will briefly suggest two applications of the principle. First, if you do provide rubrics for assignments, do not include them in the syllabus. Doing so adds unnecessarily to the

Figure 8.1 The Empire State Building illustrates the concept of the setback, by which the full volume of the building is hidden from the sidewalk view to reduce intimidation.

Photo credit: Juan Pablo Mascanfroni, on Unsplash.com.

syllabus page count with information students do not need on the first day of term. Including a lot of detail adds to the intimidation for those students already likely to be intimidated by the seriousness or volume of the course work. Instead of including rubrics or extended assignment details in the syllabus, assemble a single document with all the applicable rubrics, examples, and suggestions, and post it on the course wiki. In Appendix A, I provide sample rubrics. I did not dress these up for this book; they are exactly as they appear in the *Rubrics Document* I post on course websites.

The second application of the setback principle is this: If a significant percentage of the course grade is tied to one major assignment, produce a separate document containing the detailed instructions and specifications for that assignment. For example, describing the research paper where students have a choice among a dozen or more topics easily adds a full page to the syllabus. Some students may want to choose their topic on the first day of term but most do not. Where do such supplementary instructions go? Students find it helpful if detailed instructions or further suggestions for assignments appear with the applicable rubric in the *Rubrics Document*.

Further to the major paper that is likely due in the second half of the course, I suggest returning to that assignment on the second day of term. Students will have processed most of the syllabus detail by the second class session, and it will be possible toward the end of that class to give some time to a discussion of the character of the major assignment, its assessment, and the rubric you will be using.

Conclusion

We can build an assessment plan for our course that students find easy to understand (Chapter 6). We can make the first day of the semester a significant beginning to the course (Chapter 7). Like the entrance hall of a large public building, a well-planned first day lets people know they have come somewhere special. And, as I have described in this chapter, we can ensure that the syllabus is easy to read and understand. If we get the contents of these three chapters right, students can begin our courses with an appropriate sense that they can succeed. And their success leads to our sense that we are getting it right.

REFERENCES

Alexander, C. (1979). *The timeless way of building.* Oxford University Press.
Alexander, C., Ishikawa, S., Silverstein, M., Jacobson, M., Fiksdahl-King, I., & Angel, S. (1977). *A pattern language: Towns, buildings, construction.* Oxford University Press.
Badley, K. (2018). *Curriculum planning with design language: Building elegant courses and units.* Routledge.

Instructional Strategies
Section IV

This section begins with strategies for use at the beginnings of units or topics within a course and ends with strategies for the last day of the course. Between those two chapters are four chapters focused on four kinds of strategies. Chapter 10 offers strategies to support students in their reading. Chapter 11, which attends to writing strategies, is linked to a number of additional writing strategies that appear in Appendix B. Chapter 12 is the longest chapter in the book. It suggests a variety of ways to engage students in class discussions. Chapter 13 discusses ways to use the arts in both instruction and assessment.

Taken as a whole, Section IV of this volume offers a thorough catalog of teaching and learning strategies meant to support higher educators and the students in their classes.

DOI: 10.4324/9781003259596-12

Nine

In the early chapters of this volume, I made repeated reference to learning-centered teaching in contrast to transmission or information-transfer models of teaching. I presume that any reader who has stayed with me this far has accepted my argument that students (and maybe professors) need variety and that courses need to be divided into distinct parts. I start this chapter with an expanded argument for designing and planning courses in light of the schedule realities of students' lives. In the second half of the chapter, I offer several strategies for use on the first day of a new unit or topic within a course.

DIVIDING THE TERM

Toward the end of Chapter 8, I advocated structuring courses in light of the natural breaks in the calendar and I noted the concept of the unit, universally used by elementary and secondary teachers but not a significant part of the lexicon of higher education. In this first part of the chapter, I will expand on those ideas, beginning with the question of scheduling.

Taking Advantage of Natural Divisions

The semester or term consists of a specified number of weeks, and responsible professors plan to work through the course contents at a certain pace so that they and their students are finished their work by the end of term. Fair enough; in fact, that's precisely what's on my mind when I plan. But I want to begin this chapter by arguing briefly that if we will recognize and work within the natural breaks in the term, we will do ourselves and our students a favor. I write about natural breaks because I have observed how powerfully reading weeks, long weekends, and national holidays shape our students' thinking about their semesters and terms. Rightly, we think about our courses partly in curricular and epistemic terms: We will read this before we

DOI: 10.4324/9781003259596-13

read that; they need to understand these concepts and then we can move on to those concepts; until they have understood this problem, they won't see that other problem. As we frame the semester, such epistemic or curricular divisions may seem natural to us, but most of our students do not initially frame their courses that way, and some never do.

In *Curriculum Planning with Design Language: Building Elegant Courses and Units* (Badley, 2018), I treat the gap between curricular/epistemological framings of courses and what we might call students' phenomenological framings of courses. In that volume, I argue that we would be wise to plan semesters around those natural breaks. I grant that the structure of the discipline and the hierarchy of concepts dealt with in a given course ought to shape the course as well, but if we plan to engage living learners—learners who look forward to long weekends, for example—with our curriculum and instructional materials, then we need to take their mental schedules into serious account. In Chapter 8, I referred to planning that takes these factors into consideration *planning IRL* (planning in real life).

You could think of this approach to semester-long planning as a type of *coming to terms*; literally, we come to each fall, winter, or spring term. And we need to come to terms with our students' internal semester calendar, a calendar that takes long weekends as seriously as we may take the conceptual relations between some of the foundational ideas in our academic disciplines. Let me illustrate with reference to the typical September term in a Canadian university. As staff in the Office of the Registrar know, if classes begin before *Labour Day*, the first Monday in September, a lot of students will be unhappy. In June 2021, the federal government of Canada declared September 30 a new federal, statutory holiday, the *National Day for Truth and Reconciliation*, a day to lament and remember the sad legacy of Canada's residential schools for First Nations children. As they plan for the September 2022 semester, Canadian universities will need to decide how to recognize that day. Will holding classes but encouraging the wearing of orange shirts be enough? Should universities cancel classes? Canadian Thanksgiving (which Canadians unironically call *Thanksgiving*) falls on the second Monday of October, and no university would dare schedule classes that day. November 11 is called *Remembrance Day* in Canada; some universities schedule classes that day and some do not. To pick one date from this series of examples, the Thanksgiving long weekend is a natural break in the semester and, in my view, the wise professor plans to finish one unit (topic or block) of work before that weekend and to start another on the Tuesday after. Briefly, the professor planning January semester courses in an American college might view Martin Luther King Day, Presidents Day, Spring Break, and Easter weekend not as interruptions but as breaks that offer a way to divide the semester's work naturally.

Even professors who agree with me that such natural breaks are a real part of students' mental framing of a semester may resist coming to terms with my view that the study of the subject matter of a course should, in a sense, be constrained by a planning model that takes these breaks into such serious account. I will not argue my view further here. I will suggest only that those hesitant to plan this way try it just once, in just one course, and see if students show greater understanding of the course structure, and therefore higher levels of engagement with its contents.

The Unit, Topic, or Theme

A natural part of the lexicon of K–12 educators and therefore most undergraduates is a term largely missing from the language of those of us who work in higher education: unit. In K–12 education, units can last as long as several months or can be as short as 10 or 11 class days, depending on the subject and grade level. Besides units, K–12 educators refer to these course sections variously as topics and themes. In K–12 education, block usually refers to the divisions of a school day into periods, but some higher educators use it as I do here to refer to a portion of a semester. Undergraduates' familiarity with this model—they have worked within it for a decade before they arrive in our classes—is one reason I suggest importing unit planning to higher education.

My second reason for advocating dividing courses in higher education into units flows directly out of the previous section on natural breaks. Units are a natural way to work with the natural breaks. In fact, we can earn a kind of compound interest by designing our courses this way because many of our students also had teachers who ended units before natural breaks and started new units after those breaks. If we use a scheduling pattern with which our students are already familiar, we may increase their self-efficacy. Related also to our students' perception or reception of our planning model, unit divisions in a university course may also reduce their sense that a course is simply a term-long succession of days, with the format and content of each day barely distinguishable from the days before and after.

One final reason to consider unit planning in the college or university course is the professor's own experience of the semester. Planning units or topics of specific lengths in advance helps us keep the course on pace so that the last week of the term does not end up packed with 30% of the course's contents. Planning with this degree of detail may feel like the self-imposition of unnecessary constraints to some of the more free-spirited amongst us. But scheduling may actually be a source of liberation. As a let's-see-where-it-goes professor myself, I find such detailed planning freeing because I always know where we are headed next, and I can continuously judge our progress toward that objective, meeting Csikszentmihalyi's (1990) pre-condition of flow: Clear feedback.

The Entrance

From architecture, especially from Christopher Alexander's work on pattern languages (Alexander et al, 1977; Alexander, 1979; Chapter 3 here), I borrow the concept of the entrance and apply it here to the first day of a new unit or block. In Chapter 5 in my *Curriculum Planning with Design Language* book (2018), I treat this idea at length. In Chapter 7 herein, I offered a number of strategies that could help give the course itself an entrance. Each unit or block needs its own entrance as well. In short, we should plan the first day of a new unit so that students have a heightened sense of anticipation that what we are about to study will be interesting and worth their time.

The first time I saw the glorious entrance hall of the Chicago Art Institute I was awestruck with its grandeur. No one could ever mistake this iconic space for an auto-parts warehouse. I don't want to spoil the metaphor by suggesting that our students should be awestruck by the spectacle we prepare for the first day of a new section of our course, but I do want them to know that today and tomorrow will be different from yesterday and the day before. In what follows, I offer a few strategies to help create an entrance so students are more likely to engage with what comes next in the course.

ENGAGEMENT STRATEGIES

Having offered a warrant for making a distinct entrance, in this second section of the chapter I suggest several strategies to engage students' interest on the first day of a new unit or topic.

KWL and Its Variants

KWL stands for what I **K**now, what I **W**ould like to know (or **W**onder about or **W**ish I knew), and what I **L**earned. I recommend it for the college classroom because almost every K–12 teacher uses this strategy (or one or more of its variants) and every undergraduate knows how it works. Very simply, on the day students begin studying a new topic, they fill out the first two columns of a three-column sheet that has these three labels.

What I **K**now	What I **W**ish I knew	What I Learned

Some teachers ask their students to supply their own paper; others distribute a photo-copied sheet. In both cases, the columns are (obviously) longer than in my illustration above. Most teachers ask students to hand these sheets in so they can get a clearer picture of what their students already know about the topic and therefore identify which material requires only review and which material requires more thorough treatment. At the end of the class's treatment of a topic, educators who use KWL or its variants usually ask students to fill out the third column. This exercise helps students review and synthesize, and it helps educators assess their own teaching of the material.

Educators continue producing revisions to this instrument. In the variant below, students leave the last two columns until the class has finished dealing with the topic. The fourth column—*What I still wonder about*—helps educators plan what's next, either for the next iteration of the course in question, or for a review of the material in the next class session.

Know	Wish I knew	Learned	Still **Wonder** about

Another variant that may help students proceed with some epistemic humility labels the first column *What I Think I know*. Regardless in what directions this thinking and assessment strategy morphs in the future, I recommend it because students know how to use it and it helps them anticipate what they will learn and, later, reflect on what they have learned and still could learn. Some K–12 teachers use KWL or one of its variants to build a set of big-print, on-the-classroom-wall learning goals so that the whole class can judge their progress through the unit or topic. In higher education, where an individual professor is not the only one using a given room, this may not be possible. But a digital version of the wall poster could serve the same function, especially if it remained prominently available on the course wiki.

Mercator Surprise

As have all professors, I have taught students who resist the contents or conclusions of a given section of a course because for their whole lives they have believed the opposite, for example, that Pluto is a planet. If I may resurrect *The Matrix* for a moment (Wachowski & Wachowski, 1999), there's a red pill and a blue pill and, likely to their professors' collective dismay, some students have taken the blue pill. I once had a student claim aloud, in class, unironically, "It is literally unthinkable that members of the US government could have sold arms to Iran to fund a guerilla group in Nicaragua." I did not point out his misuse of the phrase "literally unthinkable" but I did suggest that the Iran-Contra affair was an actual fact, not an alternative fact, even if his worldview had no room for what had, in fact, happened. As our contemporary, Jonathan Haidt, has argued (2012), we believe what we believe for all kinds of reasons, some of them to do with tribal membership, and some parts of our worldviews are thoroughly fixed in place. To get at the problem Haidt identifies, and in the hope that I can persuade some students to be a bit more open to new ideas, I have my students examine their literal worldview, by using a map of the world. While showing a paper or projected Mercator projection map, I ask students to estimate, as a ratio, the relative sizes of Greenland and the continent of Africa. They are not allowed to look up the answer. I usually offer these ratios:

- Greenland is 15 times as big as Africa
- Greenland is 10 times as big as Africa

- Greenland is 5 times as big as Africa
- Greenland is about the same size as Africa
- Africa is 5 times as big as Greenland
- Africa is 10 times as big as Greenland
- Africa is 15 times as big as Greenland.

After assuring students that there will be no criticism or embarrassment for getting the wrong answer (after all, we have a class philosophy of mistakes), I poll the class to find out how many gave each of the seven possible answers. Before announcing the relative sizes, I usually ask this separate question: "How certain are you about your answers?" I usually offer a simple Likert scale for answering that question, along these lines:

Low certainty = 0, Moderate certainty = 5, High certainty = 10

After students have answered those two questions, I ask a student to look up the size of each land mass and report their findings to the class. Once these students have reported the two sizes, some quick math will reveal that Africa is about 14.3 times bigger than Greenland.

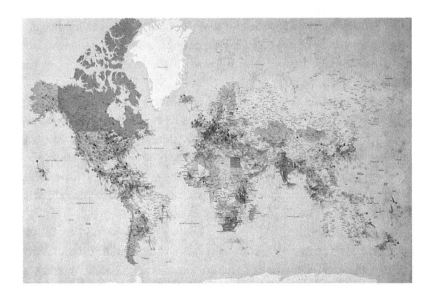

Figure 9.1 A world map, using the Mercator projection.
Map credit: Wikimedia Commons.

This opens up several discussion possibilities:

- How are our beliefs and our knowledge claims shaped by our surroundings and background?
- What else might we believe because, in a sense, we've been staring at a distorted map our whole lives?
- What do we think and how do we feel when we discover that we have misperceived something for a long time?
- How does the distortion of the Mercator projection affect our thinking about the importance of Africa in world affairs?

Almost every semester I use this strategy to get students to think more critically about their own perspectives, worldviews, and beliefs. The few students who have taken a geography course may already know about the Mercator projection's distortion of the sizes of continents, but most students will be surprised and some will experience some minor turmoil. I usually use this strategy at the start of a unit or topic where students will encounter ideas which they are likely to resist. Most of us do not want our students to descend into Cartesian doubt, but we do want them to consider the possibility that some things they believe may not be true and that this course may challenge some dearly-held beliefs, whether about politics, religion, gender, work, race, economics, history, the purposes of education, the chemical make-up of salt, or even Lady Gaga.

After some discussion, I usually show a Peters projection world map and then ask how that projection looks to students and how its use might influence political and economic thought differently in comparison to sustained use of the Mercator map. Note that one episode of *The West Wing* (search "Mercator episode west wing" on YouTube) deals with questions of worldviews. The characters in the *West Wing* clip discuss the issues raised in the bullets above.

College students in American classrooms might find a similar question interesting: What are the relative sizes of the continental United States and Australia? The correct answer is that Australia is about 95% as big as the contiguous states, significantly larger than many Americans think. The same kind of discussions I described above could follow this question.

PowerPoint Karaoke

In Chapter 4, I introduced PowerPoint karaoke as a humorous means of building classroom community. It also serves as a great way to introduce a unit or topic. In improvisational theater, those teaching or speaking are usually assigned their topic by the audience, moments before beginning. On the first day of a new topic or unit, those voluntold to teach via PowerPoint karaoke should be instructed to include a handful of developments or concepts essential to understanding the material the class will deal with in the coming day or days. As I noted in Chapter 4, I usually have available a deck of about 20 slides and I ask students to take about five or six minutes for their presentation. The engagement dividends paid on the minutes given to a PowerPoint karaoke presentation are significant, and I recommend it without reservation.

Film Clips and Case Studies

Given that I have already confessed to using film clips in every class, my readers will not be surprised that I use them on the first day of a new topic or unit. I sometimes use clips from two different films that take different approaches to the same question, trusting that in our discussion we will be able to detect some of the nuances in the two approaches and see some of the implications of the two approaches illustrated in the clips.

Another way to introduce a new unit is with a case study (Chapter 12). A shorter case can take as little as 20 minutes, including brief discussion, and can serve effectively to raise some of the key concepts or issues that students will encounter in the upcoming class or classes. A longer case usually takes about 45 minutes.

CONCLUSION

In the next four chapters, I catalogue dozens of strategies under these headings: Reading, Writing, Discussion, and Arts. Many of the strategies I list in those chapters will work effectively on the first day of a new topic or unit. Meanwhile, I offer this short chapter to encourage you, my higher education colleagues, to pump up the volume slightly so that our students know that the next topic or unit, while it may not be Cirque du Soleil, will still be interesting and challenging.

REFERENCES

Alexander, C. (1979). *The timeless way of building*. Oxford University Press.

Alexander, C., Ishikawa, S., Silverstein, M., Jacobson, M., Fiksdahl-King, I., & Angel, S. (1977). *A pattern language: Towns, buildings, construction*. Oxford University Press.

Badley, K. (2018). *Curriculum planning with design language: Building elegant courses and units*. Routledge.

Csikszentmihalyi, M. (1990). *Flow: The psychology of optimal experience*. Harper and Row.

Haidt, J. (2012). *The righteous mind: Why good people are divided by politics and religion*. Pantheon.

Wachowski, L., & Wachowski, L. (Dirs.). (1999). *The Matrix*. Warner Brothers, Village Roadshow Pictures.

Ten

Most professors, in our honest moments, admit that all our students do not read equally well. Some of our students may even have attended Derek Zoolander's Center for Kids Who Can't Read Good and Wanna' Learn to Do Other Stuff Good Too (Stiller, 2001). And, again if we are honest, we may also admit that many of our students read only a portion of what we ask them to read in a given semester. In this chapter, I offer strategies to increase engagement for all readers with the material they read and to help weaker readers read with more comprehension.

POWERFUL PASSAGES

By powerful passages, I mean those particularly poignant or important passages in a reading that deserve more attention and reflection. I structure this activity four different ways.

First, I ask students to choose a passage from anywhere in a specified page-range, read that passage to the class, and tell briefly why they found it powerful. I suggest that they select passages they have already underlined or to which they have already attached a sticky note. An adaptation of this strategy is to have them contribute their selection to a slide deck (with or without a picture) and have the class view the slide deck with all students reading their contribution to the deck. This adaptation takes more time but engages students more fully because members of the class see and hear the words instead of only hearing them. Enforcing the keep-the-commentary-brief rule can be challenging in both face-to-face and online settings, so I usually start with someone who I know will not go on too long and then I say something positive about the that person's comment being a paradigm example of the amount of commentary I hope all students will give.

DOI: 10.4324/9781003259596-14

A second approach I have used is to pre-select quotations from the textbook or reading in question, print them on card stock, and scatter them on the classroom tables. Students choose one to read aloud and tell how, for them, it catches the essence of that reading or why it struck them as highly apropos. More than one student in the class will select the same quotation because I distribute the same set of about a dozen quotations to each table. When the first student has read and commented on a given quotation, I invite other students who selected the same one to add their commentary about the significance of that passage.

Third, in online courses, I offer 30–40 quotations from the textbook and distribute or post the whole file. I then ask students to select and read one aloud, as in the paragraph above. Offering this higher number of passages reduces the chances of duplication, but where more than one student selects the same passage, I ask for all who selected a given quotation to speak in turn and invite them to address each other with questions or further commentary.

Fourth, I show a quotation from the textbook on the classroom or online screen and ask students to address a specific question. For example, I have shown the following quotation from a textbook (*The Courage to Teach*, Palmer, 1998) on the screen in both face-to-face and online education courses.

> When I was young and did not know who I was, I needed someone to model the intellectual gift that might be mine. But now, in midlife, knowing myself better, my identity demands that I use my gift in interaction and interdependence with others.
>
> (Palmer, p. 24)

I then show a second slide, which has the Palmer quotation but also the following question:

> In this statement, Palmer is talking about cultivating a personal teaching philosophy different from his mentor's. In what ways (if any) have you found yourself being inauthentic in your teaching because of the way you were being mentored during your in-school placements? What steps have you taken to counter any tendencies toward inauthenticity?

A variant on this last approach is to invite students to discuss in small groups and then share with the whole class some of the fruit of their discussion. Approaching a passage this way allows more people to respond to the passage and the question.

THINK-PAIR-SHARE

More than perhaps any other strategy I describe in this book, undergraduates will be familiar with Think–Pair–Share because their elementary and secondary teachers have used it. This strategy has students think for a moment or two about an image, a passage of text, or something someone has said, then they discuss with one partner for a couple more minutes. Some or all pairs then report to the class. I list this strategy in this chapter on reading strategies although it has wider uses. For example, some lecturers have their listeners talk briefly in pairs or small groups and then ask several to report back to the whole room. Whether or not any particular person gains new insights into the matter at hand, Think–Pair–Share implies a change of the teaching and learning mode, a benefit to those learners who become restless easily.

VIP READINGS

A quicker version of the Powerful Passages strategy is what someone has called *VIP Readings*. I cannot track down the origins of this strategy and so do not know whom to credit, but I know that I did not originate it. Simply, after reading a short passage aloud or asking students to read that passage themselves, I ask for a quick word, phrase, or sentence that stood out for them in that short bit of text. Someone who has never done this may expect the activity to produce something choppy and incoherent, but I have found that refraining from commenting myself and requiring students not to offer commentary when they say their word or phrase can yield a kind of poetic feeling in the room. Seeing or hearing a textbook passage have that effect might surprise everyone in some classrooms. This reading strategy has the potential to change students' perspective on course-related reading.

PMI: PLUS-MINUS-INTERESTING

Almost all undergraduates will be familiar with this strategy because K–12 teachers use it so frequently. Very simply, PMI involves students' appraising a bit of text, a statement on the board, an idea from history … any claim, idea, or fact, and then noting their response to it under the three headings. Students who know this strategy from their K–12 years will typically use a three-column table to list their responses.

Following is an example of an instructor-provided statement and what students might write on their PMI sheets.

Example: 17% of Americans believe Elvis, "The King," is alive. [which I made up! KB]

Plus	Minus	Interesting
What is good about this statistic?	What is bad about this statistic?	What is not bad or good, just interesting about this?
• That's good, people get a little hope without buying lotto tickets.	• That's nuts; what other crazy stuff will people believe?! • How can people claim Elvis is the "King" when Bach is?	• He was born in 1935 … he would be quite old now … would Céline Dion or Adele not have eclipsed him by now in Vegas? • How does he stay out of sight so effectively?

Obviously, PMI sheets can be used different ways. Students can meet in groups and then report to the whole class (or not). Students can hand their sheets in as a means for a professor to make a quick assessment of student thinking about a given topic or question. They can be submitted as paper or emailed exit slips (Chapter 7) as long as the instructor indicates so in advance so that students taking notes on paper do not have to submit their other class notes.

SOS: SUMMARY–OPINION–SUPPORT

Some undergraduates will be familiar with this strategy because teachers use it in middle-school and secondary classrooms. In this strategy, students read a passage and write a short **S**ummary of it. They state their **O**pinion of what the author states in the passage. They then **S**upport their opinion with evidence. Preceding whole-class discussion with a few minutes of SOS-based reflection and writing helps focus that discussion.

K–12 teachers who use this strategy usually ask their students to make a three-column table in their notebooks and fill in each column with their own answers. Following are examples students might produce in response to a work of fiction and a work in education.

Summary	Opinion	Support
By arguing that painting a fence is a particularly painstaking job and that his aunt is very fussy, Tom Sawyer fools his friends into asking him if they can help paint the fence.	• Mark Twain is pointing to the human tendency to desire what others have. • Mark Twain is pointing out how gullible humans can be. • Twain wants his readers to see what Tom's friends could not see. We actually laugh at Tom's friends.	• Tom's exaggerated language regarding his aunt and her fence-painting standards. • Tom's language about the skill demands of fence-painting. • Twain's use of superlative adjectives regarding the neighborhood children's desire to help paint.
Montessori argues that children learn best if instruction involves all five senses, rather than only sight and sound.	I am persuaded; her arguments make sense. For example, smell is very powerful but largely ignored in the modern west except by foodies, wine lovers, gardeners, and people interested in perfume.	• Montessori tells many stories about specific children who learned more deeply when more senses were involved. • The academic achievements of the orphans Montessori worked with who had been labelled *mentally deficient*.

Please note that you will not find this strategy if you search "reading strategy SOS" online. That is an early-grades spelling/reading strategy. Type "SOS summary opinion support" for more information on the strategy I have described here.

CDI: COMMONALITIES-DIFFERENCES-INSIGHTS

This comparison strategy can be used with readings or with any two contrasting claims, ideas, approaches, or theories. Again, formatting is simple. Three columns or three successive headings will facilitate the thinking process equally well. Because I cannot find this strategy online, I wonder if I developed it. Whether I did or not, I use it to help students see the complexity of ideas and issues.

I sometimes use a variant where the whole class builds a CDI page in a Google doc that shows online or on a classroom screen. When a class builds a Google doc together, students can work as individuals, or in pairs or small groups. I usually instruct the class not to repeat what another individual or group has already contributed to the document.

I ask them instead to add a plus sign in parentheses after the first contributor's comment.

TOPIC SENTENCES, WHAT QUESTION DOES EACH PARAGRAPH ANSWER?

Some middle-school and secondary teachers use this strategy for key passages and I use it in post-secondary. I have found it to be especially helpful for weaker readers. I will illustrate from a textbook I used for several years in a 100-level education course. The instructions are as follows: identify what question each paragraph in this section of your textbook answers (example from page 171 of *Educational Foundations in Canada*, Edmunds et al, 2015). A student might produce something along these lines:

- Paragraph 1: What values did education in Athens strive to realize?
- Paragraph 2: Who had access to education in Athens?
- Paragraph 3: Again about access, what about girls' and women's education?
- Paragraph 4: How important was rhetoric in ancient Athenian education?
- Paragraph 5: How important was writing in ancient Athenian education?

Writing these questions out may seem a bit like grunt-work, but it actually functions as a highly effective form of outlining or note-taking, especially for weaker students. When I re-read page 171 of the book in question (which I actually worked on in 2013) to produce the bulleted section above, I was reminded myself of some important characteristics of Athenian education.

This strategy can work as a discussion prompt for immediate use or as the basis for a written assignment. Professors in kentopia never need to give credit for reading the textbook. However, in the real world, if giving a small reward for some kind of written précis guarantees that most students will have read an important section of the text prior to our working on that section in class then, in my view, that reward is worth it.

COUNTER-ARGUMENTS AND ALTERNATIVE EXPLANATIONS

One strategy for getting students engaged with what they read is to ask, with reference to a passage of text (or a whole book or article), what evidence would support the opposite conclusion from that drawn by the author? What other ways might one make sense of the same evidence? Again, this strategy could be used as a discussion prompt or as the basis for a written assignment.

> Example: In his apparent advocacy of globalization in *The Lexus and the Olive Tree* (1999), Friedman states that no country with McDonald's has ever gone to war with any other country with McDonald's once they both had McDonald's. Some observers agree with Friedman's view and others attribute the lack of war between the many nations in question to be rooted in other soil. What are ways to frame this lack of conflict other than in terms of globalization?

This strategy helps students become more critical readers because it invites them to recognize when an author is arguing with facts or interpreting facts rather than simply stating facts. Not to make too much of what I include here only as an example, but the importance of students being able to distinguish facts from interpretation has increased dramatically since the 2017 arrival of the phrase *alternative facts* in our language.

SLOW READING AND CLOSE READING

The higher education lexicon has included the phrase *close reading* for decades, especially in senior seminars and at graduate levels, but many use it successfully in undergraduate courses as well. At its simplest, close reading involves some combination of professor and students reading deliberately, carefully, and aloud a passage of limited length, followed by discussion of the meaning of that passage. Close reading often involves repeated re-readings of the same passage.

Slow reading, close-reading's late-arriving cousin (Manguel, 2010; Miedema, 2009), overlaps with close reading at several points but differs especially in that its growth is partly connected to the slow movement in general (Honoré, 2000) and especially to the ways the internet has changed how we read and think (Badley & Badley, 2010; Carr, 2008, 2010). Carr complains in *The Shallows* that reading on screens frequently leads to our skipping parts of what is written and skimming the rest. To both professors and students who have never engaged in close reading or slow reading, these approaches to texts may seem to take up undue amounts of class time. Those who have read in these ways know that these approaches pay big dividends in student understanding of the words in front of them ... words that in typical circumstances they might not have understood or perhaps not even have read at all.

BLACKOUT POETRY

In black-out poetry, students use a photocopy or a printed photo or scan of one page of their textbook or of an assigned reading common to the whole class, and they produce a *blackout poem*. Because these are always based on published materials, I have not included an example here, but please type "blackout poetry images" into your browser to see hundreds of examples.

Students find this to be a powerful activity because they have to spend about 30 minutes on a single page of their textbook or assigned reading (really, another form of close or slow reading). Granted, they are doing a different kind of reading than they usually do when reading for comprehension. But, because they are carefully choosing words to compose something poetic and meaningful, this might be the closest reading of written text some have ever done. For both face-to-face classes and online settings, I have a student volunteer agree to sort out the technical details of hosting and building the slide deck. Once every slide is submitted (to a Google doc or to the person assembling the deck), the class watches the deck slowly. In both face-to-face and online settings, I ask students to read their own poem/slide when it appears and I ask the person advancing the slides to wait 10 or 15 seconds after each person has read their slide. Blackout poetry has provided some of the most intense "moments" I have had in class. I believe its power comes from the fact that it combines the arts, deep reading, careful attention to language, and students' personal convictions.

This strategy takes some preparation in advance. First, the professor must make sure that everyone has a paper copy of the page they're going to produce their poem on (unless they know how to design online). In face-to-face courses, I usually take a few minutes near the beginning of class to compile a list of how many copies of each needed page to produce and I then send two students to the department copier to make the copies. With online courses, I ask students to have a copy of their chosen page ready beforehand; most will have the capacity either to copy, scan, or take a picture with their phone camera and then print. Second, people need to have colored pencils or crayons available when they start. In face-to-face settings, I always bring a supply because some will inevitably forget to bring theirs.

I usually begin the activity by reviewing some of the conversations we have had about the textbook or the reading in question, and some of the ways we have read it in the previous days or weeks. I warn them that this will be a different way of reading for some and that some might want to resist because it seems soft or artsy. I invite my class to try it anyway, and I show exemplars to the class, from either a deck I have kept from a previous course or by searching online.

For my purposes in this book, I should note that blackout poetry is the last thing I do with a text, not the first. Students will have done a variety of other kinds of reading and assignments based on our textbook before we do blackout poetry as a class.

THE BOOK REVIEW

The book review appeals to some students but not to all, which is why I do not require it in undergraduate courses but do offer it as a choice (see *Tracks*, Chapter 6). Given students' range of abilities and their varied background experiences in responding to readings, I include the detailed instructions I give students and I provide a detailed grading rubric (in Appendix A, pages 202–205).

Obviously, any professor including a book review assignment could specify the course text, offer a list of several course-related titles, or leave it to students to request permission for a title they select. I have used both the first two options: The text, a choice from my list. My inclusion of the book review in undergraduate courses originally rooted itself in my observation that students usually frame the reading of their textbooks in a rather narrow—albeit understandable and important—way; their textbooks contain information that they need to pass the course. As one who has worked on eight different textbook projects and then defended textbooks in a book chapter entitled "Is There a Class in This Text?" (Badley & Antaya-Moore, 2022), I do not criticize students for taking this approach to their texts. Textbook writers write them and educators adopt them for this precise purpose. Given those purposes and the typical ways students approach their textbooks, I have found the book review a useful way to get students to frame their reading of their textbook differently. I first began using this assignment with doctoral students (whom I was trying to help get published) but, having seen their warm response to it as an assignment, I have used it as well with undergraduates and post-baccalaureate education students.

READINGS-BASED INQUIRY LEARNING

Most recent high school graduates will have had a least a little exposure to problem-based learning or inquiry learning (sometimes spelled *enquiry learning*), and some will have worked extensively with these approaches before arriving in your classroom. As well as not attempting to review the rapidly-growing literature on these approaches in what follows, I will ignore the differences between problem-based learning and inquiry learning and will focus on inquiry, a relatively new pedagogical approach that has generated a good share of controversy.

Arguably, inquiry learning is more a framework for instruction or even a philosophy of education, not simply a reading strategy. For that reason, in my planning of this book, I contemplated giving it its own chapter. Its advocates would certainly say it warrants a chapter, especially given the number of people who have written whole books about it (most of them related to elementary and secondary education). I ask you, my reader, please keep in mind my uncertainty about where to place this discussion as I delve briefly into this approach.

To begin, we must recognize the range of conceptions of inquiry learning. I illustrate this range with some examples. An educator might show the photo of the highway sign (Figure 10.1) and then ask students to respond to specific questions such as these: "What

Figure 10.1 Highway sign used as a prompt for inquiry learning.
Photo credit: Author.

does this sign tell you about the kinds of food typically available to travelers on major highways?" "Which of these chains offers the most nutritious foods?" or "Where do these chains source their foods?" I place questions like these at what I call the milder end or *educator-driven* end of the inquiry learning scale. Doubtless, framed correctly, these questions could serve as prompts for students to do careful research, to draw conclusions from their research, and to present and defend those conclusions. These questions could also lead to rich classroom discussion, both on the day the educator showed the picture and on the day students reported on their research. I therefore refrain from criticizing the educator who uses educator-driven inquiry to encourage students to reflect on nutrition, especially if the alternative to the discussion is direct instruction about the range of foods typically available to motorists.

In its stronger form, what I call *student-driven inquiry*, the educator might show the sign and then ask simply, "What research questions do you think these highway signs raise?" Students might answer that such signs raise questions about nutrition, travelers' needs, agriculture, visual communication, the economy, driving safety, and so on. In both teacher-driven and student-driven inquiry, the next steps for students would be to identify what research they would need to do to answer the questions, then to do the research and report back in.

Other examples come to mind of questions educators might raise. For example, "The United States Senate recently appointed person X to the Supreme Court. What questions are raised by the process by which this happened?" or "Sodium and chlorine are both poisons. What questions are raised by the fact that they can combine to form something that is not poisonous (salt)?" "What questions do you think are raised by the success of Brexit but the defeat of Geert Wilders in The Netherlands and Marine Le Pen in France?" In an inquiry approach to these cases, students would identify the kind of research they would need to do to answer the questions, carry out the research, and report their conclusions.

Given that students' research skills vary, I usually offer suggested directions for research. This search string and that book or journal might be good starting points. Some students need such direction and others do not. No one takes offense when a professor offers such help.

Using inquiry learning implies that there will be a degree of the kind of epistemic uncertainty I mentioned in Chapter 7. As a class, we will likely not get answers to all our questions. We need to let our students know that our goal is more to uncover questions than to cover material.

To illustrate inquiry specifically as a reading strategy, consider this instructor-driven question: In light of what Samuelson and Nordhaus have argued in your main course text (2019), what three tensions arise related to monetary policy in Chapter 2 in Levitt and Dubner's (2009) *Freakonomics*? In more student-driven inquiry, the question would be more general, likely along these lines: What are some major points of tension between Samuelson and Nordhaus's arguments in your main course text and Levitt and Dubner's approach in *Freakonomics*? Suggest directions of research one might take to resolve one or two of these points of tension.

Professors implementing inquiry learning will likely face some initial resistance, in part because inquiry asks students to do some of the work that most students ordinarily expect professors to do, work such as identifying questions, problems, and tensions that arise on inspection of a reading, event, or situation, However, when scaffolded and initiated appropriately, inquiry can become a powerful way for students to learn. I recommend to those who might consider trying it to begin small, in one class session. Furthermore, I recommend using one or more of the small-group discussion strategies I suggest in Chapter 12 to reduce students' risk of embarrassing themselves in front of the whole class.

THE JOURNAL ARTICLE RESPONSE OR SUMMARY

Most of my readers know that some students know how to read a scholarly journal article and some do not. For several reasons and without apology, I consistently invite students to read journal articles. I want them to know how scholarly research is initially disseminated. I want them to understand the difference between primary sources and secondary sources (such as their textbook). I want them to read material that pushes them closer to the limits of their reading ability and thereby creates the possibility of their getting into what Csikszentmihalyi (1990) calls the flow zone.

My wants aside for the moment, undergraduate students may need some help if they are to read articles effectively. In light of their range of knowledge about academic writing and their varied reading abilities,

I usually offer the journal article response as one of many choices (tracks, Chapter 6) in my courses so that no one is required to read an academic journal article. I also offer them a rather extensive written explanation about the structure of the typical journal article and how to read and respond to it. That description and my grading rubric for the reading response appear in Appendix A (pages 198–199).

CONCLUSION

In Chapter 12's catalog of discussion strategies, I include three more strategies that could legitimately be included here as reading strategies. The first of these is using Venn diagrams and concept maps, both of which many educators ask students to use to organize their thinking about passages of text and both of which could also be listed as arts strategies. Chapter 12 also introduces what I call the Agree–Disagree sheet, an effective tool for helping students clarify their thinking about what they have read. Chapter 13 includes a strategy called "Illustrate Your Question" and "Lunch with a Theorist," both of which could have been included here.

As I note at several points in this book, other writers would have included other strategies in a chapter such as this one. I offer these strategies, all of which I regularly use, to help you, my colleagues, help your students read more effectively and with more joy. I close with one more suggestion: Ask your own students about readings in previous courses from which they learned the most or derived the most joy. And then ask why. What were the characteristics of the readings themselves? How did their professors use those readings in the course? How did they incorporate them into the assessment schema? Such a discussion will yield valuable insights into how your students view reading. It will deepen their sense that you share important goals with them (understanding, success, enjoyment of class), thereby building classroom community. And it will likely give you more strategies to add to your repertoire—or arsenal—of approaches to teaching and learning.

REFERENCES

Badley, K., & Antaya-Moore, D. (2022). Is there a class in this text? In M. C. Hughes & K. Badley (Eds). *Joyful resilience as educational practice: Transforming teaching challenges into opportunities.* Routledge.

Badley, K. J., & Badley, K. (2010). Slow reading: Reading along "lectio" lines. (2010). https://digitalcommons.georgefox.edu/soe_faculty/35

Carr, N. (2008). Is Google making us stupid? What the Internet is doing to our brains. *The Atlantic*, (July/August). http://www.theatlantic. com/magazine/archive/2008/ 07/is-google-making-us-stupid/6868/

Carr, N. (2010). *The shallows: What the internet is doing to our brains*. Norton.

Csikszentmihalyi, M. (1990). *Flow: The psychology of optimal experience*. Harper and Row.

Edmunds, A., Nickel, J., & Badley, K. (2015). *Educational foundations in Canada*. Oxford University Press.

Friedman, T. (1999). *The Lexus and the olive tree*. Farrar, Straus, Giroux.

Honoré, C. (2000). *In praise of slowness*. Harper.

Levitt, S. D., & Dubner, S. J. (2009). *Freakonomics: A rogue economist explores the hidden side of everything*. HarperCollins.

Manguel, A. (2010). *A reader on reading*. Yale University Press.

Miedema, J. (2009). *Slow reading*. Litwin.

Palmer, R. (1998). *The courage to teach*. Jossey-Bass.

Samuelson, P. A., & Nordhaus, W. D. (2019). *Economics* (20e). McGraw-Hill.

Stiller, B. (Dir.). (2001). *Zoolander*. Village Roadshow Pictures, Paramount Pictures.

Eleven

As I suspect is the case for many of my readers, I have lamented that "scholarly effort is in decline ... as never before" (Egbert, p. 68). Knowing that Nicholas Carr, to whom I made reference in Chapter 10, will not be the last to voice this lament, nor that Egbert (of Liege, Belgium), who wrote the words above sometime in the 11th century, was not the first to make similar complaints does not reassure me. This decline seems especially apparent in students' writing ability, although that claim may well root itself more in retro-grouchiness on my own part than in actual research into students' relative writing ability in the 2020s in comparison to any other given decade. In kentopia, students need no help to become better writers. In the real universities and colleges where we teach, they do need help. Ever the realist, I have developed, adopted, borrowed, and otherwise discovered several strategies to help my students improve their writing and to present their work in more effective and engaging ways than might otherwise be the case.

In his book, On Writing, novelist Stephen King (2000) offers some useful language to frame any discussion of student writing. He distinguishes four levels of writing: bad, fair, good, and great. He attributes greatness to Shakespeare and Shaw but denies his own writing that honorific title, settling instead for good. Even that much information should sober those amongst us who consider ourselves good writers. If you read King's book, you will likely conclude that most undergraduates are fair writers, a few are bad writers, and a few are good writers. Because our situations and experiences with students' work differ so much, I will not suggest percentage breakdowns for those three categories. Perhaps the most alarming thing King reveals in his treatment of these categories is his belief that no one can move from bad to fair or from good to great. Take consolation in his belief that movement is possible from fair to good.

DOI: 10.4324/9781003259596-15

In what follows and in Appendix B, I focus on strategies meant to help all students write better organized essays and papers with stronger beginnings. These strategies may help some students develop so that they move from fair writing to good writing. Likewise, those who take King's word that, with the right help, writers have the potential to move from fair to good will want to take advantage of whatever resources are available to help students move in that direction. I want all my students to present their work as well as they are able—to be at their best—when they do submit or present their work.

Professors who take King's word as true (as I do), that no one can move from bad to fair in their writing will want to find strategies to reduce the amount of written work weak writers need to submit in a semester. That is, I want to offer alternative ways for students to show what they have learned.

HELPING STUDENTS IMPROVE THEIR WRITING

Most university Libraries, Writing Centers, or Academic Success Offices will be happy to allow someone to visit a class and help students improve their research and writing skills. I have used these resources and encourage you, my colleagues, to do the same, even if you are quite capable of leading an in-class research or writing workshop yourself. I advocate inviting these people to class for two reasons. First, inevitably, they will include ideas and strategies in their workshop that professors do not think of. Second, students who might have apprehensions about using the support services the university has on offer may find themselves less apprehensive after having met one of these resource people in person. Having recommended using people who already want to come to my class, I now confess to having developed some of my own resources. Appendix B contains materials I work through with my students as well as resources I post to the course wiki to accompany rubrics for specific writing assignments.

Students generally respond well when they learn that professional writers work through a succession of drafts before their work sees the light of day. In her wonderfully encouraging book on writing, *Bird by Bird*, Anne Lamott (1995) argues that getting the lousy first draft committed to paper is one of the hardest but most essential tasks the writer will face. In my attempts to encourage students, I use the Lamott-like metaphor of a construction site to convey the sense of brouillon, the French word for the rough first draft. Construction sites usually have piles of building material stacked here and there. Part of the building might be completed but other parts obviously remain unfinished. The ground will be messy, possibly muddy. In fact, the landscapers, who do not want forklifts driving on their freshly-laid sod, will not do their work until everything else is done. I introduce Lamott's claim, the concept of brouillon, and the metaphor of a construction site to encourage students to recognize that lousy, early drafts should not be a source of discouragement (and should also not be handed in). Rather, they are starting points, work sites. I introduce these concepts and this metaphor because I want my students to keep editing and keep editing until they are happy with their work.

In kentopia, all students are so well organized that they have time to improve their papers through repeated editing. In the actual universities and colleges where most of us teach, this is not always the case; we see more than our share of papers fueled by desperation and energy drinks. In my own real-world teaching, I carry on encouraging my students to have someone else read their papers, to print their papers out and read them aloud away from their screens, and to sleep at least once before submitting a paper so their brains have a chance to process the ideas in play before final revisions. All my students do not follow Anne Lamott's advice or my own, but I live in hope. And I have also devised and adopted a few approaches to assessment and writing that reduce some of the stresses on my students and on myself.

SUBMITTING AND PRESENTING WELL

In the introduction to the chapter I noted my desire to frame assignments so that all students can perform as successfully as possible. Regardless of the quality of the work they have produced, I want them to be able to present or submit it its best light. Following are several strategies I use to support their efforts in those directions, beginning with clear rubrics.

Because of changes in K–12 pedagogy in the last couple decades, undergraduates generally expect to see a rubric for every assignment they are asked to complete. In fact, one dean I know claims that some students view any grade on an assignment without a rubric as litigable. I have addressed rubrics already (in Chapter 6) but will repeat two comments here. First, the rubrics we use must be clear and accessible, without inflating the page count in the course syllabus. An easy way to help students get clear about our expectations for an assignment is to have them co-determine the rubric with us, as I described in Chapter 6. A second way is to have them work in groups to develop a summary of the rubric that describes the qualities we wish to see in a given assignment. Groups could present their summaries on screen as the basis for a brief class discussion.

A second strategy is to post anonymized, permitted exemplar assignments. Recognizably, posting exemplars from a previous semester on the same topic being assigned in the current semester would unduly influence some students' thinking about a topic. Therefore, exemplars need to have addressed different topics than those currently being assigned. Exemplar assignments should illustrate two or three quality ranges of research and writing. I suggest posting work in the top three grade ranges, recognizing the sensitivity needed when soliciting "B" and "C" papers from students.

Some educators use a third strategy; they ask that major assignments be submitted in stages. This approach helps less organized students inasmuch as they need to submit, for example, an enumerated thesis statement and bibliographic information for five sources by four weeks before the due date for the final project. A middle-stage submission in this approach might include 750–1000 words of writing, including the introductory paragraphs to the major sections. I recognize that the staged submission approach implies more work for professors who are already busy meeting the 40% teaching, 30% research, 30% service, 20% administration and committee, 20% grading, and 10% advising specified in their job description. My own experience with staged submission of major work is that the increased quality of students' papers is worth the investment of my time.

Daniel Coleman, a colleague at McMaster University in Ontario, has developed a variant on the staged submission. He offers a free read and light edit (with no grade) to any student submitting a paper a full week early. He returns these drafts promptly so that students can resubmit by the published due date. Papers submitted on time receive comments and a grade. Late papers get only a grade with no comments. Since learning of his strategy, I have made the same offer and have had perhaps 5% of my students take me up on it. Unfortunately, the weakest students do not have their papers drafted early enough to take advantage of this offer.

Regardless of what strategies we use to help our students improve as writers, ultimately, they need to turn in their work. Following are several ways to bring students' work to an audience wider than ourselves.

The Senior Paper or Seminar Paper

In Chapter 5, I introduced the paper presentation as a way to help move into instructor mode. Working within tightly prescribed and enforced time limits (10–12 minutes) and with strict instructions that they must not read their papers to the class, individual students present summaries of their papers to the class. This works best in senior-seminar type classes of about 15 (or fewer). In larger classes, the presentations would eat up too many course days at the end of term; in those situations, I recommend the panel, which I describe below. Professors who have used the presentation mode know that it works best if the student presenting has prepared and distributed several questions in advance to guide the discussion that follows the presentation.

The Response to the Seminar Paper

A variant on the above is to have one student prepare to make a formal, graded response (of 700–1000 words) to the presenting student's paper. Again, this works best with smaller classes at the 300-level or above. This approach does entail some logistics because the respondent needs to have access to the paper to facilitate preparing a quality response. I usually tie a percentage of the grade on the presenter's paper to its being submitted on-time to me; that increases the pressure for the student author to finish a timely draft and it reduces the amount of adjudication I have to do between conflicting accounts of when the responding student received the paper. I see high engagement when I ask respondents to raise two or three class discussion questions at the end of their response. We pursue those questions after the author of the paper has a few minutes to respond. I find that 30 minutes of class time is sufficient for the paper and the response. Following the response, the whole class can engage in discussion. Working with the nominal total of 6000 words of writing in a semester, I usually give about 10–15% course credit to a prepared response.

The Panel Presentation of Related Papers

Between three and five students who have worked on the same topic or related topics each present a prepared, written summary of their paper of about 300–400 words (two to three minutes). Panel members take a few minutes to discuss with each other before I invite the class into the conversation. I usually assign 5% course weight to students' written summaries of their own papers, a step that seems to improve the quality of the panel considerably. In Chapter 5, I also suggested the panel as a means of moving students into instructor mode. As the comment below indicates, it is much more than that.

The benefits of the panel, according to Kayla McGougan, a student in a 400-level sociology of education course at Mount Royal University:

> I absolutely love the idea of researching a topic and participating in a panel. I remember the last class of your course last semester, students actually really wanted to discuss some ideas. Unfortunately, it seems like university students are hesitant to discuss unless it's required. But I have participated in some classes where being in a panel is required and students were actually very, very eager to do it. I think it's a great way to ask thought-provoking questions that may actually shape students' views on important issues. In summary, I think a required, structured panel would be really great.

Speed Dating

Students prepare a 90-second, written summary of their paper (about 200–225 words). They meet in pairs and each student presents to the person opposite them for 90 seconds. If you allow another 90 seconds for questions in each direction, then each pair of students will have six minutes with each other. At the signal, the "chair lift" (as at a ski hill) moves one notch and people share with their next partner. Online descriptions of how to use speed dating in class do not address the logistical difficulties of getting every member of a class to present to every other member. I have found it works best if students get to present 1:1 to half their classmates. The chair lift metaphor breaks down after that.

When the class reconvenes as a whole, I suggest using at least these two discussion prompts:

- What is one interesting thing you learned from someone else's presentation?
- What is a new insight you gained into your own paper as you summarized it repeatedly to your classmates and as you engaged with their questions?

Some students might anticipate the first prompt but few will have anticipated the second. For that reason, I suggest the second. If the discussion of the second prompt leads to students confessing to significant new learning about their own papers, you might offer the option of a revision within 24 hours, with new additions to the paper indicated by a different font.

In a three-hour block, a round of speed-dating can also reflect quick, in-class research where the students' task was simply to prepare 90 seconds worth of material, not to summarize a research paper. In 50- or 75-minute classes, this version of speed-dating should occur over two class sessions.

The Book Project

Obviously, the Tracks assessment option is quite central to my thinking about the engaging classroom. As I noted in Chapter 6, the one time I listed the book project, in fall semester 2018, eight students joined me in producing a book that, in the words of one of our endorsers, "has it all ... words, sentences, paragraphs, and chapters." Another endorser wrote, "Of all the books I've read, this is the most recent." To be honest, we wrote our own endorsements but Amazon did not include them when they published the book. We presume that we were simply too funny. But seriously, the students who engaged with me in this project not only can write, but they can speak for themselves.

The following is a short reflection from one of the participants. Shauna Tunney, now a year–1 teacher in London, England, guided that

Figure 11.1 A book produced by students who elected the Book Track in a 400-level university course.

Cover design: Kristen Badley.

book project to publication on Amazon. She wrote as follows about her experience with the assignment:

> My initial hesitations when choosing this track, given that there were easier options available, was the workload. I assumed the workload would be extensive and would simply add to the busyness of a regular semester. After seeing the clear deadlines and achievable breakdown, I then worried about combining people's different experiences, writers' voices, and authenticity into one small book because I wanted to be proud of the final product we had created. After weighing the options and seeing the clear outlines that Ken had provided and the support he was willing to provide us, I decided it was a unique opportunity that would allow me to present my current experiences and understanding from a unique but valuable perspective. It also expanded my skills, making me work through the Amazon Publishing process and the creation of a cohesive project, something I carried into my inquiry-based practicum during my final year. Ultimately, this book is something I am proud of and hope to reference in my future publications.

If you have an upper-level class where you already know there are capable writers, I recommend listing this as an option. Those who participated have told me that 50% course weight (in a three-credit, semester course) was appropriate. I will stick with that course weight the next time I offer this track as an option.

GRADING LESS WEAK WRITING

My primary goal in assigning the essay or major paper always remains to increase student understanding of a topic. I want my students to know more when they finish the paper than they knew when they started. My secondary goal relates more to their becoming better researchers and writers. The realist in me knows that many of my students will never go to graduate school and will rarely need to submit unedited reports in their future workplaces. That is, while one might desire that all one's students become better researchers and writers, it is not necessary that they do so. I can do both my students and myself a favor by offering alternative ways for them to demonstrate that they have met the learning objectives for the course. In light of this brilliant logic or this egregious rationalization, I have sought ways to reduce the amount of writing I read from students who, to refer again to Stephen King's schema, are going to submit bad writing.

Smaller Written Assignments

First, at the 100- and 200-level, I have moved away from the major paper. I could couch my reasoning in grand terms but my shift relates more to my having gotten tired of reading bad papers. Any professor who has graded a few thousand essays could nuance King's category of bad writing into several sub-streams: Poor research skills, poor organizational skills, poor grasp of grammar and syntax, and perhaps other categories. Professors can frame and scaffold short writing assignments in ways that address the first two of those sub-streams. We can address research skills by telling students what they should look for in a specific page range of a book or in a specific journal article. We can address organization by recommending sectioning of the assignment, even by suggesting headings. Thus, while we may not be able to offer aid to the student who cannot recognize number disagreement (for example), we can make our grading a bit more enjoyable by providing help in these other two areas.

Editing and Other Forms of Help

Presumably, because strong writers use editors, weak writers should as well. But professors know that much of what they see comes in unedited (even not proof-read, as demonstrated by words along the lines of "put another example here," I have seen all upper-case in more than one essay). Some professors require that students submit their work with a signature or some other kind of evidence that another person has read it. According to my students, my own use of that strategy undermined the sense of classroom community so I abandoned it, leaving me back where I started, pleading with my students to have someone else read their work before submitting. Most Academic Success Offices or Writing Centers offer assistance to students who want help with specific written assignments. I have not read the research on why students do or not take advantage of these services, but I continue to remind students year after year that this help is available. In my own courses, in addition to the official confirmation of attendance, those students who follow the Research and Writing Workshops track and thereby attend four workshops given by the Writing Center or Academic Success Center need to submit a 250-word write-up summarizing what they learned. Over several years, I have read enough of these summaries to become convinced that most students who elect to attend these workshops find them helpful.

Many students struggle to write clear thesis statements and topic sentences. I provide some material in Appendix B related specifically to these two matters.

Other Assignments

My final strategy for reducing the volume of weak writing I have to read is not a writing strategy at all. I devise other ways for students to demonstrate that they have met the learning objectives of the course or a section of the course. I catalogue some of those strategies throughout this book and I recommend that my readers consider again the three questions at the heart of the Backwards by Design movement I introduced in Chapter 3: What do I want my students to know by the end of this (curriculum)? How can they show me that they have learned it (assessment)? What are the best ways for them to learn it (instruction)? Answering those questions—especially the second one—might well lead to exams, to a Tracks option, to some of the arts strategies I catalog in Chapter 13, or to a variety of other creative projects. Answering that question does not necessarily lead to more written work for our students and ourselves.

CONCLUSION

We all would love to teach classes populated with good writers. In fact, at the University of Kentopia, we restrict admission only to those in the top ranks of Stephen King's schema. In the real-world universities and colleges where most of us teach, however, most student writers need some help. I offer this chapter and Appendix B to support you, my faculty colleagues, so you can support your student writers and thereby bring more moments of actual joy and a stronger sense of accomplishment to your grading and your teaching.

Most of us in academic work believe we have responded to some kind of call. We have heard a voice and that is why we go to work in the morning (and often after dinner as well). In fact, the word *vocation* has its roots in the Latin word for *voice*. But this particular aspect of our calling—student writing—causes many of us to ask about how we use our time and energy. We wonder if there might be more life-giving ways to frame or structure our work? Among the many benefits of helping our students become better writers are these two. First, we can take some satisfaction that because of our work, some students can write better after they finished our class than they could when they began. How to word the second benefit? "Our grading can become less onerous" sounds negative. The second benefit of helping our students with their writing is that we can experience moments of joy in our grading because some of them have submitted papers that are researched, organized, and written better than they would have been had we not made the investment.

REFERENCES

Egbert of Liège. (2013). *The well-laden ship* (R. G. Babcock, trans.), Harvard University Press.

King, S. (2000). *On writing: A memoir of the craft.* Pocket Books.

Lamott, A. (1995). *Bird by bird: Some instructions on writing and life.* Anchor/Random.

Twelve

Few people have questions about how professors and students spend their time in lecture-based classes. Transmission is the business of such classes and transmitting is the mode of instruction. What about classes not based on the lecture? What do educators and students do? Part of their time will be given to discussion. Some defenders of transmission modes of teaching caricature discussion teaching as lacking direction or a pooling of ignorance. I suspect that just as there are highly engaging lectures happening on campuses, there are also directionless discussions. But in this lengthy chapter I offer strategies to help move students into discussion that has clear direction and that results in deep reflection.

The chapter is organized under five major headings: Visual organizers, top 10 lists, surveys and polls, student-developed games, case studies, feedback loop, and potpourri. I conclude the chapter with a brief discussion about discussion leadership.

Some educators appear to have an intuitive sense of how to initiate classroom discussion. Others suggest ideas or ask questions that seem to land on the floor, producing no student engagement. In what follows I offer several strategies to initiate and guide student discussion, none of which usually land on the floor. Some of these will be familiar to students from their K–12 years while others will likely be new to most.

Before beginning to describe any discussion strategies, I wish to note again the second question (from Chapter 2) I consistently ask when planning a class: "Can I get us productively engaged with this material without lecturing?" As I noted in Chapter 2, today's students compare their professors' lecturing abilities to any number of engaging speakers they can watch on the internet. One reason to listen to professors, of course, is that the internet does not grant degrees. Still, literally dozens of students have poured out their lament to me about classes where professors simply work through PowerPoint decks provided by the

DOI: 10.4324/9781003259596-16

publisher, sometimes with the paper handouts that have thumbnails of the slides and blank lines for taking notes. My unavoidable conclusion is that the lecture is simply not the preferred way most students want to learn today. In light of that conclusion, I allow myself a maximum of one lecture per semester. I confess to being uncertain that my one lecture even warrants the title because my students and I sort of talk back and forth through an outline and, at points, I even suggest that we skip a section and simply address any questions that arise for them from the next section of that outline. Even in a conference plenary speech, I usually stop and have my audience do some form of a Think-Pair-Share activity (see Chapter 10).

VISUAL ORGANIZERS

Most undergraduates arriving in our classes already have extensive experience using graphic organizers. In this section, I describe how I use two such organizers and then describe a strategy that involves using online images produced by people not connected to the class.

Venn Diagrams

Almost all undergraduates will have used Venn diagrams in their K–12 education, even from as early as their primary years. To help the small minority of students who might have arrived in your class with no knowledge of Venn diagrams I suggest showing a couple humorous examples on screen (which you can find by searching *Venn diagram jokes*). Students will engage with you more deeply if you actually conduct the search live in class, rather than prepare the humorous examples in advance.

Turning to the logical or conceptual relationships you want illustrated, obviously a professor can prepare and show a Venn diagram to a class. But students will become more engaged with the content if you ask them to create Venn diagrams in response to a prompt or question, especially one where the conceptual relationships or overlaps are not overly clear. Predictably, some students will show more overlaps between the circles in the diagram than others, revealing different understandings of the relationships under discussion and providing a basis for discussion.

Concept Maps

Most undergraduates will also have been using concept maps since their earliest grades (Hill, 2005). Look up *concept maps*, *thinking maps*, or *graphic organizers* online (in images) to see some of the many names assigned to these. Students can work alone or cooperatively to produce concept maps. As I noted in Chapter 10, these organizers are useful for responding to readings (showing an author's argument, following a plot) and for sorting through thorny conceptual issues (relationship of *justice, equality,* and *fairness,* for example).

No perfectly-suited place in this book offers itself to promote what I call flipping tables. So I recommend them here, in the context of Venn diagrams and visual organizers. Several manufacturers produce classroom and meeting-room tables that, with the release of a catch, easily convert to become vertical display surfaces. The laminate surfaces on these tables allow participants to write in erasable marker and then show their work to a class. If you have any say in how new or renovated classrooms are to be furnished, ask for these tables. These have some significant advantages compared to chart paper, notably that every member of each group can write, that groups can erase and revise as they work, and that groups can show their work to the class from where they are seated. The group thinking and discussion process prior to presentation is amazing to watch. In short, these are

Figure 12.1 A flipping table that serves as a work surface and allows groups to show their work to class.

Credit: Sophie Chardon.

a simple technology that fosters powerful pedagogy. One caution, be sure to bring your own erasable markers to class (and possibly some cleanser and rags; these do not erase as easily as whiteboards).

Online Images: Strengths and Weaknesses

I regularly ask students to search online for illustrations of some important relationship or concept, to select one to show to the class, and to point out its strengths and shortcomings. After a given student has shown a selected image and has noted some strengths and weaknesses, I ask the class to join in. Invariably, someone in the class will notice another strength or will flag a weakness of the image. It neglects this or that aspect of what it is meant to portray, or recent research has rendered it out of date because specialists now believe this or that. I ask the presenting student or anyone in the class to address the criticisms raised by suggesting modifications to the diagram on the screen. Usually, allowing three or four students to show and comment generates enough discussion to make it clear that there is a lack of agreement about what is a good curriculum model, how the water cycle works, how central banks try to influence economic velocity, and other such questions. The instructions below are lifted from a *Daily Forecast* sheet in an education course.

- Go to Google images and type in "curriculum models";
- Scroll a bit to get a sense of the overwhelming number of education professors who have put their curriculum model online … estimate the number of models you find there (seriously, don't count);
- Agree with a classmate to examine one model and see if it meets these three criteria: You can understand it; it connects theory and practice; it recognizes the three elements of the core cycle (curriculum, instruction, assessment); and it recognizes the importance of the classroom ethos.

For several reasons, this strategy has great power to pull students into a topic. First, it involves their having to choose a graphic from among the many they will find online, and it requires their brains to deal not only with words. Second, it forces them to think about the strengths and weaknesses of the models their search turns up, regardless of which model they choose (although, typically, more than one student will select the same image from among those produced by the same search string). I usually give 12–15 minutes to this exercise and then begin whatever other activity I have planned in relation to the concept or idea we will work on in that class session.

TOP TEN LISTS

Whether or not David Letterman invented the top ten list, it has become a fixture in our culture, and students engage quickly when given the opportunity to create such a list. The Top Ten List offers several benefits. It can be adapted to any topic; can be scaled down to generate a few minutes of discussion or scaled up to a graded assignment; requires little preparation; can be adapted to the entire range of available classroom technology, from none to loaded; and has the potential to pique the interest of every student in the room.

Because I teach students in a professional faculty (education), I want my students to think about the character of their own future classrooms. I regularly require that they identify the ten most important ideal characteristics of their classroom and provide up to 50 words of explanation for each ideal. This assignment could be expanded to many other subject areas:

- What are the ten features of a great novel?
- What are the ten most important qualities of a well-designed experiment in field X?
- What are the ten most important things to understand about this historical event?
- What are the ten greatest pressures on this or that system?
- What are the ten most important qualities of field research?

Obviously, others could extend the number of topics on the list. And, also obviously, the number does not need to be ten. My objective in asking my education students to identify their classroom ideals is, in part, to offer them an opportunity to write in their own voice. But the assignment also provides a basis for classroom discussion. Why did you list "noisy"? Why did you list "curiosity"? "What did you mean by the phrase minds-on?"

Education departments, schools, and teachers have generally agreed to a list of what I call threshold or baseline ideals (and recognized professional standards) that should characterize every classroom: Respect, safety, inclusion, fairness, and honesty. I ask my students not to include such baseline standards in their list but rather to list ten ideals that will set their classrooms apart from other classrooms. Even the list of baseline standards offers an opportunity for discussion. As a class, we could build that list together.

A variant on the top 10 list is what I call "The Turning Points in the Field." In this variant, students usually start by placing the events in historical order (Tennis Court Oath, Storming of the Bastille, Women's March on Versailles). Having completed the easy part, the class can then address a variety of questions such as these:

- Which are the most important events? From whose perspective?
- Which events would you identify as turning points?

Five or ten developments in any academic discipline could form the basis of a class discussion. Professors wanting to establish the knowledge baseline of their students on a given topic could carry out some form of this activity on the first day of a new section of a course. Doing so might have the added benefit that students would see more clearly the limits of their knowledge in the area.

SURVEYS AND POLLS

Numerous ways offer themselves to survey or poll a class and use the results to create class discussion or frame a written assignment.

The Agree-Disagree Sheet

This strategy consistently leads to engaging discussion. The structure is simple. Prepare a one-page handout—usually 13–15 questions—to which students respond by Agreeing or Disagreeing (as in the example below). In teaching face-to-face, the professor or a student can record the results on the board or on the projector screen. Students in both face-to-face and online classes can use an instrument such as Survey Monkey to record or a shared Google sheet to post results. Obviously, a Likert scale would work too, although the polar choice of Agree or Disagree produces livelier discussion. If one wanted to, one could use the simple model (Agree-Disagree) on a first round and then, following some discussion, repeat the exercise using a Likert scale.

Once students have completed their questionnaire and the class's responses are visible on the board or screen, discussion follows. In that discussion, I use questions along these lines:

- Why did so many indicate disagreement with #6? Would a couple people please share your thinking on that?
- Would one of the two people who agreed with #8 care to speak?
- The class is nearly unanimous in agreeing with #11. What do you think are some reasons for that unanimity?

In outlying cases, where only one person agreed or disagreed with a statement, I couch the request to share in strongly invitational language because I have no interest in traumatizing students or making them feel unsafe for holding a minority view.

Below is a portion of an Agree-Disagree sheet I have had students fill out in response to the chapter, "Big Juicy Mistakes," from William Westney's The Perfect Wrong Note (summarized herein in Chapter 6). Note that this strategy could as easily have appeared in the reading strategies chapter (Chapter 10).

1. As teachers, we should try new approaches, knowing they might now work perfectly, but knowing we can learn more about teaching. A __ D __
2. Some say that in rock-climbing if you're not falling, you're not climbing to your limits. We should encourage students to apply this view to their learning. A __ D __
3. Summative assessment is like looking at autopsy results. A __ D __
4. Summative assessment and formative assessment is too simple a binary to catch all the nuances of real-world assessment. A __ D __
5. Whether by using Westney's chapter "Big Juicy Mistakes" or by some other means, all teachers should explain and perhaps even co-develop a classroom philosophy of assessment with their classes. A __ D __

Below are the instructions I used on an Agree-Disagree sheet where students used a Likert-scale to indicate their responses:

For each statement below, indicate your degree of agreement or disagreement with a number from −5 to +5. To indicate strongest disagreement, write in a −5 or −4. For moderate disagreement, use −3 or −2. Not sure could run from −1 to 0 to +1. To indicate moderate agreement, use +2 or +3 and for strong agreement, use +4 or +5. For your information, this format for responding to statements is commonly known as a *Likert Scale*, named after the psychologist who developed it. Some of you will use such a scale in your master's research.

Sticky Notes on the Wall

This strategy, which originated in the world of project management, works very well in classroom settings. The process is simple. Students work individually or in small groups to identify themes, problems, insights, or major ideas in a reading or in response to some other prompt (film clip, still picture, poem, news item from that day, etc.). Each person or group produces a maximum of two or three sticky notes with a maximum of two words on each note. I ask students to print with large letters so the notes are readable from anywhere in the room. I also use 4" x 6" sticky notes and I bring markers to class the days I use this strategy. After a few minutes, I check on the class's progress, and

Figure 12.2 The results of a typical sticky notes exercise.
Photo credit: https://commons.wikimedia.org/wiki/File:Sticky_notes_on_the_wall_ of_the_Wikimedia_Foundation_office,_2010-10-26.jpg; Credit: Ragesoss on Wikimedia Commons, https://creativecommons.org/licenses/by/3.0/.

when almost all have completed their notes, I ask them to stick their sticky notes to the front wall. Two variants are available at this stage. They can stick their notes up randomly or they can stick them near headings that I have written on the board in advance. Both approaches work but the random placement approach engenders richer discussion.

The next step is key. I ask for one or two volunteers to help organize the sticky notes based on the themes apparent on the notes. I have always had at least one student volunteer to lead the discussion/amalgamating part of this exercise. Obviously, the professor can lead the discussion, but I have found this activity to be a powerful venue for authorizing students and moving students into instructor mode (Chapter 5). In a class of 25–35 students, the amalgamation portion of this exercise can take 10 minutes or more, in part because the one or two students who lead the process have to sort through multiple instructions about the proper locations of this or that sticky note. The richness of this process obviously stems in part because the notes' authors had to work within a word limit and the amalgamation process itself helps them clarify their thinking. This exercise, including discussion, typically takes 25–30 minutes. It can serve as scaffolding for either instruction or a writing assignment. In the latter case, having the whole class identify the main threads or themes in a reading will be of great benefit to weaker readers or writers.

The search string *brainstorming whiteboard sticky notes images* will give you some ideas about how to do this, although many of the examples shown have writing too small to read all over the room. At the time of writing, YouTube also offered some explanatory videos.

The instructions below are lifted from a *Daily Forecast* sheet for an education class:

> We will do a bit of informal research on Lockheed's Skunk Works and Building 20 at MIT, and ask how we could foster more creativity in school classrooms. We will be using a strategy that has no standardized name; I call it *stickies on the wall.* It works this way:
>
> * Each person in the room produces a maximum of three sticky notes with a maximum of two words on each sticky note (in print large enough to read anywhere in the room!!!!!).
> * We bring all the stickies together on the whiteboard to assemble a kind of class-wide conceptual map.

- Research only one or the other hotbed of creativity (the Skunk Works or Building 20), not both, and bring your sticky notes to the side of the board indicated for your research, Skunk Works on the left and Building 20 on the right.

Once everyone has their stickies on the board, we will identify what themes emerged from your research.

This particular case—research into two hotbeds of creativity—allows an extended conversation about themes. If the amalgamation portion of the exercise involved identifying the themes that emerged from the Skunk Works on one side of the whiteboard and the themes at work in Building 20 on the other, the exercise could include a second phase during which we re-organize the sticky notes to identify what themes the two centers had in common.

Building a Classroom Spread Sheet with Poker Chips

For decades I have used classroom surveys as a means of gathering a group's opinions about a vast number of questions. Following are four examples, two from education classes and two others from faculty workshops:

- What forces drive K–12 classrooms and what forces should drive classrooms?
- What qualities do teachers need to succeed as instructors?
- What are some contemporary pressures on the college curriculum?
- What are the sources of a professor's authority?

Given the availability of classroom technology, a professor can easily use an online survey instrument to take such a survey. But I have found that having students work in pairs and requiring that they allocate a set number of physical tokens (poker chips) to the various forces, qualities, pressures, or sources (to refer to the above four examples) changes the quality of thinking and conversation significantly. Maria Montessori (1912, 1972) was right when she claimed that a different kind of learning occurs when touch is involved. Figure 12.3 shows a typical sheet I photocopy for use by pairs of students. When an odd number of students is completing the exercise, I assign three students to one group and give them 50% more poker chips than the groups of two.

What Drives Ontario Education?

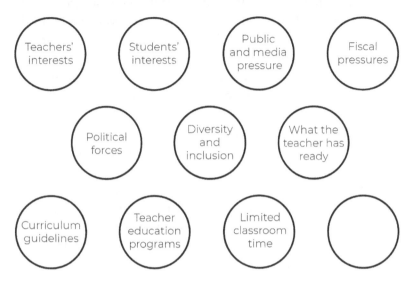

Figure 12.3 A typical worksheet used in the Classroom Spreadsheet—Poker Chips activity.

Credit: Sophie Chardon.

Notice that Figure 12.3 has one empty circle. I invite pairs of participants in this exercise to write in other categories that they believe I have missed and to allocate as many poker chips as they wish to their write-in categories.

Because each pair (or trio) of students has only a finite number of chips (usually 40 for two students) to allocate to a large number of categories, they usually engage in quite earnest discussion about their respective views. I once saw two faculty finish the activity in less than one minute. In response to the question, "What are some contemporary pressures on the college curriculum?" they allocated all their chips to a write-in category: Money. I spotted the single stack of chips from across the room before I could identify the category. That was a sobering moment, and I found out later they were telling the truth; I was never paid for the workshop. More typically, students take 15–20 minutes to agree on how to allocate 40 chips. When students have allocated their chips to the categories, they enter their numbers into a class spreadsheet and they write their write-in categories and respective allocations on the classroom board.

Literally, I have never seen this strategy flop, which is why I always buy poker chips when I see them at the thrift store. Once everyone has entered their data into the spread sheet, we discuss as a class. "Why did so many assign weight to #11?" "Note that five teams assigned zero weight to #14. Would a couple of those teams please tell us why." I usually do this exercise in two rounds. In this case, participants would already have done a first round in response to the question: "What is the situation …?" Round two would focus on the ideal, on what priorities should shape the situation. Another round of discussion thus becomes possible; why are there gaps between what is and what you think should be? This sheet can be adapted to any question in any field of inquiry or dimension of life where most people have a view about what is going on and what they wish was going on. Class-time including two discussions is usually about 60–75 minutes.

The instructions shown in the box went with the actual sheet shown in Figure 12.3.

Instructions for the Poker Chips Activity

1. With one partner, use the poker chips you have received to indicate the strength or proportional weight of your (negotiated) agreements about what ideals or learning outcomes should be prioritized in Alberta classrooms. Each of the 17 numbered circles reflects one possible ideal or purpose.

   Example: Your team may have received 40 poker chips and you agree that #1—*inclusion*—is so important that you allocate 10 of your chips to that ideal.

2. Use the empty circles on the sheet to write in other ideals or learning outcomes you believe Alberta classrooms should focus on today.

   Example: You agree that *helping students love the Calgary Flames* is a worthy ideal for classrooms, so you write that in one of the open circles and you allocate some of your chips to it.

3. Use up all the poker chips you received.

---

4. When you have allocated all your chips to various aims, write the totals for each aim on your sheet and then enter your allocations for goals #1–#17 into one column on the spreadsheet. The numbered circles on the paper sheet match the **rows** in the sheet (#1 to #17). The pairs (you and your partner) match the **columns** (A, B, C, etc.) in the order that you come to the front to enter your totals (type into the next available column).

5. Write your written-in categories and respective totals **in big, readable** letters on the chart paper and attach the paper to the wall.

Once all the teams have gone public with their numbers and written-in aims, we will discuss what to make of our profile as a group of educators.

To close the description of this strategy, it can be adapted to literally any subject matter: Most important developments, discoveries, elements, events, or ideas in the history of literally anything.

STUDENT-DEVELOPED GAMES

As is the case with several of the strategies I treat in this chapter, plentiful resources are available for the professor who wants to introduce games into teaching. Many of those resources are directed toward elementary and secondary education but some address the college and university classroom. Note an important distinction here between the professor-developed game and the student-developed game. I confess to being a gamer but I do not have the time to develop games that would meet the learning outcomes of my classes. But one of the benefits of teaching at this cultural moment is that every college class has enough gamers among its student population that the professor who lists game development as an option or Track will likely have a few takers. I have had students submit some highly creative games in the Gaming Track and have given class time to them near the end of the semester so they could demonstrate to their classmates.

The Gaming Track rubric (see Appendix A) clearly states that the game must align with one or more course learning outcomes. I do not stipulate this next condition but I do strongly encourage students to adapt a published game rather than develop one from scratch. This Track is available for those wishing to work with one other person (although I have negotiated to allow three students to work on a game). I do not limit how much time students give to the development of a game but, based on my casual questioning, I have discovered that most students give much more effort and time to developing a game than the assigned course weight (usually 20%) reflects. My students consistently report their great joy at having developed a game based on one of their own favourite board or electronic games and most do not mind the disproportionate time spent.

> This paragraph appeared in a syllabus supplement in which I provided details on all the Tracks electives in a 400-level course.
>
> > Students choosing this track will adapt a board game for K–12 student use in a specific course in the Alberta K–12 Program of Studies. It must be tied to a specific *Alberta Program of Studies* learning outcome. This game must be tested outside our class so the developer(s) know(s) that students can play it in one or two course periods. This track is available for those wishing to work alone or with one other person. Do not attempt to develop a game or simulation from scratch (because of how much time that will take, but I will not stop you if that is why you are on this earth). Students choosing this track will arrange to demonstrate their game on November 27. If you wish to select this track, please ask me for the additional resource document I have available.

As I noted, part of the genius of offering this track is that students will build the game; the professor does not need to be a game geek. Offering a Gaming Track does require trust that those students who select that track will bring their excitement and creativity to the project, as long as the purposes and parameters of the assignment are clear. Here are some sample assignments for different subject areas:

- Building a high-functioning classroom or hospital ward (education, nursing)
- Promoting a rock or pop concert in your city (business)

- Completing the next commuter rail line in our city (architecture, city planning)
- Restoring the river so the salmon come back (biology, environmental studies)

Most gamers will know the distinction between quest games and resources games (and other distinctions), and they will quickly know what kind of game would suit what subject area or topic within that subject. Most gamers will also know how to address important features of educational games such as these: Clarity of mandate and purpose; standards and assessment frameworks; identifiable steps and goals, allies and supportive people, financial structures and systems, paperflow and records systems, and rewards for successes. In Appendix A, I include several board game development resources, supplied to me by friend and serious gamer, Greg Burbidge.

One scheduling matter warrants mention. If assessment implies real work for a real audience in the real world, then students who develop a game should have the opportunity to demonstrate their game during class time and invite their classmates to participate. The November 27 date in the Track description above reflects my own commitment to this idea. I want the whole class to benefit from the work of those students who develop a game related to our course's learning outcomes.

CASE STUDIES AND VIDEO CLIPS

If you think of cases as stories, you will have less difficulty understanding why students find them engaging. Readers get hooked by plot details, ethical dilemmas, and characters. They want to know how things turn out. Of course, well-written cases, like well-written novels, are populated by people with doubts who need to navigate circumstances where no clear path seems to offer itself.

The cases that work best in university classrooms are set in familiar surroundings such as hospitals, businesses, schools, families, and voluntary associations. Engaging cases require students to identify the moral dilemmas and subterranean forces at work in the story, for it is those tensions and forces that make the dilemma difficult to resolve. What ethical, social, political, economic, and interpersonal forces were at work that complicated the situation? What historical factors constrained the actors or the situation described in the case? What policies or other contextual factors conflicted with what ideals in the story? What implications do the various possible outcomes have for the actors in the story? Questions like these make cases engaging.

Because case teaching has such a long history, numerous practical resources are available in most professional fields. These resources are supported by a robust body of scholarly research. I will not summarize that literature here, but, briefly, a quality teaching case has at least these features:

- The actors in the case need to resolve a situation and the students responding to the case need to understand the setting, including the tensions within which the actors must operate and make decisions.
- Students need to consider the case in light of recent course contents. For example, the textbook authors have suggested that in situation X, competent professionals usually take step Y. A well-written case complicates fictional situation X so that taking step Y or even identifying what step Y is becomes difficult.
- To resolve the case, students should have to define the situation, explore many variables, and recognize the possible implications of the various possible courses of action. Some educators treat the case in two phases, offering more information (possibly suggesting a resolution) in the second phase and asking students to think about the implications of that alternative.
- For effective use in about 30–45 minutes of class time, a case should have four or five questions. Those questions should force participants to probe and should reflect the reality that different people will likely wish for different outcomes. If you want to incorporate inquiry teaching into a case study, provide fewer questions and ask students to identify the questions raised by the case.
- Cases should include an introductory description of the context using language that does not favour one outcome over another
- Even after drawing conclusions and suggesting answers, students should recognize that other courses of action and other solutions to the problem are warranted. They should still have questions after the class discussion wraps up.

This brief list is a starting point only and any professor wanting to use cases will quickly discover other features that could be added to this list.

I recommend that the professor who decides to use cases consider using one or two student-developed cases late in the semester, after students have gained some experience with case teaching. I typically include the description below in a *Daily Forecast* sheet about the eighth week of a term where I have already led the discussion of a couple cases.

Case Study Development and Leadership

Develop a case study and lead a class discussion of it related to the theme of one of the next several weeks. The themes for each of the remaining weeks of the semester are listed in the syllabus. If developing a case of 400–500 words and bringing it to class interests you, please email me. We have room for two or three cases in the fifth- to second-last weeks of the term. Developing a case and leading the discussion will count as 10% course weight. Because I will need to review your case with you before you lead the class in discussion of it you will need to complete it by two days before our class meets.

Making such an offer obviously requires both clear guidance about anonymizing names and details and an assessment schema established from the start of term into which you can insert new optional assignments as the semester progresses (pages 55 and 58 in Chapter 6 illustrates such an assessment structure). Some students who have led cases in my classes have told me that 10% course weight is fair. Others have suggested that 15% would reflect better the work involved.

In online settings, case studies offer an advantage to students and professor. If you give class time for students to read and respond to the case (singly or in pairs), then you and they both get a break from being online as a whole class. Furthermore, in online settings, if you use breakout groups for discussion of a case, more people get to express their opinion (as is the case in small groups in face-to-face teaching).

The Video Clip

Framed well, the brief video clip can serve as a kind of case study. Because video is a natural language for students, they engage readily with a well-scaffolded film clip. By *well-scaffolded*, I mean that professors have made clear on a handout or on the screen why they are showing the clip and what they want students to notice as they view it. I usually provide about four lines of scaffolding so they know a bit about the film and they understand what to watch for. The example in the box (from a *Daily Forecast* sheet) illustrates both those.

> Film clip: *Taare Zameen Par* (*Like Stars on Earth*, India) (Khan, 2007).
>
> Scaffolding: Today we will be exploring metaphors for teachers, learning, students, curriculum, instruction, and schools. In this clip we see substitute teacher Ram Shankar Nikumbh interact with his student, Ishaan, in ways that reveal that he views this troubled student differently from how Ishaan's family, the teachers at his previous school, and the other teachers in his current school have viewed him.
>
> Discussion or writing prompts: Dig underneath the scene we see to get at the metaphor at work. What do you think might be some of Ram Shankar Nikumbh's metaphors for instruction and students? What might his metaphors be for the purposes of schools?

Most Canadian education students do not know of the film in the example above. By design, I look for film clips with which my students are less familiar so that they have to watch carefully. I typically use only four or five minutes to begin the discussion. To reduce my paperwork year to year, I store my scaffolding and prompt notes for all the films I use in one file. I use at least one film clip in every three-hour class, and students regularly tell me that those clips became an important part of their learning and, aside from class, change the way they watch films.

FEEDBACK LOOP

As professors, we have multiple ways to find out how well our students are grasping the course contents and meeting the course's learning objectives. Tests and written assignments are obvious ways. Having a few students respond to the professor's offer to select the Leadership and Planning Track described in Chapter 6 is another way. The exit slip (Chapter 7) offers a way to solicit feedback from all students on any given days. I recommend it again here as a way to find out what questions students were left with at the end of class that we might take up at the start of the next class or clarify on the course wiki.

Here are some typical guiding questions for students to address on an exit slip:

Identify one or two questions raised for me by the session that we could pursue in our next class.

Identify an appropriate exam question arising out of today's class that would require both subject matter expertise and critical thinking to answer. This type of exit slip is actually required of students who select the Final Exam Track.

What are two implications of today's class for practice or for possible directions of future research?

Exit slips are also an excellent venue for students to use Venn diagrams (Chapter 7). Students can incorporate a Venn diagram into an exit slip at the end of a class that illustrates the overlaps and differences they noted during the class discussion (the same question could form the basis for an exit slip following a lecture). Such exit slips can serve at the start of the next class session as the basis for a quick reminder of where the class left off last day.

POTPOURRI

Other discussion strategies are available besides those I have suggested in the above sections. In this section I offer several more, beginning with several ways to use Wikipedia.

Wikipedia

Some claim that the Wikipedia war is over and others claim it is still on. Members of the latter group may frown at my inclusion of these strategies, which I began using in 2016. I have developed several ways to use Wikipedia.

First, students can summarize a Wikipedia article, noting its strengths and weaknesses. I suggest encouraging students to employ some of the reading strategies I describe in Chapter 10, for example, Plus–Minus–Interesting (PMI, pages 109–110), and Summary–Opinion–Support (SOS, pages 110–111) if such strategies would aid students in structuring their appraisal of the article.

In a variant of the above assignments, I require that they add to the article, submitting before and after screen-shots as evidence of their work. If you accept that assessment should include real work for a real audience in the real world, then I suggest this variant on the variant: They show the article to the class and explain why they made the changes they did. Students who have taken up the invitation to add to Wikipedia have found great satisfaction in doing so (even if, as has happened in some cases, editors later removed their contributions). For that reason, I connect this assignment to student self-efficacy (Chapter 5). When they add to Wikipedia, they feel smart because they have contributed to human knowledge.

Another variant involves having students write a critical comparison of a relevant Wikipedia article to the treatment of that topic in the course text. Or, have students compare two Wikipedia articles on related topics. The Commonalities–Differences–Insights strategy (CDI, Chapter 10) works perfectly for this kind of task. See the instructions below for a compare/contrast assignment:

> Based on the Wikipedia articles ("Education in Ancient Greece" and "Education in Ancient Rome") and whatever other sources you wish to use, write a 500-word comparison/contrast paper of the values that drove ancient education in those two places and the values that, in your view, drive contemporary education. (Value: 10%; Rubric: #1; Course Learning Outcomes: 4, 5.)

As are my readers, I am aware that Wikipedia is not the only resource available to students. But if increasing students' sense of their self-efficacy is a concern, then, in my view, Wikipedia is an obvious resource to have students use.

Debates

Because of the human instinct to want to be right, debates can spark interest in a topic. I do not recommend attaching grades to debates; rather, I give a few minutes for the whole class to outline arguments for both sides and then arbitrarily assign two students to each team. That is, debates in my classes are informal and nearly impromptu. If students end up defending a position, they do not themselves hold, then, in my view, that is for the good because it demands that they consider perspectives different from their own, fostering critical thought on their parts.

Below are four topics that illustrate the uses to which I put spontaneous debates. In each case, I could introduce the relevant conceptual or policy question in a vast variety of ways. Starting a discussion with debates guarantees quick interest and high student engagement.

- Be it resolved that the Bachelor of Education program at Mount Royal University is a teacher education program, not a teacher training program.

- Be it resolved that all school jurisdictions should follow France's lead and forbid school students from using phones while at school.
- Be it resolved that Alberta schools should follow Finland's model and abolish homework.
- Be it resolved that the Alberta Schools Act should be changed so that Alberta students must complete grade 12 before they are allowed to leave school.

These four debate topics illustrate one of the necessary (and obvious) features of debate: Topics must be selected that are nearly guaranteed to generate debate.

Wicked Problems

After a brief explanation of what researchers and policy specialists call a wicked problem (perhaps with a definition on the screen), ask students to identify wicked problems in the field of study of which that class is a part. Problems could range from major, unresolved disciplinary issues to questions about the meaning of a key passage in a reading. I suggest using small groups initially so that more students can participate in the initial conversation. Identifying a Top 10 or Top 5 list of wicked problems in the field could lead to further discussion or to a written assignment related to what kind of research or conceptual breakthrough would be necessary to resolve one or more of the wicked problems identified.

Metaphors in the Field

Every academic discipline employs metaphors to shed light on its respective subject matter. In *Metaphors We Live By*, Lakoff and Johnson (1980) present a strong view of metaphors, by which I mean that metaphors are not just helpful; they actually shape how we see the world and we cannot think without them. In my own work, I have found that having pre-service teachers examine common metaphors for such important ideas in education as curriculum, instruction, and assessment yields new insights for them about the ways they think about the work they plan to do. Such examination also provides the basis for rich discussion in class.

The best way to begin using class time for an examination of metaphors is with a brief, whole-class discussion in which the class identifies the most popular metaphors in the field. For example, when education students identify metaphors for assessment, they often mention hitting targets, measuring, outcomes, and they list words such as *standards, top, bottom, struggling, strong,* and *weak.* Once the class has developed its list of common metaphors for a field, I assign different metaphors to groups of students, typically asking them to answer these questions about the particular metaphor I have assigned their group:

- What are some of the strengths of this metaphor?
- What aspects of the subject does this metaphor highlight?
- What aspects of the subject does this metaphor downplay or miss altogether?
- What aspects of this metaphor does your group judge to be illogical or ill-considered?

Alternatively, one can have students use a three-column, Plus–Minus–Interesting structure to appraise the strengths and weaknesses of their assigned metaphor.

World War I—Who Was at Fault?

One result of my long fascination with metaphors has been that I ask my students to unpack the metaphors at work in our thinking about important questions. A second result is that I regularly look for metaphors to help students engage more deeply with course contents. For example, when I taught secondary history, I asked students to use the rules of hockey to determine how many penalty minutes would be given to the various belligerent nations in World War I. Who started the fight? Who was on the ice at the time and joined the fight? Who came off the bench to join the fight? In their attempts to agree on which participating nations deserved two minutes, five minutes, and ten minutes, my students—I admit it, they were high school students and hockey is Canada's official religion—would argue heatedly about the relative guilt of the respective belligerents. In other words, they engaged critically with what could have been a rather boring recitation of dates and facts.

Typically, I ask students to prepare a slide of their work on metaphors for presentation to the class (and I give very clear instructions about brevity). As with the case with many of the discussion strategies I catalogue in this chapter, this metaphor activity can become the basis of a graded assignment. In that case, individual students take their own groups' work and develop it into a written submission.

Pick the Right Decade

In this strategy, the professor asks students to identify the decade in which various developments in the academic discipline took place. This could be applied to inventions, ideas, or events. I admit that I developed the strategy only after playing the table game *Timeline* for the first time. In the example below, I asked education students to identify the decade in which educators first introduced five important ideas. In each case, I listed every decade from 1800 to 2020 (lists I omit here). As it happens, our class did the exercise on the day of a Canadian federal election.

Pick the Decade

For each idea below, mark with an X the decade in which you think it was first introduced. Hey, it's just like voting, which you had BETTER do today!!!

1. instruction should involve manipulatives
2. art instruction should be based on actual objects instead of theory and imitation of great works
3. materials and plants in the schoolyard should be a resource in nature study and geography
4. deduction and teaching from theory are less effective than building instruction upward from the children's own sense experiences
5. teachers must scaffold new learning into/onto what students already know

This activity takes only a few minutes and has the potential to lead students to new understandings about how old or new are some developments in their field.

DE-TEACHERING DISCUSSION

My Microsoft Word speller reluctantly accepted my addition of the first word in this section's title to its dictionary. I introduce this neologism intentionally to bring our focus to an important aspect of class discussion: Our perceptions of our own role and our responses to students' contributions. The key question running through the idea of de-teaching is this: Are professors—or any discussion leaders—aware of how their body language, facial expressions, tone, and word choices invite more discussion or close discussion down. For reasons such as a shortage of time or a group having reached a resolution to a problem, it may be appropriate for a discussion leader or professor to push toward closure. And it may also be appropriate to continue. In what follows, I point to some of the ways that professors may inadvertently close discussion.

To begin, consider the difference between the first and second sets of bulleted questions below. The first questions typically have the effect of opening up further conversation. The second may have the opposite effect.

- What do you think of how so-and-so interprets what happened?
- How do you feel about/respond to this?
- How would you say this fits in with what so-and-so said earlier?

The person asking questions such as the next two may mean to invite more conversation but the wording may produce the opposite effect.

- Thank you. I think you've hit the nail on the head with your observation.
- You've got it. That's precisely what Famous Author said in an *Important Book*.

The speaker offering these latter two responses obviously means to be positive. My concern is that the comments may lead discussion participants to conclude that nothing more needs saying. The two comments below might also be misconstrued. Depending on many factors, including the speaker or professor's tone, someone making these comments might hear them as simple checks for understanding. But a listener might hear them as the starting points of a grilling or interrogation.

Instructional Strategies

- So are you saying then that this is the case?
- So you seem to be taking a/an XYZ position then. Is that right?

Below, I offer more comments in the genre of the first list above, comments meant to extend conversation and invite more participation.

- Can you explain more what you mean when you say that please.
- So what would you say that implies about this?
- What reasons do you think support your view on that?
- What do you think might be the counter position to what you have just given?
- How do others in the room respond to that idea?

Literally thousands of others have addressed what I have opened up in this short treatment of discussion leadership. I offer this only to flag the fact that the strategies we might choose to generate classroom discussion are only a part of what will produce good discussion or cause our attempts to land on the floor. On most topics in our courses, we will be the experts. But we may need to put our expertise slightly into the background if we want class discussions to generate deep, critical thinking among our students. *Profsplaining* is already in the cultural lexicon. We need to form invitational speech habits, not so that no one will accuse us of profsplaining but because we want our students to participate in classroom discussions.

CONCLUSION

What I have given here is incomplete. The chapter is complete but, again, if a dozen colleagues had co-written this with me it would be longer and much richer. Still, I offer these strategies because they work so effectively and I invite you, my colleagues, to try some of them. None of us can reinvent our teaching program in one week, but we can try this strategy in one class this month and another strategy in another class next month. I welcome you to appropriate some of these and make them your own.

REFERENCES

Hill, L. H. (2005). Concept mapping to encourage meaningful student learning. *Adult Learning*, 16(3/4), 7–13.

Khan, A. (Dir.). (2007). *Taare Zameen Par* [*Like Stars on Earth*]. UTV Entertainment.

Lakoff, G., & Johnson, M. (1980). *Metaphors we live by*. University of Chicago Press.

Montessori, M. (1912). *The Montessori method: Scientific pedagogy as applied to child education in "the children's houses"* (A. E. George, trans.). Frederick A. Stokes.

Montessori, M. (1972). *The discovery of the child* (M. J. Costelloe, trans.). Ballantine.

Phillips, L. V. (1987). Closure the fine art of making learning stick. *Instructor, 97*, 3.

Thirteen

As is the case with many of the strategies I offer in this volume, many higher educators tend to view arts strategies as soft or, in some cases, even as a complete waste of instructional time. The question I ask about all strategies, including arts strategies, is how much my students will learn by using them. Will they meet the learning objectives for that class or will they move closer to meeting one or more of the learning objectives for that course? I have consistently been able to answer "yes" to those questions when I have used the strategies and so I offer and describe them in this chapter.

THE SUBWAY MAP

This idea struck me when I first saw Simon Patterson's *The Great Bear* in the Tate Modern Gallery in London (Patterson, 1992). Patterson used the iconic London Underground map to trace important figures in 20th century culture. Using the same idea, the London Underground Museum Shop now sells a Black History Poster based on the same Underground map (Black Cultural Archives, 2021). Part of the power of these maps derives from their having crossed the boundary between two genres: Transit maps with station names and lists of important historical or cultural figures. From a distance, *The Great Bear* looks like a standard Tube map. The viewer who gets up close realizes it is a different way to present a who's who of culture.

Taken by the creativity of this genre-bending idea, I have been asking education students for a decade to use transit maps (of Prague, Moscow, Vancouver, or Toronto) to trace their call into the profession of teaching. They base their maps on questions adapted from Parker Palmer's *The Courage to Teach* (1998). They consistently report to me that renaming stations on a transit map after people, fiction and non-fiction book titles, film titles, experiences, and life events brings influences to mind that they simply would not have thought of had they been answering these

DOI: 10.4324/9781003259596-17

159 **Arts Strategies**

questions by typing on a keyboard or even by writing in a journal. The artists among us would say, "of course." Such is the power of the arts.

In face-to-face courses I offer students a choice of a digital map (in several formats) or an 11" x 17" paper map with the train lines colored as they are in the actual transit maps from the respective city. In both cases, I have already stripped the map legends and station names from the maps. In face-to-face classes I also distribute black and white copies of the maps for students' use as working copies. The Prague, Vancouver, and Toronto maps all have three or four lines; Moscow has ten. I regularly offer the Moscow map for those students who want to turn this assignment into a major occasion for life reflection and review. But I recommend to students that they use one of the maps with fewer lines.

To illustrate how this activity works, Figure 13.1 shows a portion of the Toronto subway system with some of my own literary and philosophical influences. For my purposes here, I show only half the subway line in question, having given the other half to another topic (my mentors, whose names I omit here). I encourage students who want to respond to more questions than there are lines on a transit map to split a line at some major point and use half the line for one question and half for another. Typically, a few students respond to the invitation to outline the trajectory they hope to follow in their profession. Urban transit planners use dashed lines to indicate projected routes for future subway lines or light-rapid train lines. Similarly, students wanting to illustrate their anticipated professional trajectory use a dashed line for that portion of their map, often including such steps as "master's degree" and "department leadership."

I have used this activity with undergraduates, graduates, doctoral students, and, jointly with my colleague, Amy Dee, with faculty. A tiny minority of students knock this map off as simply another assignment they are required to complete if they want to pass a course. For the overwhelming majority of students, however, this activity becomes an occasion for deep reflection and often gratitude. I believe it has power to engage students for the same reasons Simon Patterson's *The Great Bear* originally engaged me in London: The combination of the unfamiliar—the surprise of using a map to answer such questions—with the familiar—the most famous subway map in the world (London) or the subway map from a well-known city in one's own country. Appendix A contains detailed instructions and the rubric for a subway map assignment.

Important
steps on my
way into teaching
(not done in
this example)

Authors who shaped me

J. Tolkien
D. L. Sayers
J. Conrad
W. Shakespeare
G. Greene
J. Milton
J. Irving
L. Penney
J. Conrad
B. Shaw
C. S. Lewis
L. Tolstoy
F. Dostoevsky

Figure 13.1 A portion of a Toronto transit system map showing one half of "The Bloor Street Line," representing the author's influential authors. Credit: Sophie Chardon.

I always require a written component so I can be clear about some of the details on students' maps, especially mentors' names. Instructions for this written component also appear in Appendix A. My strong recommendation to readers who decide to use an activity like this with a class: Complete such a map yourself before assigning it to your class.

The Student-Built Slide Deck

Students respond warmly to the idea of building a slide deck, a strategy that can be adapted to any topic. Each student contributes one slide. As I described in Chapter 10, students build a slide-deck with the Black-out Poetry and, as I describe in what follows, I use it to develop a quick overview of the ideas of some important philosophers and philosophers of education. Part of the beauty of this exercise is its flexibility; it can be used in any academic discipline. A professor can construct the list—the most significant concepts, people, dates, or developments in the history of a nation, movement, or research field—and thereby guarantee that the subjects of the slides suit the learning outcomes of the course. I do not edit the slides produced by my students, and therefore can neither stop aspiring comedians nor guarantee the quality of the contents, but I have been disappointed only infrequently so far, and the higher level of student engagement with student-produced slides compensates for those limitations.

The example below contains the instructions and list of 40 names I recently made available to 31 students in a 500-level philosophy of education course. You will see names here that you would not ordinarily associate with philosophy of education, but I want my students to understand that it is not just dead male philosophers who have envisioned the good life; I want them to see that everyone has a worldview and lives out of a vision of human flourishing. The following instructions to students are lifted from a *Daily Forecast* sheet distributed in an online course.

Philosophers of Education: Slide Deck Instructions

Pick one name from the list below and immediately highlight it in the Google doc so no two people end up working on the same person. Produce a slide with the person's picture (from Google Images, Wikipedia, etc.) and summarize that person's worldview or their educational philosophy in 30 words or less. To help your classmates be able to see this easily when we see the slide show, please put the words in big font, as in the John Krasinski example I have on the slide I showed you a moment ago.

Socrates	Tina Fey	Plato	Oprah Winfrey
Homer Simpson	The Buddha	J. P. Sartre	Mother Teresa
Confucius	Gandhi	Guru Nanak	Jimmy Kimmel
M. Montessori	J. Dewey	J. Piaget	Howard Gardner
J. A. Comenius	N. Noddings	B. F. Skinner	Wm. James
J. J. Rousseau	J. Pestalozzi	J. F. Herbart	Miss Frizzle
F. Froebel	E. Ryerson	Aristotle	Taylor Swift
Beyoncé	Jesus	Mohammed	Chris Pratt
R. Steiner	Drake	T. Hobbes	R. S. Peters
Bill Nye	D. Umbridge	Dewey Finn	M. McGonagall

Take 15–20 minutes to research your summary and produce your slide. Please edit your summary for clarity and smoothness. When you have completed your slide, please email it to your classmate who agreed to assemble the slide deck at their.email@someserver.com.

This last bit of instruction is important. I recommend you find a tech-savvy student volunteer the day before you plan to use this exercise. While that volunteer manages building the slide deck, you are free to answer questions and interact with those students who have completed their slides. This activity usually takes about 40–45 minutes, for instructions, construction, and showing the slide deck. As I noted in the description of Black-out Poetry (Chapter 10), I ask the person showing the slides to pause for 10–15 seconds after each person has read their slide.

The Performance Track

In the chapter on assessment (Chapter 6), I introduced the idea of Tracks, typically the 20% of a course grade where I invite students to work in area of their interest and strength. One of those tracks involves preparing a performance related to the course objectives and contents. Performances can include drama and readers' theatre, song, spoken word, and poetry. Besides giving the performance, students choosing this track must include a brief essay that justifies the performance and explains what they are trying to accomplish with it. I also require that they develop a clear rubric that will help both them and me judge the success of the performance.

The following instructions are from the *Rubrics Document* available to students:

> Students choosing this track may work in pairs. If you need more people than two for your performance, you will need to persuade friends and/or classmates to participate, but the assignment's credit cannot go to more than two people. Students choosing this track will arrange to perform their work on November 27.

"I Really Want to Direct" is a variant of the performance track suggested to me by Angela Farrington-Thompson, a teacher in Toronto. She describes it this way:

> Write a monologue/poem that expresses something learned, and become a director for a partner who delivers it! This is an exchange assignment.

In other words, students partner up: I write a monologue/poem about my topic, and direct my partner as they deliver it. They direct me, as I deliver theirs. Through the process of creating, revising, sharing, and performing/delivering the material, a lot of growth and meaningful learning happens. This can work for multiple subject areas/topics—and gives both verbal/writing learners as well as artistic learners a wonderful entry point to express their learning.

A Line From a Song or Film

Because students respond so readily to people they recognize, especially actors and singers, I often use a line from a song or film to begin discussion of the theme of a given day's class. Such lines have far more discussion-generating capacity when they appear with the image of the person who sang or spoke them. I am not permitted to reproduce the slide here I often use in class to spark discussion with education students about the perception that teaching is not most young adults' *Plan A*. I use a still shot from *Bad Teacher* (Kasdan, 2011), a film in which Cameron Diaz, playing Elizabeth Halsey, asks what she is going to do with her life now that all vocational and relational doors seem to have closed. That single image never fails to produce discussion. Also, it leads to an important conversation about how the lives, joys, and sorrows of *reel teachers* (teachers in film) compare to the lives, joys, and sorrows of real teachers. Lines from songs and still images from films have the potential to foster such conversation about professionals in many fields. And, as I noted in Chapter 4, words and images on a slide can also serve as prompts for class meetings and circle meetings.

Illustrate Your Question

In Chapter 5, I briefly described this way of pulling students into what I called instructor mode. This strategy is a corollary of the Line From a Song or Film slide created by a professor. To illustrate, I turn to the economics concept of *competitive advantage*. For generations, economics students have wrestled with this concept. By Illustrate Your Question, I mean something quite personal, as shown in Figure 13.2. A student in an economics class might ask aloud, "Why is competitive advantage so difficult to understand." That same sentence on an image of a stressed student has much more poignancy. With very modest graphic skills and Microsoft Paint, I created Figure 13.2 in three minutes.

WHY IS THE CONCEPT OF COMPARATIVE ADVANTAGE SO HARD TO UNDERSTAND?

Figure 13.2 A student-produced graphic that illustrates an economics question.
Credit: jeshoots.com at Unsplash.

I recommend that professors invite their students to create similar slides to make public their struggles with some of the thornier conceptual issues in their courses. As I have argued at several points in the book and throughout this chapter, the visual adds great power to the verbal. I cannot guarantee that students would engage more deeply in a discussion of comparative advantage prompted by Figure 13.2 than they would if their professor simply asked for a student to define it for the class. But my own experience (in another discipline) leads me to want to offer such a guarantee.

Thought Bubble Video

Some students will usually take up the invitation to produce a short series of still shots from some currently popular television show or movie where, by means of thought bubbles, the characters appear to express or summarize key points in a reading from the text or another source. These mini-productions must be shown in class. If a student chose to use images from *The Simpsons*, for example, the key points or sayings the student chose to include would appear as thought bubbles above various Simpsons' characters' heads.

For a mix of reasons I do and do not understand, class members love watching and pay close attention to such presentations. After all, it is one of their classmates who produced it. The genre itself has a kind of ironic foundation, suiting the generation of students we now teach. Why am I still surprised when students report that they now, finally, understand this or that after watching such a presentation. I did not know that characters from The Simpsons or Downton Abbey had such pedagogical skill.

Film Festival

If students are required to produce a short video or elect to do so because they chose the Performance or Video Production Track, those videos could be shown in face-to-face or in online classes as a film festival. Suitable situations, topics and genres for a film festival include these:

- Students' summaries of the biographies/ideas/reception of/critiques of historical or literary figures;
- Students' visual interpretations or outlines of a portion of reading;
- Students' work in the Performance Track (certainly in online courses where they cannot perform in class);
- Recorded performances of students who prefer not to perform live in front of a class.

Such videos have the capacity to bring great joy to both students and to professors. My own pleasure is usually tempered by my knowledge of how many hours some students spend producing a short video that carries only 20% course weight.

Lunch with a Theorist and Channeling an Author

Lunch with a theorist involves students' creation of a script for a conversation with a theorist in an academic discipline or practitioner in a professional field. That conversation focuses on a particular theory and the benefits and difficulties of applying that theory to a specific problem in practice. Lunch with a theorist has obvious similarities to an activity where an author of the students' textbook plays different roles in scripts written by students. I use the assignment in the box in a course where we use The Courage to Teach (Palmer, 1998) as our course text.

Channeling Parker Palmer

For one of the bulleted scenes below, work with one partner to develop a brief sketch where you play the two roles indicated. The Palmer character needs to say wise and deep Palmer-ish things and should try to incorporate materials from the book. The other person should truly inhabit the other role named and not break the fourth wall during the performance.

You are Parker Palmer, a mentor teacher in a Calgary school that takes interns from Mount Royal University, and you are in conversation with an MRU education student who …

- … just taught a great lesson today, and knows it, and is expecting mostly lavish praise [1]
- … just taught a major flop of a lesson and is thinking of giving up on the idea of professional teaching [2]
- … is doing well in her placement but thinking of dropping out of the education program in favour of another field [3]

You are Parker Palmer, a school principal, in conversation with one of your teaching staff, who …

- … was described in Brie's case last week and you need to have "the talk" [4]
- … has just been described in Wendy's case this morning [5]
- … you have just seen in Freedom Writers [6] (LaGravenese, 2007)
- … you have just seen in Stand and Deliver [7] (Menéndez, 1998)
- … is a mid-career teacher, 38 years old, doing a good job, but bored with teaching grade 5–6 science and math, and regularly compares teaching to the torture machine in The Princess Bride (Reiner, 1987). [8]
- … is a first-year teacher and is absolutely swamped with day-to-day preparation, keeping up with grading and administration, trying to have at least a bit of life outside of work [9]

The original list as I offered it to students has been truncated for brevity but the idea is clear: Students must write a script where one character speaks in character as a well-known person in a research or professional field.

I thank nursing professor Sarah Hanson, from the University of Northern British Columbia, for bringing the "lunch with a theorist" strategy to my attention in late 2020 and for pointing me to Sherri Melrose's (2011) article in *Nursing Educator* and Shannon Shah's TEDx talk (2013), both listed at the end of this chapter.

Visual Journals and Sketchnoting

Former students of mine, both now teachers, have written about the benefits of these two strategies. As is the case with many of the strategies I catalogue in this volume, K–12 educators have begun to use these approaches, and many undergraduate students will therefore know what to do if they have the opportunity to demonstrate their learning by using one of these approaches.

Visual journals. One assignment that I found highly engaging was creating a visual journal to reflect on my learnings about assessment in a course strictly about assessment. As an education student, I did not enter the field with big dreams of assessing students, so this course is not the most exciting, though it is very important for a future teacher. What made this assignment so engaging was the fact that it was so open. Students were given the opportunity to express what they had learned using a visual representation of their choice: some made infographics, some made paintings with a written description, some made videos, one person made a claymation video, and I made a guide book using an extended metaphor. Once I got started, I felt like I didn't want to stop because I was enjoying making an aesthetically pleasing document in which I was able to demonstrate my learning however I wanted to. This assignment was also beneficial to students because it allowed students who struggle with writing an opportunity for success, while still allowing students who enjoy writing assignments to write as much as they wanted to.

Credit goes to Janaye Keys for permission to quote this personal account of using a visual journal.

Sketchnoting has obvious similarities to visual journals and can be an effective way for students to summarize oral or written material. I will not give space to a long explanation of it here but will note that a simple online search of the string *sketchnoting* will produce over a million hits and will reveal to some of my readers that it may simply be a new name for the way they have taken notes for years. That is, many of us already doodle, use visual organizers, and mind-maps as we read or listen.

In one of the workshops in late 2020 that led to my proposing this book, Maegahn Smith introduced me to this strategy. Maegahn is one of the student authors of the book project described in Chapter 11. Following is her permitted description of how it might be used in higher education.

> **Sketchnoting.** A typical use of sketchnoting in the college classroom would be to assign each student or small group of students the task of producing a single slide sketchnote summary of a section of the textbook chapter. When the slide deck is shown, students have a minute or two to explain their slide and another minute to answer questions that arise. Professors wanting to build a short written assignment onto a sketchnoting activity can have students produce a short written explanation of their slide, noting how they would revise it in light of their classmates' comments and questions.

As a doodler myself (and as one who has trouble understanding information presented orally), I recommend these approaches.

Conclusion

Throughout the book, I have suggested strategies that I could have legitimately included in this chapter instead of in the chapters where I placed them. These include:

- PowerPoint karaoke (Chapters 4, 5, 9)
- Musicians in disguise (Chapter 5)
- Mocked-up book covers and posters (Chapter 5)
- Video clips (Chapter 5)
- Black-out poetry (Chapter 10)
- Venn diagrams and concept maps (Chapter 12).

An age-old debate among K–12 educators focuses on whether the arts are a frill or are basic. We could nuance that question into two questions. Do we mean having students study the fine arts as part of the curriculum? Or do we mean that we should incorporate the arts into instruction in all the subject areas? I will not attempt to answer the first question here. But I have seen the power of incorporating the arts into instruction in other subject areas. I have kept using the strategies I have catalogued here because they increase student engagement and deepen student learning. To quote a bumper sticker I once saw on a colleague's ring-binder, Art Is Basic.

I close by proposing another kind of arts strategy altogether, one I have already mentioned repeatedly in this book and will not repeat at length here. That is, that we use aesthetic and design principles in our planning of our courses and units. Students have reported to me for years that my course structures make sense and they suit (a word one does not ordinarily expect to hear in course evaluations). Such reports should not surprise us. After all, the aesthetic dimension—the design dimension—is part of what makes us human, and professors who shape their courses in light of aesthetic and design principles should expect to create courses more suited to the humans who enroll in those courses. So, I invite you to consider incorporating aesthetic principles—the word arts doesn't quite fit here—into your planning. Incorporating Alexander's work on pattern languages into my own course and unit planning revolutionized my teaching (Alexander et al, 1977; Alexander, 1979; Badley, 2018; Badley et al, 2021), and I believe it could revolutionize yours. Start with Alexander's work or start with mine, but please consider reframing planning along design lines.

To all, including those who will not explore Christopher Alexander's idea of pattern languages, I offer the arts strategies I have described here. Because they involve the visual, these strategies increase engagement. Furthermore, some of them are downright fun.

REFERENCES

Alexander, C. (1979). *The timeless way of building.* Oxford University Press.

Alexander, C., Ishikawa, S., Silverstein, M., Jacobson, M., Fiksdahl-King, I., & Angel, S. (1977). *A pattern language: Towns, buildings, construction.* Oxford University Press.

Badley, K. (2018). *Curriculum planning with design language: Building elegant courses and units.* Routledge.

Badley, K., Ayer, N., Cloutier, D., Daniel, D., Flood, E., Keys, J., Laing, D., MacIsaac, K., McManaman, D., Reid, B., & Scovoranski, A. (2021). By using architectural principles can teachers become curriculum designers, not simply instructional planners. In M. Jacobsen & J. Nickel (Eds.), *Preparing teachers as curriculum designers,* (pp. 222–246). Canadian Association for Teacher Education. https://cate-acfe.ca/wp-content/uploads/2021/04/Preparing-Teachers-as-Curriculum-Designers_ebook_FINAL.pdf

Black Cultural Archives & London Underground Museum Shop. *Black history tube map*. https://www.ltmuseumshop.co.uk/black-history-tube-map

Kasdan, J., (Dir.). (2011). *Bad teacher*. Columbia Pictures.

LaGravenese, R. (Dir.). (2007). *Freedom writers*. MTV Films, Jersey Films, Paramount Pictures.

Melrose, S. (2006). Lunch with the theorists: A clinical learning assignment. *Nursing Educator*, 31(4), 147–148. https://journals.lww.com/nurseeducatoronline/fulltext/2006/07000/lunch_with_the_theorists__a_clinical_learning.4.aspx

Menéndez, R. R. (Dir.). (1998). *Stand and deliver*. Warner Brothers Studios.

Palmer, P. (1998). *The courage to teach*. Jossey-Bass.

Patterson, S. (1992). *The great bear*. Tate Modern Gallery. https://www.tate.org.uk/art/artworks/patterson-the-great-bear-p77880

Reiner, R. (Dir.) (1987). *The princess bride*. 20th Century Fox, Vestron Pictures.

Shah, S. (2013) Bringing theory to practice: Let's have lunch (TEDx talk). https://www.youtube.com/watch?v=qAOuZMKGNyo

Fourteen

When I introduced Christopher Alexander's work (Alexander et al, 1977; Alexander, 1979) on pattern languages in Chapter 5, I mentioned his concern that the physical spaces we inhabit have easily identifiable entrances and exits. I returned (metaphorically) to entrances in my treatment of course design and unit planning (in Chapter 9). Alexander also concerned himself with exits, as do I. From my student years, I recall several courses where the professor rushed through the last three weeks of content in the last couple hours, kept us past the nominal end time for class, and then exited the room after a cursory expression of best wishes for our futures. In this chapter, I want to propose that we do things differently from those classes to which I refer. I argue there that we should close our classes with intentionality and not simply end them, to use Yonge, Lee, and Luhanga's distinction (Yonge et al, 2006).

Given that the last scheduled day of class constitutes a perfectly obvious finish to a course, this chapter may seem unnecessary. But this whole book is meant to help higher educators build a certain kind of classroom ethos or climate. And, for me, that climate implies that we do not simply teach till the clock indicates that class is over and then remind students of the final exam schedule. Rather, we draw the final class—and, implicitly, the course—to a close.

The research literature on finishing courses is thin. Not surprisingly, given that they have written about it, those who do address the matter of ending the course largely agree with each other that the finish is important (Aoh, 2019; Hansen, 2019; Yonge et al, 2006). And, given that I am writing about it as well, one could surmise correctly that I agree with them. I find Aoh's vision of the course ending especially interesting because he would have us reminding our students that our course fits into the big picture, in his case, the biological big picture.

DOI: 10.4324/9781003259596-18

Replace his phrase *big picture* with the phrase *grand vision* and you catch some of what I try to impart to my students on each successive last day of class.

Appropriately, those who might want to close their courses on a high note will ask how to do so. What strategies are available to close a course and not simply end it? In what follows I describe some of the strategies I use to close my own courses. As has been the case so many times in this book, I wish I could guarantee that these approaches would work for everyone. I can say in truth only that they consistently work for me.

DESIGNING AND PLANNING THE WHOLE SEMESTER

My reference above to the rushed ending is not incidental to my purposes in this chapter. If I have designed the whole semester carefully and followed my own suggestions about planning, there will be no need to rush on the last day. If I have listened to my students' comments about our progress and if I have assessed their learning accurately throughout the semester, we should all be satisfied by the end of the course that we have completed the work we set out to do. Thus, successfully closing the course and finishing it in a big picture way imply taking the right steps throughout the semester. These steps—this designing, planning, and checking the class's pace and progress—are obviously not strategies one implements on the last day. Rather, they are strategies one follows through the whole semester that open up the time and create the conditions for the kind of last day I describe in what follows.

FOOD AND DRINK

As I do all semester, I bring food and coffee on the last day. More than once, students have brought food as well. Having aimed at being hospitable and building community all semester, it would seem unusual not to bring treats on the last day. No more explanation needed.

THE LAST CIRCLE MEETING

For the last time in this book, I recommend the circle meeting. In this last-class circle meeting, I give some strict instructions and I gently remind the class of them when students fail to follow them. Those instructions—and recommendations—are as follows:

- Students are not allowed to talk about me or my teaching.
- They are encouraged to name things they have learned.
- They are encouraged to name someone they met for the first time.
- They can share an idea that another student gave them.
- They are encouraged to share something they learned from the course readings.
- They are encouraged to encourage other students to aim high.

For this final circle meeting of the semester, I ask everyone to speak but I do not require that they do so. I understand that a university class is not an encounter group or a group therapy session, but when I have worked hard to build community all semester and have asked my students to help build it with me, I consider it appropriate to have students make kind and personal comments to each other.

At the end of the circle meeting, I encourage students to take the needed steps in the following weeks to form Professional Learning Communities (PLCs) with each other. I emphasize that PLCs cannot simply be coffee groups; they should explore professional topics together and support each other's professional development. I encourage students to invite people they met recently (in class) to be part of a PLC and not just to gather their oldest friends. In my view, a PLC that continues to meet after the end of a semester is a natural outgrowth of the kind of classroom community we have created together.

PERFORMANCES

Normally, students who elect the Performance Track usually have their performance ready for their classmates to see by the second-last week of class (my usual due date). If everyone is ready by that date, I may ask for volunteers to perform in the first segment of the final class. On those days we hear and see those performances after we have finished the circle meeting.

PROTECTING AND NURTURING OUR VOCATIONS

Of course, students are relieved when another semester draws to a close. But that relief is often mixed with some apprehension. What will the rest

of my course grades be? What will next semester be like? Will I ultimately find work and satisfaction in my field? Although our role among
our students is not to be psychologists, we can still be encouraging.
During the final class session, I distribute a paper called "Nurturing Your
Personal and Professional Core to Protect Your Vocation." Following the
title on the handout is this question: How can teachers stay vital into
late career so they can keep their ideals and continue to believe that
they are doing what they are supposed to be doing? Professors wanting
to encourage their students could word a parallel question for any academic discipline. After briefly noting a couple pieces of research related
to long-time vocational vitality, I work with them through a list of
20 strategies that other educators have used to stay alive vocationally,
inviting their questions, commentary, and concerns. I will not reproduce the entire list here but do offer these sample items:

• Deliberately can put yourself in the path of mentors.
• Set a research agenda.
• Plan ahead for the year you start your next degree.
• Five years in, swap jobs for a year with another teacher (locally or
  internationally).
• Get involved in a service-teaching trip as part of a team, but read
  Ivan Illich's essay "To Hell with Good Intentions" (Illich, 1968)
  on the web before running off to save the world. And please watch
  "Who Wants to be a Volunteer?" (SAIH, 2014) as well.
• To help keep your brain alive, change about 7–15% of your course
  contents per year (new lessons, new assignments, new assessments
  annually in every unit).
• Plan a once-in-a lifetime trip (examples: Morocco, Yukon River).

As you can see, the throughline in this list of strategies is that the
end of the semester or the end of the degree is not the end, it is only
the beginning. But no one should take long-time career vitality for
granted; thus the tile, "Protecting and Nurturing Our Vocations."

TWO PIECES OF POETRY

On the last page of the handout on which the bulleted points above
are printed, I print two poetry passages. The first is from "A Summer
Day," a poem by American poet, Mary Oliver (1990). The line I quote

is this: "Tell me, what is it you plan to do with your one wild and precious life?" The other poem, "To Build a Swing," comes from Hafiz (also spelled Hafez), the 14th-century Sufi poet from present-day Iran (Hafiz, 1999). I show the full text of that poem to class but am not able to reproduce it here (there are many copies of it online). The gist of "To Build a Swing" is that we have all the materials required to make a good life and we need to use them well. My summary sounds like the kind of self-help one might hear on day-time television but in the hands (or words) of Hafiz, "To Build a Swing" sounds distinctly big picture.

With both these poems I want to encourage my students with the same throughline: They need to keep their heads up and keep moving toward worthwhile professional and personal goals.

THE CHALLENGE

While not a spoken word artist by any means, I have written an extended spoken word piece (of about 1100 words) which I regularly perform for my students on the last day of class. Because one of the requirements of my religion is that we be kind to other people, I want to give my students an encouraging word in the final class and I want to send them out (it might sound more religious if I said "send them forth"). Thus far, I have succeeded in keeping my spoken word performance off the internet, and I do not wish to publish it here. But, in summary, I try one final time to build up my students' self-efficacy and I tell them to go and change the world.

THE LAST EXIT SLIP

My students know that the course they have been in has been shaped in part by previous generations of students. I invite them to help me improve the course for the next cohort by writing honestly on a final exit slip. I usually hand out a paper slip and provide an online form of the same slip so that students can leave their slip with me as they leave the room or email it to me. I word the questions so they can criticize the shape and contents of the course without feeling like they are doing so. Typical questions on the final day exit slip usually run along these lines:

- What could there have been more of in this course?
- What could there have been less of in this course?

- What topics did you think we would address in this course that we did not address?
- What was the most important thing you learned in this course?
- What was the most important question this class raised for you and how did you resolve it, if you did?
- What print or online resources do you know of that I could incorporate into this course in future semesters?

I vary the questions from term to term, depending on how each course goes, but the usual themes of the last-day exit slip are apparent in the above bulleted questions.

Figure 14.1 The last slide shown on the last day of a course, meant to offer lighthearted encouragement to students.

Art credit: Sophie Chardon. The photo she used for 14.1 was Outserspace: https://unsplash.com/photos/E0AHdsENmDg; Credit: Jeremy Thomas.

CONCLUSION: MAY THE COURSE BE WITH YOU

When it is obvious that everyone has said everything they want to say, I put a slide on the screen with an image of that course's textbook and the words "May the course be with you" in Star Wars Font (full disclosure, my daughter is a graphic designer and can do magic). Because I would rather spend my time reading than litigating, I will not show here the actual slide that has the cover of Parker Palmer's *The Courage to Teach* on it. In its place, I have substituted in a cover of a book of my own, which I described earlier as an homage to architect Christopher Alexander (Badley, 2018).

With that slide showing, I circulate through the room to complete the round of handshakes and farewells, doing my best to greet every student by name one final time.

REFERENCES

Alexander, C. (1979). *The timeless way of building*. Oxford University Press.

Alexander, C., Ishikawa, S., Silverstein, M., Jacobson, M., Fiksdahl-King, I., & Angel, S. (1977). *A pattern language: Towns, buildings, construction*. Oxford University Press.

Aoh, Q. L. (2018). Biology in the news: Beginning and ending the semester with the big picture. *Journal of College Science Teaching, 48*(1), 51–54.

Badley, K. (2018). *Curriculum planning with design language: Building elegant courses and units*. Routledge.

Hafiz. (1999). *The Gift: Poems by Hafiz, the great Sufi master*. (D. Ladinsky, trans.). Penguin Compass.

Hansen, B. L. *Teaching music appreciation online* Oxford University Press.

Illich, I. (1968). To hell with good intentions. Conference on InterAmerican Student Projects, Cuernavaca, Mexico. file:///C:/Users/Owner/AppData/Local/Temp/To%20Hell%20with%20Good%20Intentions.pdf

Oliver, M. (1990. *House of light*. Beacon.

Palmer, P. (1998). *The courage to teach*. Jossey-Bass.

SAIH, Norwegian Students and Academics Assistance Fund. (2014). *Saving Africa: Who wants to be a volunteer?* ikind Media, NEFDT Films. https://www.youtube.com/watch?v=ymcflrj_rRc

Yonge, O., Lee, H., & Luhanga, F. (2006). Closing and not just ending a course. *Nurse Educator, 31*(4), 151–152.

Conclusion

Section V

Stepping back from instructional strategies, the second-last chapter of the book invites professors to implement strategies for assessing their own teaching. Instructional improvement roots itself in different soil for different people. But consistently assessing one's own teaching and taking the necessary steps indicated by such assessment is a means of improvement open to all. The chapter lists several sources of assessment data. The final chapter encourages those who rely on the lecture to try some of the strategies catalogued in this volume. And it encourages all professors, including those already oriented toward learning-centered instruction, to embrace those patterns and practices that lead to improvement.

DOI: 10.4324/9781003259596-19

Fifteen

In this chapter, I address the question of assessing our own teaching. How do we know how well we are doing? How do we find out what to drop, what to add, what to approach differently? This kind of assessment can involve formal or informal evaluations conducted by colleagues and supervisors. In various ways, we can also gather information from our students. The kind of ongoing assessment I advocate in this chapter makes the most sense when we view our overall work as educators in a specific frame or curriculum model, and I begin by introducing that model.

A CURRICULUM MODEL

If you type the string *curriculum model images* into your browser, as I regularly ask my education students to do, you will find dozens of models of how the component parts of teaching connect to each other (most of the models from education professors' course wiki posts and handouts). Figure 15.1 shows a portion of my own curriculum model. Later in this chapter, I will offer a more expansive model, but this diagram catches some of the key elements of my approach to my work in the classroom and of my view of assessment of my own teaching. The three key words in the shaded box represent the three main elements of most educators' work, what I consider to be the core cycle of educational work. We have a curriculum—a subject, course contents, materials—that we need to teach. We engage in instruction so that our students can learn the contents of the curriculum. We assess their learning. Educators repeat this core cycle of work or parts of it in physical spaces such as classrooms, offices, subway cars, living rooms, and committee rooms. Those parts we do in classrooms we also do in a social and relational space, in an ethos or climate. Because of my belief that curriculum, instruction, and assessment do not happen in a vacuum, I have given over some of this book to the creation of that climate. I have given much more of the book over to instruction and

DOI: 10.4324/9781003259596-20

CLASSROOM ETHOS

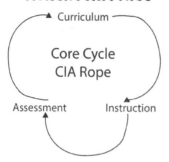

Figure 15.1 The Core Cycle of curriculum, instruction, and assessment. Credit: Kristen Badley.

assessment. Years ago, when I presented an early iteration of this diagram in a workshop, a colleague suggested that curriculum, instruction, and assessment are like a three-strand rope. None of the three is sufficient by itself, and they are strongest together. That colleague also came up with the clever acronym—CIA—which, she pointed out, no other process or agency in the world uses.

Especially important for my purposes in this chapter is the arrow in the upper left corner of the shaded box. It runs from assessment back up to curriculum and, implicitly, back to instruction. That is, educators recalibrate and make adjustments based on their assessment of their students' learning and whatever other data they can gather about their teaching. I included the word *recalibration* in my model for several years but dropped it in favour of the simple arrow that you now see in Figure 15.1. If we want to teach better next year than we did this year, then our students' assignments—our assessments of their work— become very important to us. Those assignments and assessments become sources of key information about how well we taught. Baldly, if everyone in my class answered #17 wrongly on a mid-term, it should not be too hard to identify the source of the confusion.

When I taught my first college class, I had students complete assignments or take tests, the main purpose of which was to supply a set of grades to the Office of the Registrar. I don't recall if I had the secondary purpose of finding out what my students had learned. As Figure 15.1 shows, things have changed. Now I primarily want to know the degree to which my students have met the learning outcomes for the course. What have they learned? Secondarily, I want to know how well I taught the course. What did I get right? What do I need to do differently next time. Now, my tertiary purpose is to get grades to the Registrar's Office (which I sometimes do only after getting a friendly email reminder that they were due the previous Friday).

The more expansive curriculum model I promised appears as Figure 15.2. There, I situate the core cycle of curriculum, instruction, assessment, and the classroom ethos in a wider context. That context involves answers to three questions. Starting in the upper right-hand corner, I must teach who they—my students—are, by which I mean that both individuals and generational cohorts have characteristics which I must take into account. I cannot simply teach my courses into a vacuum. The individual students I teach come to class with a variety of learning strengths and challenges (as I noted in Chapter 6). And as cohorts, my students have characteristics. I taught a generation that knew Duran Duran. I taught a generation that downloaded music illegally from Napster. And I now teach a generation that loves Ed Sheeran and

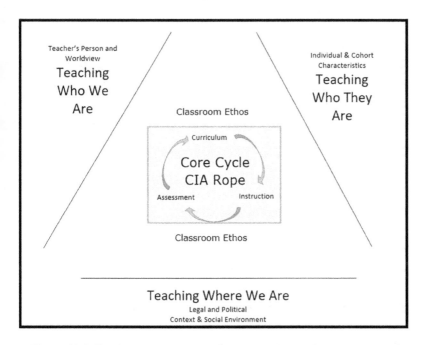

Figure 15.2 The Core Cycle of curriculum, instruction, and assessment set in three major contexts.

Credit: Sophie Chardon.

Taylor Swift. These generations each have unique characteristics. Given that my goal is to engage them in learning, I need to know their generational characteristics and do my best to work with rather than against those characteristics.

Moving to the bottom centre of Figure 15.2, my employment in a formal, institutional context implies that I have professional and legal obligations. A monthly or bi-monthly auto-deposit should remind me that my contract requires me to teach, grade, conduct research, attend department and committee meetings, do academic advising, and so on. Beyond my classes and department, my being in academic work implies that society expects certain things of me. We teach where we are.

The upper left corner of Figure 15.2 implies that I am not a robot whose main job is to press PgDn on successive decks of PowerPoint slides. My students want me to be a person who teaches people. This dimension of teaching runs as a throughline through this book and I will not argue the case again. But, within limits (of course), my students want *me* to teach them. Yes, they want me, the experienced educator with the degrees, the experience, and the books. But they also want me the canoeist, me the carpenter, me who still listens to the Beatles, me who reads Dorothy Sayers, Fyodor Dostoevsky, and John Irving, me who brings food to class, and me who brags about my children. At the time of writing, the search string *teach who we are* yielded over 300,000 hits, some of which are along the lines I have sketched out here.

Arguably, this chapter would survive without my including and explaining Figure 15.2. But I offer the diagram and this brief explanation because they may help you, my reader, grasp how I understand the context in which I view assessment of my teaching and the continuous challenge of improving my teaching. We must see the significance of the arrow in the upper left corner of the central shaded area. If we move every semester from curriculum to instruction to assessment without ever recalibrating, we may simply be repeating our mistakes. Gathering the requisite data for careful evaluation of our teaching and then recalibrating in view of those data is one key to year-on-year improvement. In what follows, I suggest two clusters of strategies to gather that needed data.

FORMAL EVALUATIONS AND COLLEGIAL HELP

In some colleges and universities, untenured professors may undergo required observations by a department chair or dean. Such observations may lead to a conversation, a written evaluation, or both. In some cases, the supervisor may also recommend or require that the faculty member seek the support of the Teaching Development Center (by whatever name). Such observations and evaluations can be sources of significant professional growth if we can view them the way I portrayed our assessment of our students' work (in Chapter 6), as formative rather than summative. That is, we should view these formal evaluations as stepping-stones for our own professional development.

Two other paths to this kind of instructional development are open to professors with a desire to improve and a secure sense of self. The first is the self-initiated review by a supervisor or colleague. Unfortunately, few instruments are available that focus on teaching in higher education. But several educators have offered frameworks for evaluation of K–12 educators, including Robert Marzano (Marzano, 2001; Marzano et al, 2007) and Charlotte Danielson (2013). Teaching in higher education and teaching in K–12 education have enough overlaps that Danielson's and Marzano's frameworks will serve the professor wanting to improve quite well. In 2014, I requested that a colleague evaluate my own teaching using Danielson's evaluation instrument. Her framework includes four domains, as follows:

- Planning and Preparation.
- Classroom Environment.
- Instruction.
- Professional Responsibility.

Even though Danielson's instrument was intended for the evaluation of elementary and secondary educators, the evaluation I received gave me a great deal to reflect on as a professor (in a doctoral program at that time). My evaluator identified areas of strength and areas for improvement. I found it humbling to listen as my colleague worked through the many sub-headings in the 40-page summary of my teaching evaluation.

Another approach to the self-initiated evaluation of teaching is to approach the Teaching or Teaching Development Center at the university and ask staff there for assistance. I have met many staff members of these offices and, to a person, they are warm and helpful, not at all heavy-handed in their approach to our professional development. With reference to the teaching portion of the portfolio one assembles for a Tenure and Promotion Committee, these staff would also know the criteria professors in their institution are expected to meet. I suspect that my readers desire to improve in their teaching for reasons beyond promotion and tenure, but such institutional realities will inevitably and understandably be in view for some.

End-of-Semester Student Evaluations

I end this half of the chapter by briefly addressing student evaluations as a form of assessment of our teaching. The scholarly research on student evaluations is inconclusive, with researchers finding various kinds of bias related, for example, to both students' and professors' gender and race. Factors such as course easiness and even time of day affect ratings of teaching quality. This topic could fill books (for example, Chilson, 2008), and so I will not say more here. My own strategy with student evaluations typically involves ignoring the comments from the 10% of students who think I walk on water and the 10% who think the university must have recruited me through Craigslist. I look for specifics in the middle 80% and try to build from there.

OTHER DATA SOURCES

Students are our second source of information about our teaching quality. If we frame their exams and submitted work the right way, we can recognize that, in a sense, they already tell us what they are learning and, implicitly, how well we are teaching. But there are other ways to get them to give us the kind of information we need if we want to assess our teaching. In what follows, I suggest several such ways.

The Daily Exit Slip

Repeatedly in this book, I have recommended the exit slip. Again, most undergraduates will have used these during their K–12 school years and will not think it unusual to tell a professor that they still do not understand this or that concept, or that the professor omitted a topic or failed to make a topic clear. That is, they view making such observations or registering such concerns simply as comments about learning and teaching, not as insults or criticisms leveled at us. We must view them the same way.

Consistently asking for exit slips that include any observations about what a student does not understand or what a class should have included lowers the temperature for the student. To my point in this chapter, it directly addresses the question of how well I taught, of how well I have the contents organized, and of the strategies we use for students to learn those contents.

Without typing in all caps here, I want to invite my readers who have never tried an exit slip to try it. Specifying that students finish a sentence beginning with words such as "Something I still don't understand is …" will have the primary benefit of helping you know the likely place to start the next class session. But it will bring a secondary benefit: Students will feel more comfortable in your class because you used a strategy they know from their high-school years. In plain English, they will likely think your class is a better place to be than they previously thought.

The Mid-Course Correction Exit Slip

In a 13-week semester, I usually give an extended explanation of a unique exit slip I call the "Mid-Course Correction." Figure 15.3 shows a portion of the Saskatchewan grid road system near where I grew up. The dark, east–west, line is what Saskatchewan people call a correction line road. Grid roads running east and west were originally built two miles north or south of each other. North–south grid roads were originally built one mile east and west of each other. North–south roads need to run true north for the purposes of the square mile grid (one square mile = one section of farmland) that served as the basis for land titles, but of course the world is not flat, it is round. To compensate for the earth's being round, surveyors re-aligned north-south roads to true north every 18 miles north and south. The east-west roads where these re-alignments took place are known as correction lines. Thus, the correction line road was, in effect, the road where everything started over. As a side note, I have no idea how flat-earthers account for the need for correction lines but there may be a comedy sketch waiting in there somewhere.

I call the mid-course evaluation form a correction-line as a way to lower the stakes for students. I want them to feel free to write honestly

Figure 15.3 A segment of a map of Saskatchewan illustrating a correction line road.

Source: The background image the artist used is from here: Figure 15.3 Segment of map: https://unsplash.com/photos/EXlUnZKb9s0. Credit: Tim Mossholder, Sophie Chardon.

about the class. I explain that no one will fail the course and no one will get fired from their professor job based on this evaluation; it is simply an opportunity to get the class pointed north again. I underline that the correction line is necessary not because the world is messed up but because the world is round. The indented text below is adapted from instructions I give to my students.

> This is the middle day of the course (#7 of 13). If we're not heading straight north in this class, we should make whatever corrections we need to so the course works for all of us. Below, please write anything you want about the class, with or without your name.

In face-to-face classes, I do this exercise on paper. In online courses, I ask students to email one of their classmates (who has agreed in advance) to amalgamate and anonymize the comments and send them to me. I usually use headings such as these:

- What are we getting right?
- Any highlights so far?
- What there could be more of?
- What there could be less of?

My language in the indented paragraph—phrases such as *straight north* and *correction line* and the words *we* and *us*—is purposeful. I want the instructions to make clear that I do want to hear from my students and, as I have noted several times in this book, that our class truly is ours, not just mine.

The Leadership and Planning Track

In Chapter 6, I noted this track as one of the options, saying that I ordinarily do not list it in the syllabus, but rather invite specific students to follow that track. Consistently, the students who have followed the Leadership and Planning Track with me have contributed to the quality of the course. Obviously, they have sources of information to which I have no access. Without needing to feel at all like spies, they can give me a sense of the mood among their classmates, thus helping me know how to proceed week to week. That is, they serve as a valuable source of information for my efforts to assess my teaching. Additionally, they are staked on their own success in the course, they usually contribute ideas to me about how we should proceed with this or that upcoming topic, and they sometimes suggest alternative activities to those I had planned. I strongly recommend offering such an opportunity to students. And I do so knowing the risks that any students following that track could be subject to criticism for being the professor's chosen ones.

Assessing Critical and Creative Thinking

My own teaching ideals include my desire for my students to do critical and creative thinking. But how can I tell if they are doing that? Among the self-evaluation tools I have found helpful is this list of quite specific questions. I ask myself where in my course I require students to do the following:

• Pose questions and propose hypotheses?
• Gather and analyze data?
• Make arguments?
• Ponder enigmas and mysteries in the field?
• Wrestle with the inter-connected puzzles of this discipline?
• Ponder unresolved questions and controversial theses in the field?
• Challenge assumptions and explore alternate explanations?
• Experience cognitive dissonance?
• Struggle over the meaning of a key passage in a reading?
• Wonder because something is highly counter-intuitive?
• Encounter problems that they cannot themselves resolve unless they take these steps?
• Formulate and justify their own thesis in response to a problem?

These questions help me assess my teaching with reference to my stated goal of fostering my students' critical engagement with the course materials and their sense that university courses are, in fact, venues to think creatively. These questions help me see if I am designing instruction that moves them in those directions.

These questions can guide professorial reflection on a single class session, on a unit, or on a whole course. And they can also serve as prompts on an exit slip, or as the basis for in-class conversation with students. Unfortunately, I do not recall the source of this list. I have searched several of the individual items with quotation marks but without success, and therefore wonder if I developed this list myself. Whatever its origins, I recommend adapting this list for use as a teaching assessment tool.

CONCLUSION

It is likely that only a minority of us relish the idea of having our teaching assessed. It is also likely that only a minority of us will improve without such assessment. Because of the second likelihood, I strongly suggest that we become more imaginative about using the data that we already receive from students. And to those who wonder if you have the courage to walk into the Teaching Development Center in your college or university, I say this: There is only one way to find out.

REFERENCES

Chilson, F. (2008). *Faculty perceptions of student online course evaluations.* VDM Verlag.

Danielson, C. (2013). *The framework for teaching evaluation instrument.* Charlotte Danielson.

Marzano, R. J. (2007). *The art and science of teaching: A comprehensive framework for effective instruction.* ASCD.

Marzano, R. J., Piockering, D., & Pollock, J. (2001). *Classroom instruction that works: Research-based strategies for increasing student achievement.* ASCD.

Sixteen

About a year ago, my doctor's office urged me strongly to attend a presentation at a local hospital about a screening program for cancer. I dutifully attended. After a brief introduction by a hospital staff member, the lights in the room were dimmed slightly and those of us in attendance watched a 20-minute PowerPoint presentation. I can summarize the subject matter in seven words: Do these things or you could die. Frankly, I don't know that I've taught anything that important in my whole career. But, the importance—the vital importance—of the subject-matter notwithstanding, I became bored within minutes and found myself wondering if it would be rude to walk out. After all, I could read about this subject matter. I wondered why we didn't start with participants' questions. I wondered if the presenters could have used a story or a case study to pique our interest.

Then—mentally leaving the presentation and the room I was sitting in—I began to wonder about the millions of students who watch hours of PowerPoint presentations every week, and I wondered about what they wonder about when they get bored. I wondered especially about students in classes where professors have uploaded the slide decks to their respective course wikis. Would these students not wonder as I was doing then why they bothered attending? How could they possibly resist checking their social media feeds? This book was not borne out of my cancer-screening seminar, but that seminar did confirm to me that a significant percentage of our students learn better by means others than the lecture.

By this point in the book, you will understand that I consider the curriculum materials—the course contents—to be important. But I always begin my planning of a course or class by asking how my students can best learn the course contents rather than by asking how much of my metaphorical ring binder I can work through in a

DOI: 10.4324/9781003259596-21

192 **Conclusion**

given amount of time, how many PowerPoint slides are needed for a 50-minute class, a 75-minute class, or a 3-hour class with a 15-minute break? In essence, asking "how can they best learn this?" is what I mean by learning-centred instruction.

Throughout this book I have repeatedly disavowed any interest in arguing at length that the strategies I have presented are superior to the lecture method. As much as that argument has a kind of perverse appeal, I will avoid it here as well. Despite my having written this book for another kind of class, some of the strategies I suggest here could work within the class lecture. And I invite anyone who believes deeply in the efficacy of the lecture to try one or two of the strategies I describe here.

John Dewey's critics have had a century to twist his use of the phrase *students' interests*. He called on educators to start not with some concept or principle central to the subject matter but to start with something of interest to our students. But he did not say to end there. In fact it would not be at all in our students' interests if we started and ended only with those topics that interest them. If teachers started and ended only with topics our students find interesting, my grandson's class would be all dinosaurs all the time. And some university classes I have taught would be all Taylor Swift all the time. Dewey said that once we had piqued our students' interest, we could move with them into the curriculum contents. That is, their interests are the door into the contents.

I view the strategies I have catalogued in this book through this Deweyan lens. I dearly want my students to meet the specified learning outcomes of a course or class; indeed, that's why my department pays me. But my questions are always the same: What is the best way to go at that task? How can they learn this material without my lecturing? I do not want to sound argumentative here, but I have concluded that simply telling students what I know—even when they need to know it—is not the best way for them to learn it. The cancer screening people were giving me information that could mean the difference between life and death, and I contemplated walking out. There must be more effective ways for people to learn. Because I believe there are more effective ways than telling, I have borrowed, adopted, adapted, developed, devised, and otherwise created the dozens of strategies I offer in this book.

My wish for you, my readers and colleagues, is that you will find some of what I have offered in this volume helpful in your own professional development as educators. Patrick Allen, a long-time university provost, colleague, co-author, and friend used to say to his faculty, "We're good but we could be better." I suspect that anyone who has read to this point in this book is already good and wants to get better. I commend you for having travelled as far as you have on the teaching journey, and I wish you success as you continue to create courses, units, and classes that engage students and as you invite them to think critically and creatively about the issues you set before them. May the practices and patterns you adopt as professors give you great satisfaction in this rewarding but immensely complicated vocation.

Appendix A

This Appendix includes documents meant to support various chapters in the book. It includes the following documents and resources:

1. Rubrics and instructions lifted from a course Rubrics Document.
2. More extensive descriptions of tracks than those offered in Chapter 6.
3. A sample *Daily Forecast* sheet.
4. A sample detailed semester calendar/schedule lifted from a 2021 syllabus.
5. A sample case study for use in an undergraduate classroom.
6. A catalog of gaming resources provided by a gamer.

In the acknowledgments, I noted the work of Kristina Hedlund, who worked through hundreds of course-related computer files to find the most appropriate materials for inclusion in this book. What she found could easily have filled an appendix many times the length of this one. I thank her again for her work, and I offer these samples to you, my colleagues. May you find the material here of use in your work. Also, I thank Greg Burbidge for supplying the section of this appendix related to gaming. Without his willingness to share his expertise, that section would not have appeared in the book.

1. RUBRICS AND INSTRUCTIONS

Following are six rubrics meant to illustrate the clarity of assessment grading structures and clarity of language that should characterize rubrics. Note, that I use four columns in all my rubrics. I regularly bring that to my students' attention, followed by the semi-snide remark that I would be happy anytime to add a column called "Redefines Expectations" if someone can invent the equivalent of a stealth aircraft or point out how NASA has been misinterpreting data from the International Space Station.

The rubrics included are these:

- Original Documents and Policy Papers.
- Reading Response (article, chapter).
- Film Review.
- Book Review.
- Major Paper/Research Essay.
- Subway Map.

Notes [supplied to students]

When you get assignments back from me, I will have attached the appropriate rubric as the last page. In digital assignments, I will have highlighted in yellow the cells that, from my reading, best describe your paper. I sometimes highlight two cells side by side because I believe your paper lies somewhere along the border of the two cells.

Rubrics in this document are all/100 and therefore do not equal a given assignment's weight in the course. While entering grades, I convert grades to the respective weight the assignment has in the course.

Formatting of written assignments: Please use APA formatting for all references, including films. You do <u>not</u> need to purchase the APA manual. Search "Owl at Purdue" or type https://owl.english.purdue.edu/ to get to Purdue University's Online Writing Center. This website has samples of APA-formatted entries for every kind of source.

Original Documents and Policy Papers Rubric

The purposes of assigning you original materials include these:

- To push you to use original sources rather than or at least in addition to secondary sources. Original sources in any field are usually harder to read; readers must persist. But the reader usually gets substantial rewards from difficult and slow reading.
- Original documents bring you into the conversation on the ground floor, so to speak. Original documents and policy papers are good examples of carefully reasoned and worded statements about an issue, the complete opposite of the rant-like comments that typically

follow a blog or news item online. But this careful wording has another side: The organization publishing the document wants to project a positive image of themselves and their own purposes.

- Success in reading original and policy documents implies understanding what the organization in question is most concerned to achieve, how and how well they argue their views, how their views and concerns fit the contemporary context, and what the documents imply for policy and practice.

Notes: Please write responses to these documents in formal English prose, using paragraphs and sentences.

Quote sparingly if at all. Every time you quote, you remove your voice, and your work needs to be in your voice.

Criteria	Excellent	Good	Adequate	Unsatisfactory
Demonstrates understanding of document's thesis and conclusions (25%)	Thorough grasp of contents and approach.	Understands the article.	Shows shaky grasp of article.	Demonstrates little or no understanding.
Critical reading ... is able to discuss strengths and weaknesses of the document's approach to the topic (25%)	Mature critical reading demonstrated throughout.	General critical abilities demonstrated in response.	Some appraisal of quality of the article.	Critical reading not apparent.
Interacts with the article in his or her own voice (15%)	Comfortable writing voice without dominating.	Periodic appearance of writer's voice.	Rare appearance of voice. Writing mechanical and reportive, not interactive.	No voice.
Thesis statement, organization, coherence, and flow (15%)	Direction and tone of response clear from beginning.	Direction and tone generally apparent and consistent.	Direction and tone fuzzy. Organization bumpy at points.	Poorly organized. Hard to follow.
Sees and draws connections to educational policy, teachers' work, or classroom practice (10%)	Clear and compelling connections.	Sees some implications and draws some connections.	Sees or makes a few connections ... thin connections.	Sees/makes no connections.

Recognizes format, grammar, syntax, and punctuation conventions (10%)	Written without error and with grace and style.	Error free.	Some errors.	Errors throughout.

Reading Response Rubric

These are the purposes of assigning you a response to an article or book chapter:

- In the case of articles, to give you a sense of what academic research looks like presented in raw form instead of summarized in a text book. This puts you right in the room where academic conversation is happening, rather than hearing about the conversation second-hand from a textbook author.
- In the case of book chapters, to give you quick access to a summary of an area and quick entry to a conversation that has already been underway for some time.
- Success in reading implies understanding what the author has said, seeing both the strengths and weaknesses of the writing, and seeing what the writing implies for future research, policy, and practice.

The rubric below is almost identical to the rubric for original documents and policy papers.

Criteria	Excellent	Good	Adequate	Unsatisfactory
Demonstrates understanding of article's thesis and conclusions. (25%)	Thorough grasp of contents and approach.	Understands the article.	Shows shaky grasp of article.	Demonstrates no understanding.
Critical reading ... is able to discuss strengths and weaknesses of the author's approach to the research or topic. (25%)	Mature critical reading demonstrated throughout.	General critical abilities demonstrated in response.	Some appraisal of quality of the article.	Critical reading not apparent.
Interacts with the article in his or her own voice. (15%)	Comfortable writing voice without dominating.	Periodic appearance of writer's voice.	Rare appearance of voice. Writing mechanical and reportive, not interactive.	No voice.

Thesis statement, organization, coherence, and flow. (15%)	Direction and tone of response clear from beginning.	Direction and tone generally apparent and consistent.	Direction and tone fuzzy. Organization bumpy at points.	Poorly organized. Hard to follow.
Draws connections to educational policy, teachers' work, or classroom practice. (10%)	Clear and compelling connections.	Sees some implications and draws some connections.	Sees or makes a few connections … thin connections.	Sees/makes no connections.
Recognizes format, grammar, syntax, and punctuation conventions. (10%)	Written without error and with grace and style.	Error free.	Some errors.	Errors throughout.

Notes:

Please write article and chapter responses in formal English prose, using paragraphs and sentences.

Quote sparingly if at all. Every time you quote, you remove your voice, and your work needs to be in your voice.

Be sure you response has a thesis statement, not a question, and not only a statement of your topic.

Film Review Rubric

You have the opportunity to complete two film reviews in this course (Assignments 8, 17). Why films? In important and sometimes very twisted ways, screen portrayals of teachers shape real teachers' and students' understandings of the teaching vocation and of teachers' work. Your study of a film should attend to such matters as these:

- relevant vocational themes or threads in the film
- how those themes or threads inform your own emerging identity as a teacher
- portrayals of the teaching vocation; what kind of people go into teaching?
- portrayals of the nature of classroom work
- portrayals of the classroom ethos; what kind of place is it socially and relationally?

For any given film you might choose, please look at other people's reviews, which you can find online. Do interact with other reviewers BUT ONLY AFTER YOU HAVE SEEN THE FILM or they will unduly shape your viewing of it. Agree, disagree, add to, and subtract from other reviewers' assessments but please do not quote more than 10–15 words total from other reviewers in your review. Your main job is to interact with and respond to the film yourself. I note other reviews simply because the temptation to plagiarize is great when all that material is sitting there. I want you to know that I know about it, and I want you to interact with it.

Criteria	Excellent	Good	Adequate	Unsatisfactory
Conversation, voice, and ideas (70%)				
The reviewer's voice is appropriately present. (15%)	Voice present and clear.	Voice present throughout.	Timid or periodic presence.	Reviewer's voice not apparent.
The reviewer treats the film, its director and actors fairly and responsibly, engaging them in conversation and allowing them to speak. (15%)	Review is an engaging conversation between film, reviewer, and reader.	Interactive tone through review.	Some interaction with film-makers and actors.	Cherry picks flaws/strengths. Rants about flaws or gives uncritical praise.
The review explores and discusses the worldview of the teacher portrayed. (20%)	In-depth exploration of teacher's worldview with frequent reference to film.	Shows good understanding of worldview concept and works with material from film.	Shows some understanding of worldview concept and limited ability to see it in film.	Little understanding demonstrated of this aspect.
The review includes an appropriate amount of summary of the film's contents and an appropriate mix of detail & generalization. (10%)	The mix makes clear to the reader the style, point, plot and direction of the film.	Appropriate mix of detail and generalization. Enough information about contents.	Some summary but reader of review remains unsure about film's point or direction. Too much detail.	Rote repetition of contents. Too much detailed retelling at cost of other review functions.

The review appropriately assesses the film's success at addressing & reaching its intended audience in view of its apparent purpose. (10%)	Review makes clear the film's audience and purpose, and judges its success.	Review assesses film's audience and purpose, and director's success.	Little assessment or timid, incomplete assessment.	Assessment absent from review or overwhelms the review.

Writing, language, and format conventions (20%)

The review contains complete bibliographic material. (5%)	Complete information.	Complete information.	Incomplete information.	Incomplete information.
The review follows format conventions, including respecting the 700–900 word limits. (5%)	Follows format conventions precisely throughout.	Review largely follows format conventions.	Review mostly follows some format conventions.	Review largely fails to follow format conventions.
The review follows relevant punctuation, syntax, sentence & paragraph conventions, creating readable prose. 5%)	Writing has grace and style beyond conventions.	One or two lapses.	Five or more lapses in the review.	Lapses throughout.
The review employs vocabulary appropriate to the film being reviewed and the intended audience of the review. (5%)	Vocabulary use contributes to readable and enjoyable review.	Vocabulary level contributes to good style and easy readability of review.	Vocabulary level periodically appropriate for audience.	Vocabulary level markedly inappropriate for audience.

Global sense of review's quality (10%)

Global sense of review's quality. (10%)	An inviting review.	Informative and readable review.	Understandable with effort.	Confused and/or unreadable.

Book Review Rubric

Criteria	Excellent	Good	Adequate	Unsatisfactory
The reviewer's voice is appropriately present. Reviewer notes his or her personal response to the book and its effect on him or her. (20%)	Voice present and clear.	Voice present throughout.	Timid or periodic presence.	Reviewer's voice not apparent.
The reviewer treats the book and its book author responsibly and fairly, engaging the author in conversation and allowing the author to speak. (25%)	Review is an engaging conversation between author, reviewer and reader.	Interactive tone through review.	Some interaction with author.	Cherry picks flaws/ strengths. Rants about flaws or gives uncritical praise.
The review includes an appropriate amount of summary of the book's contents and an appropriate mix of quotation, paraphrase, summary and mention. (15%)	The mix makes clear to the reader the style and direction of the book.	Appropriate mix of quotation, paraphrase, summary and mention. Enough information re contents.	Some summary but reader of review remains unsure about book's contents. Too much quotation.	Rote repetition of contents. Too much quotation or summation at cost of other review functions.
The review appropriately assesses the author's success at addressing & reaching her or his intended audience in view of the book's purpose. (15%)	Review makes clear the book's audience and purpose, and author's success.	Review assesses books' audience and purpose, and author's success.	Little assessment or timid, incomplete assessment.	Assessment absent from review or overwhelms the review.
The review follows format conventions and includes complete bibliographic material. (5%)	Follows format conventions precisely throughout.	Review largely follows format conventions.	Review mostly follows some format conventions.	Review largely fails to follow format conventions.

Review follows the relevant punctuation, syntax, sentence & paragraph conventions, creating readable prose. (5%)	Writing has grace and style beyond conventions.	One or two lapses.	Five or more lapses in the review.	Lapses throughout.
The review employs vocabulary appropriate to the book being reviewed and the intended audience of the review. (5%)	Vocabulary use contributes to readable and enjoyable review.	Vocabulary level contributes to good style & readability of review.	Vocabulary level periodically appropriate for audience.	Vocabulary level markedly inappropriate for audience.
Global sense of review's quality. (10%)	An inviting review.	Informative and readable review.	Understandable with effort.	Confused and/or unreadable.

Readers, please note that I usually include more hints and instructions in the *Rubrics Document* than I have done here. The following indented text usually accompanies the rubric for the book review.

Write a review of *The Courage to Teach* of about 900–1000 words. I've been around classrooms long enough to know how much reading actual students complete in the average textbook. In light of the fact that you plan to teach, I urge you to understand the importance of reading every page of this book, not only for this assignment but to survive teaching. Your review should reflect reading of the whole book, by interacting with Palmer's themes and ideas, not by inserting a word here and there with a page number.

The book reviewer has three jobs. First you should tell what you think the writer was trying to say. For example, David Elkind said in several books that he thought we should allow children to have a childhood. Malcolm Gladwell seems to argue in *Outliers* that once people have worked for 10,000 hours at something, they get good. I've been brief here (almost as brief as Gladwell's books) but you get my point: Why did the writer write the book, to entertain, to expose, to explain, to correct a misperception, to recount, to convince the reader to change views, to protect? And for what audience did he or she write it? The audience question is often answered in the foreword and then confirmed or disconfirmed in the text. My suspicion, worded most generally, is that Palmer wanted to encourage teachers to keep at it, but you have to say more than that.

Your second job is to tell your readers how the writer went about making his or her case. Stories (anything by Thomas Friedman)? Argument (almost anything in philosophy)? Facts, figures, and tables (The Spirit Level by Wilkinson and Pickett)? Humor? Humility/arrogance? Does the author move quickly or slowly? What kind of sentences, what level of writing? Is it accessible, impenetrable? What are the author's assumptions and conclusions?

Finally, you need to tell your own readers to what degree you think that author succeeded in his or her intended task, that is, whether your readers should read the book or not (to be really blunt). If so, why? Does it have great writing, wit, illustrations, or importance, or is the author the sole person addressing the question, one who resolves several outstanding issues, or one with new, great insights, etc.? If you do not recommend it, why not. Giving your view—writing in your own voice—may be frowned on in some university courses, but it is necessary in the book review, so please do it. And please don't think this job is done if you tip your hand in the opening sentence or make an explicit recommendation in the last few sentences. Adjectives and adverbs are appropriate as ways of embedding your judgments of the author's work throughout the review.

Combining the Three Tasks

The three tasks, while inseparable, do sort of move in an order, although not a lock-step order, starting with what the author said they set out to do or, if that is not clear, what you think they were trying to do. You weave together your précis of the contents with your own clear voiceover about how they go about it and also, more quietly, your own assessment of how well they do it. As you move toward the end, you state clearly whether you recommend it and to whom, likely while still making reference to the contents and approach.

Contra some academic writing where quotation is verboten, please do include quotations from the book to enrich your review and to give the book's author more voice in your review. That said, I suggest a maximum of one extended quotation in a single-book review, given our overall word limit, but of course welcome you to include several single words or phrases. Provide page references either by working the page number into your running text ("As Palmer notes on page 61, children need food …") or with an abbreviated notation system following the cited material (p. 61) with a character space following the "p" not (p.61) or (p61). Page references at the end of a sentence are formatted in APA style, with the final punctuation "… outside the citation and reference, like so" (p. 61). Remember that the word *quote* is a verb and *quotation* is a noun. Given that the whole review is about Palmer's book, you don't need to keep typing "Palmer" in your references; once is enough.

Major Paper/Research Essay Rubric

Course weight: 35%. Due April 9 at the start of class on paper or as an MS Word document attached to an email sent by the start of class. Approximately 1000 words.

This reflection will be structured as a response to the interview questions "Can education make the world a better place?" and "How do you see the relationship between education and democratic life?" You are to imagine that you are talking to two school principals who want to know how you view the role of education in relation to social and political issues such as human rights, peace, social justice, poverty, and the like. It is essential that you specify specific concepts we have examined in the course and that you offer your interpretation of how those concepts inform and will inform your own teaching.

Criteria	Excellent	Good	Adequate	Unsatisfactory
Argumentation (29/40)				
Use of sources (15%)	Interacts responsibly with prior discussions.	Uses sources responsibly to present or support their argument.	Uses sources but without nuance or interaction.	Uses no sources; misrepresents others' arguments.

Thesis statement (5%)	Clear thesis statement that structures the paper.	Comes to a clear conclusion.	Expresses thoughts on a general topic.	Paper has no apparent direction.
Writer perspective (15%)	Clear and consistent, but unobtrusive presence.	General presence.	Uneven presence.	Writer's perspective is unstated or dominates.
Bibliography (5%)	Sources representative of the prior discussion; diverse sources.	Uses responsible sources.	Uses adequate resources.	No evidence of the contours of the discussion.
Structure of argument (20%)	Sound and compelling.	Focused and generally persuasive.	Lacks precision; unsystematic; somewhat persuasive.	Muddled and unfocused; not compelling.
Examples/ illustrations (20%)	Judiciously chosen examples; integral to the argument; used appropriately.	Relevant examples chosen; application fairly well established.	Examples are somewhat appropriate; incomplete demonstration of their relevance.	Examples dominate the paper; undeveloped connection to the argument.

Writing, language, and format conventions (11/40)

Grammar and spelling (5%)	No errors.	Rare errors.	Some errors.	Errors throughout.
Sentences & paragraphs (10%)	Varied sentence complexity; well-formed paragraphs; creative style; graceful prose.	Sound and clear sentences and paragraphs; meaning is clear.	Some unclear sentences and paragraphs; reader has to re-read for meaning.	Unclear or incomplete sentences and paragraphs.
Reference conventions (5%)	No errors in documenting sources.	No errors in documenting sources.	Few errors documenting sources.	Conventions ignored.

Mapping Assignment Rubric

Because hundreds of students have told me how much they enjoyed this assignment, I provide here the rubric and extensive commentary regarding its use, including instructions I usually provide to students. The next three paragraphs appeared on a recent syllabus.

This mapping assignment is meant to allow you to explore your own biography to produce a (literally) graphic understanding of what moved you toward teaching and shaped you as a teacher. This is an intensely personal exercise, requiring that you go slow, re-read or write in your journal, reflect, and meditate.

This assignment leans very heavily toward reflection. Obviously, you can crank it out like any other assignment made meaningless by taking the cynical approach. But it can generate reflection on the deepest questions of the teaching vocation. Also, this exercise can force those who usually default toward language and critical discourse—that's most teachers—to awaken our aesthetic/artistic selves and engage the affective dimension. By making a map, we use other faculties and abilities than language and argument.

The questions on the assignment outline ask us to remember people, authors and books, formative events, moments in classrooms where, as students or student teachers, we saw things that inspired or repelled us. For sure, memories have a cognitive component, but they also have a reflective, affective component. In view of that, if you are willing to let yourself into this assignment fully, rather than knocking it off, you may find ways to re-inscribe, to re-write, to re-remember your story and thereby to reframe your current posture toward teaching.

Criteria	Excellent	Good	Adequate	Unsatisfactory
Written component				
Writing shows thoughtful reflection and is clearly in author's voice. (20%)	Comfortable writing voice without dominating.	General presence of writer's voice.	Mechanical and reportive writing, not interactive.	No voice.
Writing follows format, grammar, syntax, and punctuation conventions. (10%)	No errors, graceful and powerful writing.	No errors clear writing.	Some errors.	Many errors, distract and slow down reading.
Writing has thesis statement, clear organization, coherence, and flow (10%) **See note below.	Direction and tone of commentary/narrative clear from beginning.	Direction and tone generally apparent and consistent.	Direction and tone fuzzy. Bumpy organization at points.	Poorly organized. Hard to follow.
Cartographic component				
Map demonstrates artistic attention and care. (25%)	Compelling! Did a person do this?!	Map demonstrates care throughout.	Map generally careful.	Lapses throughout.

Map is clear, readable, and easy to follow. (25%)	Inviting and completely easy to understand.	Throughout, map is understandable.	Map is generally understandable.	Difficult to follow.
Works creatively with the limitations of a subway map (specific # of lines, specific # of stations on each line) as a way to inscribe life's events and influences. (10%)	Creative, inviting exploration of life narrative despite map's limitations.	Uses map to advantage with no apparent struggles.	Mostly uses map to advantage. A few apparent struggles.	Unable to use map to visualize relevant events and influences.

** A thesis sentence for this assignment could be as simple as these examples, both of which happen to be enumerated:

> As my Prague subway map shows, three distinct kinds of influences have led me into teaching: mentors, fiction, and early teaching experiences.
>
> Among the many forces and influences on my life so far, my friends and family, my reading, this education program, and several mentors have most powerfully confirmed my calling to teach.

Notes to readers about in-class use of the subway map assignment

The prompts I offer students are left or adapted from the course text, Parker Palmer's, *The Courage to Teach* (Palmer, 1998). If you keep a journal, I recommend a retreat based on some of these questions. I also strongly recommend Palmer's book, available as a review assignment later in the course. Don't try to respond to all these prompts; rather, decide whether you would like to work with a map of Vancouver, Prague, Toronto, or Moscow.

- Who were my mentors?
- Vignettes and moments when I knew I wanted to teach.
- What life events have shaped who I am becoming as a teacher?
- People, events, and forces that have helped me keep my heart open to teaching.
- Teaching moments that helped shape my sense of integrity or identity as a teacher.
- Assignments you completed as a student that shaped your own understanding of students, curriculum, instruction, the purposes of schools, etc.

- Some of your favorite sayings, proverbs, distinctions.
- Brilliant days of teaching and utter flops.
- Works of fiction and non-fiction that have shaped my understanding of teaching.
- The characteristics of my desired teaching space.
- Surprises students, colleagues, and family members have given me along the way.
- Metaphors and images that enrich and give vision to my teaching self.
- Some of the tensions I anticipate facing as a teacher?

I take pains to make clear that a subway map—of Prague, for example—with only three lines can be used to respond to three, four, five, or six prompts. Students need only split one of the subway lines in two to respond to two prompts on one line. I usually show an example like the Toronto map (in Chapter 13) to illustrate how to do this. In that example, I split the green (Bloor Street) line into two halves and listed some authors who influenced me on the western half of that line. The other half of that line, not reproduced in the book, listed the names of several of my mentors. Without reservation, I recommend to you, my colleagues, that you find a way to adapt a transit map assignment to a course.

2. TRACKS PARAGRAPH DESCRIPTIONS

In this section, I include parts of the expanded descriptions of the various assessment tracks I introduced in Chapter 6. For the purposes of this book, I have edited these descriptions for length. To be clear, I have never offered all these tracks in any single course but I usually offer five or six of them. The tracks described here are these:

- Research and Writing.
- Mentorship.
- Performance.
- Gaming.
- Maker.
- Film Review and Discussion Leadership.
- Exam.
- Writing Center Workshops.
- Tri-fold Brochure.
- Website of Annotated Resources.

- Book Project.
- Leadership and Planning.
- Service and Practices.

Except for the Book Project Track and the Research and Writing Track, I now assign 20% course weight to these tracks, which students have consistently reported as fair. I usually assign 35% to the Research and Writing Track. As I noted earlier, I assigned 50% course weight to the Book Project Track the one time I offered it.

Research and Writing Track

Write a major paper on one of the boxed topics on the next page (3000–4000 words including reference list). As per the syllabus, this is due April 2 and includes ungraded participation in a panel of students who wrote on related papers (April 2 or 9, to be decided according to topics and number of students who wrote various papers). That role on a panel includes a very brief summary (3–4 minutes), Q&A with others on panel, Q&A with the class.

This paper requires deep engagement with the scholarly conversation in the respective field. Students choosing this track must submit an intermediate draft of their work of at least 1500 words (including a complete outline) before the February break. In this paper, you should interact with other voices in the conversation but should write in your own voice (which means using the pronoun "I" and giving your view). Inevitably, someone asks "How many sources?" That depends on the quality of your interaction. If you're just going to block and copy bits of text from here, there, and everywhere, then 80 sources please (and I can assign your grade now: 60%). If you're actually going to report on the state of the scholarly conversation before you arrived and then argue your view of the conversation, then 5 or 10 or 15 sources will suffice. Note: Your paper requires a written or e-signature of one other person confirming that they edited your paper before submission. Major essays are graded according to the "Major Paper" rubric in the Rubrics Document.

Mentorship Track

A fourth-year student and a second-year student will work together to implement content related to this course in one unit from the Alberta K–12 Program of Studies. I strongly suggest that you do not build a unit from scratch but rather that you use one the fourth-year student has already developed or you download one from another educator. Both students of any pair on the mentorship track will write 2–3 pages of reflection (due December 11) about the joys and challenges of working in a mentoring relationship. This track obviously involves a pair of people working together. Students choosing this track will arrange to show their final work to the class on December 11.

Performance Track

Students electing this track will prepare a performance related to the course objectives and contents. Performances may include drama, readers' theater, song, spoken word, and poetry. With the performance, those choosing this track must include a brief essay (500 words) that justifies the performance and explains what you are trying to accomplish with it, as well as a clear rubric that will help both you and me know the degree to which you have succeeded. Students choosing this track may work in pairs. If they need more people than two for their performance, they will need to persuade friends or classmates to participate, but the assignment's credit cannot go to more than two people. Students choosing this track will arrange to perform their work on November 27.

Gaming Track

Students choosing this track will adapt a board game to the contents of this course. This game must be tested outside of class to ensure that members of the class can play it in 50 minutes or less. This track is available for those wishing to work alone or with one other person. Do not attempt to develop a game or simulation from scratch (because of how much time that will take ... but I will not stop you if that is why you are on this earth). Students choosing this track will arrange to demonstrate their game on November 27. If you wish to select this track, please see the additional *Gaming Resource Document* posted on Blackboard.

Maker Track

If you do not know the meaning of this word, it is not for you. Students choosing this track will arrange to show their work on December 4 and must provide a 400–500 word Guide for Dummies + rubric so both you and I can judge your success with reference to the course objectives.

Film Review and Discussion Leadership Track

Students in this track will view two or three school/education documentaries and one feature film related to the objectives and themes of this course. They will write a single review essay of 2000–3000 words. Films must be from the list available on Blackboard. The film review rubric makes clear that a film review is not a rehearsal of plot details; it is a critical appraisal of the screenwriter's and director's work, and of the actors' abilities to convey a story. The review must include reference to at last 4 academic and 4 popular articles about how teachers and schools are portrayed in film. Students choosing this track will arrange to present one or two clips from the films they chose and lead 10–15 minutes' discussion of the clips on December 4.

Exam Track

Students may elect to write take-home, essay-style mid-term and final exams. Students electing this track will submit exit slips on at least 10 days between September 12 and December 5. These slips will contain one or more exam questions authentically related to each day's content. These questions must meet the two usual baseline criteria: Requiring that the student know the subject matter to answer the question successfully, and requiring students to raise critical questions, and develop and defend propositions related to that subject matter in their answers (that is: Critical thinking and writing). The exams will incorporate material from exit slips submitted by students but will also include questions not raised by students.

Writing Center Workshops

Attend at least four writing and research workshops given by the Academic Development Center and submit the published brochure certifying that you attended. Note, confirmed attendance at four *Academic Success Workshops* will count for 10% course weight but the grade assigned will be pro-rated from the rest of the semester's graded work.

Because the tracks portion of the course is weighted at 20% and the workshops count only as 10%, students following the Workshops and Writing Track must complete reading responses to two academic articles listed in the bibliography on the syllabus. Those responses will be graded using the Reading Response Rubric in the *Rubrics Document*.

Tri-fold Brochure Track

The typical tri-fold brochure both invites and informs. It includes basic information and pictures, without becoming too text-heavy. In this assignment, you make the brochure with a maximum of about 200 words and you produce an accompanying commentary for me, explaining what's behind the brochure. What are the foundations of this school you are about to start and in which you ask people to enroll their children (maximum word-count on the accompanying commentary is 1000 words). [Note: I always post a complete sample brochure on Moodle or Blackboard with the brochure rubric.]

Website of Annotated Resources Track

Two students may elect this track together and produce a website with at least 20 annotated resources. If two students work together, they will receive the same grade for this track. [Note: I always include links to student-built websites from previous years so current students can see examples.]

Book Project Track

Students electing this track will contribute to an edited book in the 125–150 page range (35,000 to 45,000 words). My goal is to see students produce the book you wish you had during your first year of your degree or during your first major school placement. This book will be published directly on Amazon. It must relate clearly to the learning objectives of this course. Participating in this project will entail the following intermediate steps:

- Attending planning meetings to agree on theme, thesis, and the tone of the book.
- Drafting 6000–8000 words.
- Having your work edited repeatedly.
- Editing chapters written by your co-authors.

Disclaimer: There is enough work to do in this class that we do not need to make a book. If we are to make a book, we need at least eight people. It would still work with as many as ten. Do NOT feel pressured to join this just because others have expressed interest. It will be hard work and you should not commit to it unless you are really serious.

Leadership and Planning Track

Responsibilities include …

- review and revision of the course syllabus before the semester begins
- track and evaluate the professor's teaching on September 11, 18, and 25 and October 2

- leading group discussions throughout the semester including the evaluations of student-led classes in weeks 5–6 and 8–9. You will have about ¼ of the class members in your group
- participating in leadership of week 10's discussion
- meeting three times to assess class progress, suggest corrections, revisions, directions.

Students choosing this track will write a final report on their experience of being involved in university class planning and leadership, noting applications to their anticipated work in K–12 classrooms. [Note: This description does not appear in the syllabus. I invite students to participate in this track.]

Service and Practices Track

Aristotle said in his *Ethics* that a favorable disposition toward an action often follows our doing the action. That is, we can change our mind by practicing. This track involves such action. Arrange at least 10 visits to one place of service (such as Boys and Girls Clubs of Calgary, a place of worship, a school, a food bank, a community center, or other non-profit agency) and serve in whatever capacity that place asks you to serve. You are not allowed to do anything that might be construed as research in this place, nor can your service be part of meeting the requirements of another course. The written assignment, due at the start of class on December 11, will focus on how implementing a practice affected your thinking and your dispositions. That is, what did you learn by engaging in service?

3. SAMPLE *FORECAST SHEET*

Time	Mode	Activity
9:00 – 10:00 Block 1	Offline	It's a flipped classroom!! Please prepare for blocks 3 and 5 by reading the document: 2021 *Day 1 Block 5 Worldviews*, including doing some writing in response to the questions about *The Truman Show* and about your associate teacher (top of p. 6)
10:00 – 11:00 Block 2	Zoom	1. Q&A with the teacher … because you spent a lot of money for this class and you had better check me out! 2. Attendance: Stuck in an elevator with Montessori, Dewey, Piaget, Gardner … which one? 3. Course DNA diagram and response (to come during session)
11:00 – 11:15		**Break**

11:15 – 12:15	Zoom	4. My desired learning outcomes ... and yours
Block 3		5. Syllabus questions
12:15 – 1:15		**Lunch Break**
1:15 – 2:30	Offline&	1. June Madness (see the file by that name): As a class we need to
Block 4	then	compile a list of 16 of the most important educators, dead or
	on	alive. Over this class's 2 weeks we will vote 15 times to narrow
	Zoom	our list down to the one most important educator. Of course

our voting will not change the world ... but we will all learn a
new instructional strategy and we will have fun. Instructions for
today's activity are in the June Madness file.

2. June Madness: Vote #1

3. Philosophies of reel teachers (teachers in film)

Pressure Cooker, (USA, 2009; documentary, 0:00 – 3:10) and
discussion of Wilma Stephenson's practice.

<u>Scaffolding</u>: Wilma Stephenson teaches cooking in inner-city
Philadelphia. Her graduating grade 12s regularly win hundreds
of thousands of dollars in scholarship money to chef schools.
Our worldviews are revealed in our practices and our practices
also shape and mold our worldview.

<u>Prompts</u>: What are some characteristics of her practice? She presents
on the stern end of the continuum but the question is ... is
there a theory/practice gap? What can we extrapolate about
Wilma Stephenson's educational philosophy or worldview
[I know it's a brief clip!]?

Finding Forrester (USA, 2000), 1:32:20 – 1:36:35

<u>Scaffolding</u>: Reclusive, once-famous novelist Forrester (played by Sean
Connery), mentors Jamal, an African-American secondary student,
in writing. Professor Crawford (played by Murray Abraham) deeply
dislikes Jamal and works hard to make his life miserable.

<u>Prompt</u>: If you, as a Tyndale field placement supervisor, were
having a post-sample-lesson conversation with Professor
Crawford, what issues would you raise about his teaching?

2:30 – 2:45		**Break**
2:45 – 4:30	Zoom	1. Worldviews ... a geography exercise, including a url I can't send
Block 5		you yet because it will spoil things.
(with a mini-		2. Worldviews discussion & clarifications based on 2021 *Day 1 Block*
break @		5 (*Worldviews* document posted on Moodle)
time to be		3. June Madness: Vote #1
decided by		4 e-Exit slip: A question I still have about the syllabus or something I
us as we go)		wish we had discussed today about the class or about worldviews.

Notes:

1. This *Forecast Sheet* represents a full day in an intensive course.
2. In face-to-face courses, I distribute the *Daily Forecast* sheet on standard copier paper. This example has been reformatted to fit the page dimensions of this book.
3. The 2021 *Day 1 Block 5 Worldviews* document this *Forecast Sheet* refers to in Block 5, item 2 is the closest I come to a lecture in this course. Notice in Block 1 that I ask students to read this document in advance because we'will have a flipped classroom (Chapter 3). Well, not quite

flipped; I have found that in intensive courses that meet for the full day, giving students time offline helps them and me last through the day. Thus, we did take class time for the reading. A side point, I taught this online course from Calgary, during lockdown, for a university in Toronto. Calgary is two time zones behind Toronto, and I could not start teaching at 7:00 a.m. each day.

4. SAMPLE COURSE CALENDAR AND SCHEDULE

In Chapter 6, I promised to include a more detailed calendar than the abbreviated one I reproduced there. The calendar below is lifted verbatim from a June, 2021 syllabus at Tyndale University in Toronto. Following standard Canadian nomenclature, the teaching licensure degree is called a Bachelor of Education degree whether it is a students' first or second degree. Tyndale's BEd is a post-baccalaureate degree. I teaching one foundations course there annually, toward the end of my students' four-semester program. The following calendar and schedule represent an intensive, two-week course, and a "block" is approximately 1.5 hours in length.

Date	Topics	Assignments
June 7, Block 1	Worldviews, maps, and seating arrangements	
June 7, Block 2	The course syllabus and expectations	
Lunch break		
June 7, Block 3 Vote #1	June Madness ... Filling the bracket: Sixteen thinkers in education	
June 7, Block 4 Vote #2	Seeing the world, worldviews	
June 8, Block 1 Vote #3	Worldviews and curriculum orientations	Assignment #1 due, 9:00 a.m. 10 Classroom Ideals
June 8, Block 2 Vote #4	Parker Palmer and *The Courage to Teach* – initial reflections	
June 9, Block 1 Vote #5	Religious worldviews and Christian worldviews	Assignment #2 due 9:00 a.m. Palmer chs 1–2
June 9, Block 2 Vote #6	Worldviews, educational ideals, and metaphors	
June 10, Block 1 Vote #7	Worldviews and classroom ideals	
June 10, Block 2 Vote #8	Metaphors continued	
June 11, Block 1	Circle meeting / morning meeting	
June 11, Block 2	Expressing faith appropriately in public settings	

June 14, Block 1 Vote #9	Expressing faith appropriately in public settings	
June 14, Block 2 Vote #10	Realizing classroom ideals: Case study 1 – A visit to Room 232	
June 15, Block 1 Vote #11	Minding the gap 1: Theory and practice	Assignment 3, Subway map, due 9:00 a.m.
June 15, Block 2 Vote #12	Minding the gap 2: Ideals and classroom realities	
June 16, Block 1	Parker Palmer – *The Courage to Teach* – Powerful passages	Assignment 4 <u>optional due</u> <u>date</u> 9:00 a.m.
June 16, Block 2	Parker Palmer – *The Courage to Teach* –Blackout poetry The Bracket in other subject areas	
June 17, Block 1 Vote #13	Democracies' expectations of schools: Metaphors, worldviews, ideals, Ontario College of Teachers standards in context	
June 17, Block 2 Vote #14	What drives Ontario education? Realizing ideals in Ontario curriculum units	
June 18, Block 1 Vote #15	Religious worldviews in democracies. Responding to difference: Case study	Assignment 4, <u>non-optional</u> <u>date</u> – 9:00 a.m.
June 18, Block 2	Protecting and nurturing your personal professional core.	

I include this calendar to help make the case that clear syllabi are a key way to increase student self-efficacy starting on the first day of the term. In my course syllabi, I typically have another column that lists the readings due for each day. I omitted that column so that the calendar would fit in the page-width of this volume.

5. SAMPLE CASE FOR CLASSROOM USE

Taking Serious Differences Seriously: Using Cases to Treat Controversial Issues

In her 12 years of teaching senior-high social studies, Sarah D. has heard her share of classroom outbursts about liberals, unemployed persons, African-Americans, capitalists, Indo-Canadians, socialists, Latinos and other immigrants, the homeless, the aged and other groups identifiable by any number of characteristics. But she has rarely had to deal with persistent, nearly term-long arguments from one individual student (Sean O.) like she is dealing with this term.

The essence of the argument that she faces is simple: "We" should send all "them" back home.

The student in question brooks no opposition to his views. Sarah tried to explore with Sean what she considered to be a bomb-proof argument based on the twin ideas of equality and the fact that people of European descent were not the original residents of what is now British Columbia. He retreated to a nation/race argument and claimed that his nation belonged only to his race. She tried rights arguments (natural rights, UN Charter, etc.), legal arguments (federal laws, etc.), and even pragmatic arguments ("they're" here and you may as well figure out how to live with some joy in the circumstances, etc.). For every argument, Sean had answers, most of which were nasty, patently racist, white supremacist, and illogical. But his stance looked sound from his perspective (as stances are known to do), and there was no convincing him otherwise. In fact, Sarah detected that Sean entrenched himself further with each of her approaches to the question.

After the fourth in-class outburst, Sarah contacted Sean's parents, only to discover that they held the same views. She sought the help of teacher colleagues who had taught or were currently teaching the same student. She read intensely for a couple weeks on the topic and then decided to try a case study approach. She adapted some materials that she found and developed a small unit called "The Immigrant Experience."

In her unit, each student was to research their own forebears' history in North American and then write a case to highlight some of their struggles as newcomers. In the course of completing his research, Sean became deeply interested in the story of his great-grandparents' (father's side) immigration after WWI from Ireland to Nova Scotia, then Montreal, then San Francisco, where his father's parents were born. His mother's grandparents, also Irish, and one of whom was still living, had left Ontario for Washington State.

Sean wrote an interesting story of prejudice against Irish. Inspired by the movie, The Gangs of New York, he developed a background to his story detailing some of the opposition faced by many Irish immigrants in Canada and the United States. Sean's final essay and the 300-word case he wrote for class discussion both had a kind of "Oh, the poor Irish," and "Oh, poor me" tone, albeit mixed with some powerful anecdotes about taking risks and working hard.

Sean, while bright in some ways, didn't see that he had set his own trap. When his turn came to present to the class, he showed several pictures to the class and then handed out the single page with his case write-up and four discussion questions. When he informed his classmates that they had five minutes to read the case and respond to the first question, Sarah told him he could tack his pictures to the bulletin board. His posting area stood adjacent to that of a Sikh classmate. Sean began stapling his pictures onto the bulletin board. When he stapled his last picture up—a photo of his great-grandparents debarking ship in Halifax in 1921 (with four rectangular suitcases), he noticed for the first time the immediately adjacent photo in Monahar S.'s display: his grandparents landing in Vancouver airport in 1959 (with four rectangular suitcases).

For the briefest moment, Sean apprehended how similar were the stories of all those descended from immigrants. He never made another outburst about immigrants in class. But, interestingly, he also refused to speak to any of his classmates that fit into his category of persons who "belonged back where they came from."

Questions for reflection and discussion

1. What mistakes, if any, do you identify in Sarah's handling of this situation?
2. What suggestions would you make to Sarah regarding her handling of Sean's new understanding and behavior (following his case presentation)?
3. This case could have ended better. What interventions or steps do you think might have moved it that way?
4. This case could have ended worse. Describe a couple ways that this case could have gone completely off the rails, and what steps might have prevented its having done so.
5. In your own teaching experience, how have you approached situations parallel to this one? Talk about successes and failures here.

Notes

1. I have used this case with both in-service teachers and with education students on the university campus.
2. The discussion of this case can be handled in several ways. One can move immediately to full-class discussion. In this approach, the percentage of students who usually refrain from speaking aloud in class will not get to participate. For that reason, I usually use small

groups or some version of Think–Pair–Share (Chapter 10) so that students have an opportunity to speak with one other classmate before the class reconvenes as a whole. In online classes, I used breakout rooms for the initial discussion of the case.

6. GAMING RESOURCES

By Greg Burbidge

In Chapter 6, I listed the Gaming Track as an elective for 20% course weight. I play a board game almost daily but consider myself no expert. At my request, Greg Burbidge, a Calgary friend and serious gamer, has supplied the following to me about adapting games for educational purposes. Higher educators should take his caveat that most games already adapted for educational use are directed toward K–12 settings. But if I may add a codicil to his caveat, if we have seriously asked our students to imagine themselves at Lockheed's Skunk Works or at Building 20 at MIT, then they will be able to build games suited to our course contents and learning outcomes. The rest of the section is directly from Greg Burbidge.

Many games are already available in college subject areas, a majority of them directed toward a secondary or middle-school market. Here are a few examples:

Freedom: The Underground Railroad. *Freedom* is a card-driven, cooperative game for one to four players in which the group is working for the abolitionist movement to help bring an end to slavery in the United States. The players use a combination of cards, which feature figures and events spanning from Early Independence until the Civil War, along with action tokens and the benefits of their role to impact the game. Players need to strike the right balance between freeing slaves from plantations in the South and raising funds which are desperately needed to allow the group to continue their abolitionist activities as well as strengthen the cause.

- Rise Up: The Game of People and Power: Lead a march of thousands of people. Write a protest song that goes viral. Fight for what you believe in. Rise Up is a cooperative board game about building people power and taking on oppressive systems to create change. In *Rise Up*, the game weaves a story about your movement, which can either be based in reality (like stopping an oil pipeline) or fictional (like fighting for dragon rights). But "the System" is hard at work, too, maneuvering to crush your efforts through tactics like setting up surveillance, making arrests, or causing infighting. In order to win, players must collaborate to build a movement that scores more victories than the system.

- Keep Cool: With *Keep Cool*, each player takes a role within global climate politics. You have to put through economic interests—e.g., of the USA and its partners or of the Developing Countries—yet you must not forget the strong lobby groups in your country like the oil industry or environmental groups as they also decide whether you win or lose. Within each round of the game you have to decide between measures for climate protection good for all and egoistic decisions just for your own sake. The risk: catastrophes like droughts, floods, or pandemics. The chance: welfare and a stable global climate. Whoever reaches his targets first wins, yet if you are not cooperative enough, all players might lose due to a collapse of the world climate.
- Civio, A Civil Right Game: Each player starts as an intern at a law firm specializing in civil rights. Using a handful of cards representing laws, Supreme Court decisions, constitutional amendments, key issues, rights and freedoms, players race to combine these cards into precedents.

Resources for social justice game design:

- Designing Games for Social Change
- Developing a Board Game to Engage People in Social Justice Issues
- Fast Company Article on Rise Up

General board game design resources:

- Board Game Design Wiki
- Stonemaier Games How to Design a Board Game
- How to Learn Board Game Design and Development
- Cardboard Edison Tumbler
- Games Precipice
- Meta: Designing a Board Game as Curriculum

Popular games that have been re-themed
- Carcassonne became Carcassonne Star Wars
- Cards Against Humanity became Cards Against Colonialism
- Pandemic became Pandemic Cthulhu, Pandemic Iberia
- Love Letter became Love Letter Santa, Love Letter Batman, Love Letter Lord of the Rings…

Simple/Gateway Games for Converting
- Carcassonne: "This simple tile-laying game was one of the original gateway Euro games—one so elegantly designed that people who've only played Clue and Monopoly should have no problem picking it up. In Carcassonne, players place various tiles on the table according to certain rules in order to build castles, claim land, and score points."
- Dominion: "Dominion isn't technically a boardgame, but it's an excellent card game that feels as deep and strategic as any game with a big board to put on the table. Dominion features a mechanism called 'deck-building' that the game made popular in modern boardgames. It's simple to learn: just draw five cards from the top of your deck, play cards, and purchase ones from the shared piles to go into your deck. It's had a huge impact on boardgame design, now being implemented in all games from all kinds of genres."
- Pandemic: In Pandemic, several virulent diseases have broken out simultaneously all over the world! The players are disease-fighting specialists whose mission is to treat disease hotspots while researching cures for each of four plagues before they get out of hand.

Ticket to Ride: With elegantly simple gameplay, Ticket to Ride can be learned in under 15 minutes, while providing players with intense strategic and tactical decisions every turn. Players collect cards of various types of train cars they then use to claim railway routes in North America. The longer the routes, the more points they earn. Additional points come to those who fulfill Destination Tickets—goal cards that connect distant cities; and to the player who builds the longest continuous route.

REFERENCE

Palmer, P. (1998). The courage to teach. Jossey-Bass.

Appendix B

In Chapter 11, I outlined some of the ways I have tried to help my students develop as writers. I begin this appendix by offering materials I use with my students to help them distinguish thesis statements from other openings that fall short of the thesis. In the second section of the appendix, I return to the rubric for the major paper and research essay I introduced in Appendix A. In this case, I offer an elaborated version of the rubric I work through with my students. After all I have written in the rest of this book, it should be obvious to my readers that I do not lecture on this rubric. I usually break students into small groups and have different groups lead the discussion about each line of the rubric and the commentary associated with it. I answer questions as needed but they explain each line as they understand it and ask me to clarify those parts they do not understand. Periodically, they complain about my criteria. I have used this exercise as a prelude to our co-determining the rubric for the major paper (as I described it in Chapter 6).

The materials below are as I handed them out to students. I welcome my colleagues to use and adapt this material in any way you wish.

1. TOPICS AND THESIS STATEMENTS

The Point

If you were on the phone with an aging grandparent who still used a phone to talk, and they asked you this question, "What is the point of your paper?" what would you say? In a maximum of 40 words ...

Examples:

1. I'm arguing that most schools want to alleviate inequality but standardized testing sabotages that purpose.
2. I want to persuade my old professor that he needs to scale back his view of sharing authority with students because some students

don't learn as well in democratic classrooms as they do in more controlled classrooms.

3. That schools need to recognize the many issues that affect immigrant students' learning.
4. It's about how inequality affects some students' ability to learn.
5. It's about classroom authority.
6. It's about the factors that affect immigrant students' learning.

Notice the wording of the above six examples

First, notice that #s 4–6 are only announcements of topics, not statements of what point you are trying to make in your paper. Unlike the last three examples, the first three would clearly inform your aging, phone-using grandparent what point you were trying to make in your paper. Still, in print form rather than in conversation, the first three would need some cleaning up.

How do we turn those first three into clean thesis statements?

1. I'm arguing that most schools want to alleviate inequality but standardized testing sabotages that purpose.

Cleaned up and making the main point the subject of the sentence yields this thesis statement: *Standardized testing sabotages schools' attempts to alleviate inequality.*

2. I want to persuade my old professor that he needs to scale back his view becomes: Those who believe strongly in sharing authority with students need to exercise caution because some students don't learn as well in democratic classrooms as they do in more controlled classrooms.

We won't clean this one up further because you can already see what I did. But do notice how I softened the *scale back* to *exercise caution* in the revision.

3. That schools need to recognize the many issues that affect immigrant students' learning.

Presto! It's done, transformed from a relative clause into a sentence.

Using formal prose, turn what you wrote about your own paper in the box on the top of the other side of this sheet into a single sentence—a thesis statement—that would work in your paper.

Enumeration

Enumerating (listing) the points to come provides your readers with cognitive signposts and will increase their understanding of the paper in one reading.

Example from #1 above:: *Standardized testing sabotages schools' attempts to alleviate inequality* can be enumerated in several ways, the two most common being these:

- *Standardized testing sabotages schools' attempts to alleviate inequality because children in poverty experience schools and school practices as foreign and because many tests are standardized using middle-class populations resident near universities where test developers work.*
- *For three reasons [in three ways], standardized testing sabotages schools' attempts to alleviate inequality. These are way one, way two, and way three.*

The main difference between the two enumerations is obvious: The first uses one sentence and the second uses two. Writing purists generally accept both forms of the thesis statement.

Enumerating your thesis statement

In formal prose, using the trial thesis statement you wrote in the box on the reverse side of this sheet, and following one of the two patterns demonstrated just above, write an enumerated thesis statement that would work for your paper.

More examples of topics and thesis statements

Note these four topics for major papers:

- Residential schools.
- Gender in education.
- Roman Catholic education.
- The achievement gap.

225 **Supporting Students' Writing**

You need to be clear on the differences between topics, as above, thesis statements, and plain old questions. Below are parallel questions for each of the above topics:

- What are some of the effects of residential schools?
- What roles does gender play in Canadian education?
- To what degree is Roman Catholic education in an identity crisis at this time?
- What are some of the sources of the achievement gap for children in poverty?

You may legitimately (and sparingly) ask questions in a paper, but do not confuse questions for thesis statements.

Below are thesis statements embedded in opening paragraphs. In these examples, the italicized text preceding the thesis is introduction and set-up, and some of it may be repeated in a later paragraph of the paper's introduction. The thesis statements are bolded. The underlined passages following the thesis statements are announcements to the reader about structure. These announcements are legitimate as long as you have stated the thesis. Note that the first and third theses below are enumerated; that is, the sections are listed in the thesis statement.

Residential schools

The Canadian government, like the governments of Australia and the United States, used residential schools as one means of implementing a policy of cultural assimilation of Aboriginal peoples. In Canada, this policy remained in effect from the late 1800s until 1969, although many schools had already closed by that date. **The narratives of those who attended Canadian residential schools and academic researchers reveal three dominant effects of residential schools: effect 1, effect 2, and effect 3.** <u>In what follows, I briefly treat the first two and then focus on the third. I conclude my paper with recommendations for future research, for policy, and for practice, all related to the third effect of residential education.</u>

Gender in education

Changing understandings of gender, especially the idea of equality, over the last century have led to nearly industrial-scale research into the role of gender in education. Among other topics, researchers have studied achievement differences between boys and girls, the proportions of female and male teachers in elementary classrooms, textbooks' portrayals of gender roles, and a host of other aspects of gender in educational settings. A persistent issue related to gender is the funding of school sports. **Because of the cost of running a football program, funding for sports in secondary education schools goes disproportionately and unjustly to boys.** By examining four actual school budgets, I demonstrate what typical high school football programs cost compared to other programs, and I argue that school boards and schools should redress this imbalance.

Roman Catholic education

Throughout the 1980s and 1990s, Roman Catholic schools in Ontario, Saskatchewan, and Alberta answered the charge that they should not be funded because they were just like public schools by becoming more explicitly Catholic. Meanwhile, recent immigration to Canada has meant that many parents from other world religions want their children to attend Catholic schools because those schools take religion seriously. **Catholic schools today must work in a tension between the core need to be fully Catholic and the need to welcome many students from other faiths. That tension reveals itself in three ways: Whether to provide worship or meditation space for followers of other faiths, whether to require chapel attendance of followers of other faiths, and whether to provide alternative curriculum materials at points of key Catholic teaching.** In this paper I survey school board documents from several Catholic school districts in the three provinces where Catholic schools are funded, examining their admission policies for students whose families do not attend Catholic churches.

Achievement gap

Some weeks ago, we viewed a short video (narrated by Morgan Freeman) about the achievement gap and how it grows. That video confirmed a hunch I have had since my placement in second year at Such-and-Such School. I noticed in that placement that even in kindergarten and grade 1, children from some homes seemed to lag behind children from other homes, despite showing every

version 1 ... sign that they were equally intelligent. **The achievement gap affects lower income students in four distinct ways.** I begin with a survey of the research into the achievement gap and then focus on the four major effects of the gap.

version 2 ... sign that they were equally intelligent. **The achievement gap affects lower income students in four distinct ways**. I begin with a survey of the research into the achievement gap and then focus on the four major effects of the gap. Those effects are affect 1, affect 2, affect 3, and affect 4.

Notice

1. The low word count on my set-up/intros. You do not need many words to bring your reader into what you plan to do in your paper.
2. The one-sentence thesis in the first, second, and last paragraphs. I used two sentences in the third example.

2. AN ANNOTATED RUBRIC FOR THE MAJOR PAPER

Appendix A included the rubric for the major paper or research essay. I have lifted the material below from my own annotated version of the rubric I usually post on Moodle or Blackboard. Because I dearly want my students to read the annotated version of the rubric, I sprinkled in two tablespoons of snark.

Criteria	Excellent	Good	Adequate	Unsatisfactory
Argumentation (/80)				
Use of Sources (15%)	Interacts responsibly with prior discussions.	Uses sources responsibly to present or support their argument.	Uses sources but without nuance or interaction.	Uses no sources; misrepresents others' arguments.

Notice the wording in the Excellent cell in this row. In my view, *interacts* implies that you don't just stack a bunch of quotations in your paper to support your view. You create a conversation among people with whom you agree and with whom you disagree. Face it, they've been arguing with each other before you walked into the room. *Responsibly* implies that you demonstrate in your paper that you have actually read carefully and understood what the others in this conversation have been saying. *Responsibly* also implies that you treat them with respect … that you really struggle to honor what's been said so far that is worthwhile and also that you treat charitably those with whom you disagree … unless they are clearly idiotic.

Thesis statement (5%)	Clear thesis statement that structures the paper.	Comes to a clear conclusion.	Expresses thoughts on a general topic.	Paper has no apparent direction.

A thesis is not an announcement. It is a claim that indicates to your reader the direction your paper will take. In some cases, it also tells the reader how many sections the paper will have (in the descriptions below, I use the standard word *enumerated* to discuss that aspect of the thesis). The material below is from another rubric in the rubrics booklet.

** By "thesis" I simply mean that this assignment, like all expository writing, needs a sentence or two to indicate to the reader what angle you plan to go in your paper, even in one this short.

It could be one sentence, in this case a somewhat mild thesis, and not one that is enumerated:

> "In their article, so and so present three lines of evidence that Y is the case." [obviously the underlined part could be any kind of judgment, and, just as obviously, you don't have to enumerate.]

It could be two sentences, in this case a bit stronger, and not enumerated:

> "In their article, so and so argue that Y is the case. While they demonstrate that they did careful research, I do not find their conclusions compelling."

This is **not** a thesis; it is an announcement:

> "In this paper, I will summarize article X."

Writer perspective (15%)	Clear and consistent, but unobtrusive presence.	General presence.	Uneven presence.	Writer's perspective is unstated or dominates.

This is your paper and I want to hear you in it. All academic writers experience tension between honoring the prior conversation (which I discussed above with reference to "Use of sources") and writing in their own voice. I don't want to read your diary any more than I want to read a string of quotations from sources. Under "use of sources" I said that you must honor those in the conversation before you got there. But I want you to join the conversation, too … what's your take on what people have been saying? What's your contribution? What do you think needs to happen in our thinking, in policy or in practice?

Bibliography (5%)	Sources representative of the prior discussion; diverse sources.	Uses responsible sources.	Uses adequate resources.	No evidence of the contours of the discussion.

I refuse to tell you how many sources you need but I do have the word adequate in the *Adequate* cell in this row. At minimum, you need to work with some peer-reviewed research articles in academic journals. And you need to recognize the varied quality of websites ... ranging from Covid-denying nutters to government- and university-sponsored repositories of original, historical materials. See the two words highlighted in the *Excellent* cell above ... these need to be diverse voices that, if you're honest in your reading and your writing, will bring you into the conversation and will allow you to show your reader that you've read responsibly.

Structure of argument (20%)	Sound and compelling.	Focused and generally persuasive.	Lacks precision; unsystematic; somewhat persuasive.	Muddled and unfocused; not compelling.

I need to be able to follow where you go. So ... headings, subheadings, topic sentences in paragraphs. Transition words and phrases such as *first, second, for example, another example, on the other hand, more-over, furthermore, to conclude,* etc.

Examples/ illustrations (20%)	Judiciously chosen examples; integral to the argument; used appropriately.	Relevant examples chosen; application fairly well established.	Examples are somewhat appropriate; incomplete demonstration of their relevance.	Examples dominate the paper; undeveloped connection to the argument.

↑

To make a good argument, you have to point to examples, you have to have evidence.

Grammar and spelling (5%)	No errors.	Rare errors.	Some errors.	Errors throughout.

↑

Rule #1 of the Write Club: There is such a thing as Write Club.

Rule #2 of the Write Club: Turn on all the grammar and spelling switches in MS Word under File/Options/Proofing.

Rule #3 of the Write Club: Get someone else to read your work.

Sentences & paragraphs (10%)	Varied sentence complexity; well-formed paragraphs; creative style; graceful prose.	Sound and clear sentences and paragraphs; meaning is clear.	Some unclear sentences and paragraphs; reader has to re-read for meaning.	Unclear or incomplete sentences and paragraphs.

↑

Rule #4 of the Write Club: See rule #3.

Reference conventions (5%)	No errors in documenting sources.	No errors in documenting sources.	Few errors documenting sources.	Conventions ignored.

↑

If you don't know APA format, go to "Owl at Purdue" (https://owl.english.purdue.edu/owl/) for examples of every kind of reference formatted for the American Psychological Association format.

To my readers, as I noted at the start of the Appendix, please adapt any of the above to your own subject areas and purposes. These words all came from keyboard; none of them came to me in a blinding flash of light.

In Chapter 11, I made reference to Stephen King's four-category schema of writing quality. We all share the responsibility of helping our students move ahead in their writing. On King's account, such movement will most likely be from fair to good. My hope is that this material helps if a few professors move a few students toward good writing.

Index

Lightning Source UK Ltd.
Milton Keynes UK
UKHW020700261122
412817UK00016B/129

9 781032 195230